Cases in
ONLINE INTERVIEW
Research

For Hannah, Zac, Sammy, Alex and Oliver—May you find the answers you seek and make real connections in the digitally connected world where you will grow up.

Cases in
ONLINE INTERVIEW
Research

Janet Salmons

Vision2Lead, Inc. and Capella University School of Business and Technology

Editor

Los Angeles | London | New Delhi
Singapore | Washington DC

Los Angeles | London | New Delhi
Singapore | Washington DC

FOR INFORMATION:

SAGE Publications, Inc.

2455 Teller Road

Thousand Oaks, California 91320

E-mail: order@sagepub.com

SAGE Publications Ltd.

1 Oliver's Yard

55 City Road

London EC1Y 1SP

United Kingdom

SAGE Publications India Pvt. Ltd.

B 1/I 1 Mohan Cooperative Industrial Area

Mathura Road, New Delhi 110 044

India

SAGE Publications Asia-Pacific Pte. Ltd.

33 Pekin Street #02-01

Far East Square

Singapore 048763

Acquisitions Editor: Vicki Knight

Assistant Editor: Lauren Habib

Editorial Assistant: Kalie Koscielak

Production Editor: Astrid Virding

Copy Editor: Taryn Bigelow

Typesetter: C&M Digitals (P) Ltd.

Proofreader: Ellen Brink

Indexer: Kathleen Paparchontis

Cover Designers: Anupama Krishnan and
Candice Harman

Marketing Manager: Helen Salmon

Permissions Editor: Adele Hutchinson

Printed in the United States of America

Library of Congress Cataloging-in-Publication Data

Cases in online interview research/edited by Janet Salmons.

p. cm.
Includes bibliographical references and index.

ISBN 978-1-4129-9180-3 (pbk. : alk. paper) ✓

1. Interviewing. 2. Telematics. 3. Online chat groups. 4. Qualitative research. 5. Research— Methodology. I. Salmons, Janet, 1952-

H61.28.C38 201
2001.4,33—dc23   2011032018

This book is printed on acid-free paper.

11 12 13 14 15 10 9 8 7 6 5 4 3 2 1

Contents

List of Figures

List of Tables

Foreword

First, pick up this book. Second, don't put it down. These case studies provide a wealth of lived experience about the process of doing research in online contexts. Ostensibly focused on online interviewing, the cases reveal much more than a simple set of techniques or strategies and move far beyond interviewing. As the authors describe their premises, choices, and dilemmas, we readers get closer to the interplay of research—the experimental and recursive processes of applying qualitative epistemologies to define field boundaries and engage with participants; the challenges of negotiating with external ethics review boards; and the discoveries and decisions made in the middle of studies when the technologies, participants, or one's own research strategies present unanticipated surprises. These key moments, mostly absent from formal research reports, teach us about the difficulties and joys of doing qualitative inquiry. Salmons and her contributors offer us a rare glimpse into the actual work of doing research.

The book invites dialogue. The cases can be read as retrospective narratives, through which we gain valuable insight about the authors' decision-making practices, successes and failures, and inductive strategies. Each case includes a response by another contributor as well as commentary by Janet Salmons. The responses complicate as well as clarify, serving as vital tools for further inquiry. Read as a whole, these dialogues emphasize the need for flexibility and adaptation as these practices are enacted and negotiated in various technologically mediated environments. This understanding of the emergent characteristics of qualitative research practice is augmented by the conversational tone of the book.

The scope of this book would be challenging for any editor and the range of cases was intentionally broad. Janet Salmons' ability to weave a framework throughout the book is a remarkable achievement, considering the natural yet daunting number of issues raised within and across the cases. At the end of the book, she shares her own meta-synthesis of the cases, looping back to the keen set of metaphors offered at the outset for situating the researcher within the frame of traveler, gardener, or miner.

When I conducted my first online interviews via e-mail, instant messaging, and game spaces in 1995, there were very few guides to help me grapple with myriad challenges that would emerge before, during, and after these interviews. Now, more than a decade has passed and online interviews have been used by thousands of scholars across the spectrum of disciplines. Still, there are relatively few detailed treatments of online interviewing. This case collection is a vital tool for helping one avoid or anticipate situations and to lessen the perceived need to reinvent the wheel. Whether one agrees with the various authors' decisions and strategies or not, these cases enrich the conversation concerning the complexity, premises, practices, and consequences of online interviewing.

Annette N. Markham
Guest Professor,
Centre for Internet Research and the Institute
for Communication and Media Studies
Aarhus University

Preface

With a nothing-special laptop and an Internet connection, I can converse with people around the world. We can hold a written conversation or see each other while we talk. We can share files, pictures, or URLs. Or, we can traipse around a virtual environment with our avatars. I can pull a smart phone out of my purse and send all kinds of verbal or written messages, or send photos or videos of the circumstances around me—with quality that is good enough to show on television. The communication capacities of fairly low-cost, easy-to-use hardware and software are not lost on faraway grandparents, deployed military personnel, business travelers, citizen journalists, and telecommuters—or on researchers. For researchers, the benefit works both ways: Researchers have more potential ways to communicate with research participants, and more potential participants have access to an array of information and communications technologies (ICTs). This beneficial interplay is of utmost value to researchers who rely on in-depth interviews.

More so than other types of data collection, the interviewer and interviewee must communicate. The interviewer must actively engage the interviewee to gain personal trust and build mutual respect to elicit information-rich responses. Some level of relationship is inherent in the exchange, if only for the time period of the interview. When interviews occur online, researchers must devise and learn new ways to build trust and motivate individuals to share thoughts and observations and reveal personal views or experiences. Online interview researchers must also devise and learn new ways to design studies, recruit participants, and meet ethical research guidelines.

"ONLINE INTERVIEWS" DEFINED

For the purpose of this book, the term *online interviews* refers to interviews conducted with information and communications technologies (ICTs). The primary focus is on interviews conducted with synchronous technologies including text messaging, videoconferencing or video calls, multichannel meetings, or 3-D immersive environments. Asynchronous technologies such as e-mail, blogs, forums, wikis, social networks, or websites are used to prepare for, conduct, or follow up on the interview. Scholarly online interviews are conducted in accordance with ethical research guidelines; verifiable research participants provide informed consent before participating in any interview.

While researchers are now taking advantage of emerging technologies to conduct interviews and are publishing the results of these studies, few have taken the time to examine the online interview data collection process itself. This is the purpose of the present book.

In *Online Interviews in Real Time* I started to analyze some of the particular characteristics of data collection from interviews conducted with information and communications technologies (ICTs), including text-based, videoconference, multichannel meeting space, or immersive environments. I interviewed other researchers and wrote about their experiences and lessons learned in a "Researchers' Notebook" for each chapter. Based on that experience, I recruited e-interview researchers to contribute in-depth explanations of their work. Ten researchers were invited to create case studies about the online interviews they had conducted. Their cases offer the opportunity to scrutinize the inner workings of their research from design steps, decisions, joys and frustrations, to discoveries.

So that readers could compare the proverbial apples to apples, contributors were asked to organize the case using the same outline (with the understanding that not every case would include every item). They were provided with a glossary of common terms, so consistent language could be used throughout the collection of cases.

CASE STUDY OUTLINE

- Research purpose and questions
- Research design overview
  - Epistemologies, guiding theories

- o Methodology (phenomenology, case study, grounded theory, etc.)
- o Sampling approach
- o Data collection (interview style and approach)
- o Data analysis
- Technology choices and rationale
  - o Kinds of communication, such as written, audio, and/or visual
- Ethical issues and approaches
  - o Experiences with institutional review boards, ethics reviews, committees, or funding-related reviews
- Interview experience and challenges
- Research findings
- Lessons learned and recommendations

While everyone had the same guidelines, the research they used as the basis for the cases could hardly be more diverse. Represented disciplines include business, psychology and sociology, education and museum education, environmental policy and health studies. Methodologies include grounded theory, ethnography, phenomenology, case study, and action research. Thus, each researcher or research team had to negotiate the particularities of emergent interview methods in the context of existing methodological and disciplinary conventions. Taken together, we have the chance to learn something about approaches to research across disciplines.

Fostering meaningful discourse about emergent online interview research approaches is a central goal of this book. To spur discussion, each contributor was asked to comment on another case. They were not asked to carry out a critical "peer review," but rather to bring up points of interest and/or similarities or distinctions with their own research. Some of them met (online of course!) to talk about their cases or to pose questions. I hope you will join in and extend the dialogue—in your mentor/adviser and student conversations and in classrooms, conferences or meetings, or online discussion forums. Please communicate with me about how you use the ideas presented in this book—and your discoveries.

Chapter and Case Overviews

Chapter 1 introduces an *E-Interview Research Framework*. This conceptual framework is intended as a multidimensional way to understand e-interview research. The term *understand* is intentional here to encompass evaluative, instructional, and consumer purposes. Sometimes we dissect a research design or completed study to appraise its quality or judge its merit, completeness, or ethical considerations. Sometimes we use them to teach or learn, other times we simply read to acquire new knowledge about the topic. In any of these situations, we need first to understand the elements and context of the study. Other disciplinary and methodology-specific criteria and frameworks can be used to understand the study more generally; this framework offers a set of models and questions that can be used to look at the "e" part of e-research.

Contributors received a draft of the E-Interview Research Framework when they were preparing their cases. I used this E-Interview Research Framework to organize after-case commentaries and a final meta-synthesis. I hope this framework will provide you with additional ways to look at and understand these and other studies (including your own . . . or your students').

Understanding the alignment of key research elements—theory, epistemology, methodology, and methods—is important when trying to dissect any research design, and particularly essential for understanding online interview research (see Figure P.1). We need to know the rationale for using online interview methods to determine whether and how the data collected accomplish the purpose of the study.

The E-Interview Research Framework review cycle begins with an examination of the key elements of the study and consideration of the overall alignment of the study's purpose, methodology, and e-research methods. A snapshot of these research design elements in the context of each case is presented here to introduce the study (and pique your curiosity about each chapter).

The **Chapter 2** case is "Blog Like An Egyptian" by Sally Bishai (see Figure P.2). This grounded theory study used data collected through text-based online interviews as well as document analysis of participants' writings on blogs. To pursue research interests in psychology, communications, and culture, the study was designed to explore three areas: (1) the acculturation strategies of Egyptians in the diaspora; (2) current attitudes, anxieties, and/or dreams held by Egyptians (living in Egypt or the diaspora); and (3) manifestations of the dialogical model of acculturation through an examination of three communication dimensions (identification, cultural orientation, and communication style). Findings included a proposed theory, a dialogical model of acculturation.

The **Chapter 3** case is "Stranger in a Strange Land: The Challenges and Benefits of Online Interviews in the Social Networking Space"

Figure P.1 Research design map.

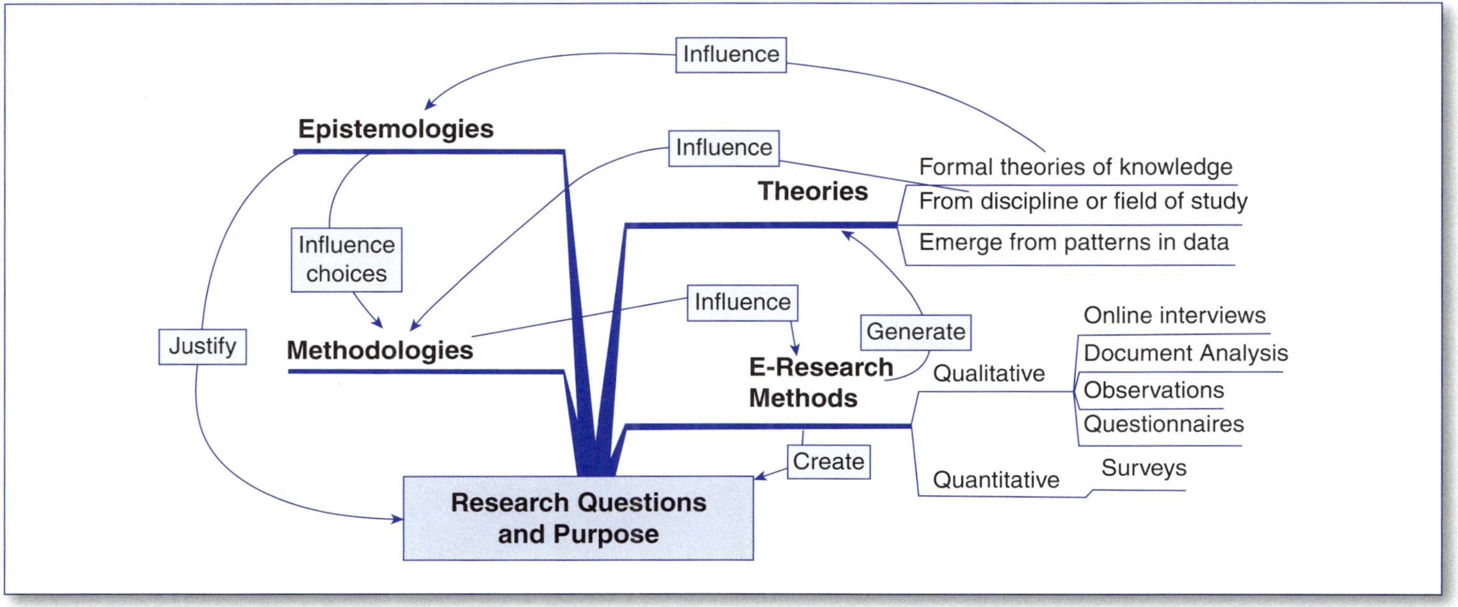

Figure P.2 Research map for "Blog Like an Egyptian."

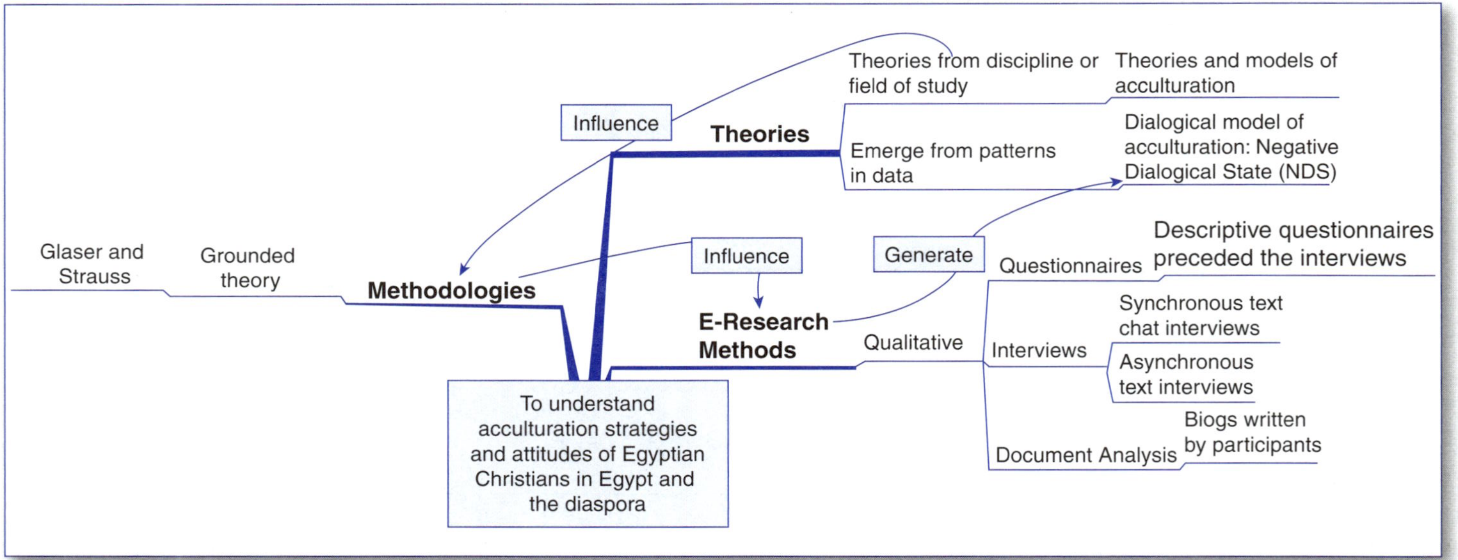

Figure P.3 Research map for "Stranger in a Strange Land: Online Interviews Within the Social Networking Space."

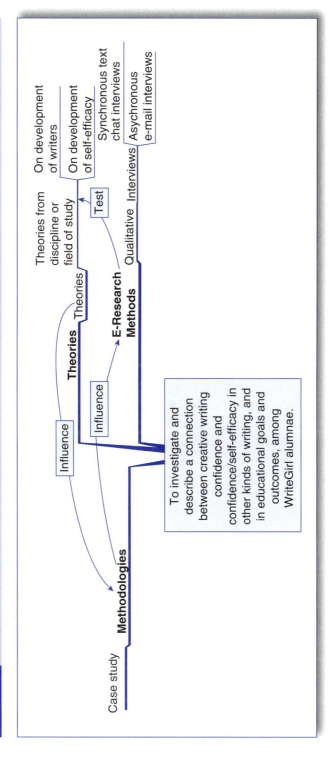

by Allison Deegan (see Figure P.3). To pursue research interests in education, this case study used data collected through text-based online interviews conducted on Facebook. The purpose of the study was to examine the development of confidence in creative writing abilities by adolescents who were participants in an out-of-school-time (OST) creative writing and mentoring program. The study found that most participants developed confidence in their creative writing abilities through their membership in WriteGirl, and some who believed themselves to be strong writers when they joined, developed confidence in other areas of their lives. Many found that the supportive environment they experienced as youth writers in the program contrasted sharply with the environments they encountered in college courses, and that change impacted their confidence.

The **Chapter 4** case is "Interviewing in Virtual Worlds: An Application of Best Practices" by Jonathan Cabiria (see Figure P.4). The main purposes of this virtual-world study were (1) to discover if virtual-world engagement can be used for therapeutic purposes by psychologists who treated marginalized people dealing with social stigma and its related psychological effects, and (2) whether engagement in virtual worlds produced any transferrable effects to the physical world. This grounded theory qualitative study indicated that regular engagement with similar others in virtual environments first created awareness of the gap between authentic and inauthentic living, creating increasing discomfort with one's physical world presentation of self, thus leading to changes in one's real-world presentation that were more in line with the desired virtual-world identity. It was proposed that use of virtual-world spaces by psychologists could be a useful therapeutic process for some clients seeking identity reformation as a result of stigmas that marginalized them.

The **Chapter 5** case is "Beneficial Interview Effects in Virtual Worlds: A Case Study" by Ann Randall (see Figure P.5). To pursue research interests in education, this interpretive, qualitative study used data collected through text-based online interviews conducted in Second Life. The purpose of the study was to investigate positive effects of qualitative interviews on interviewees—an effect referred to throughout this chapter as *beneficial interview effects*. Randall's analysis of the interviews suggested that the beneficial interview effects phenomenon did indeed occur in virtual-world text-based interviews.

The **Chapter 6** case is "Learning to Work In-World: Conducting Qualitative Research in Virtual Worlds Using In-Depth Interviews" by Taryn Stanko and Jonathon Richter (see Figure P.6). To pursue

Figure P.4 Research map for "Interviewing in Virtual Worlds: An Application of Best Practices."

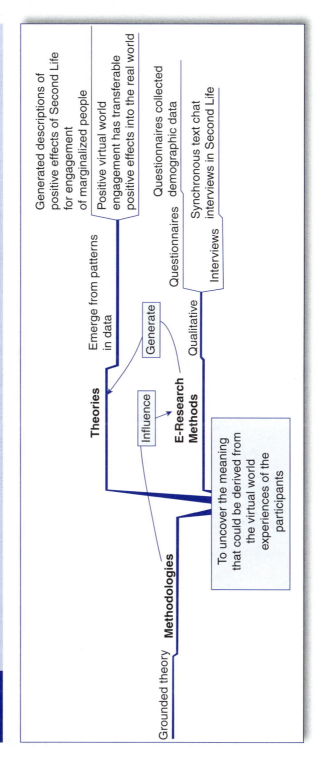

Figure P.5 Research map for "Beneficial Interview Effects in Virtual Worlds: A Case Study."

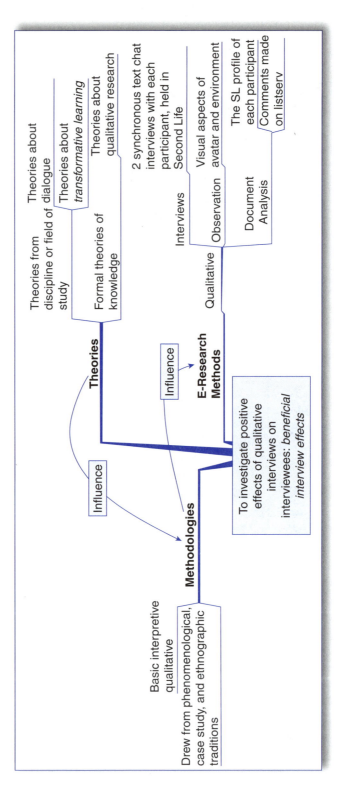

research interests in business, this grounded theory study used data collected through text-based and verbal online interviews, as well as photographs and machinima media, all conducted in the virtual worlds Second Life and Wonderland. While investigating the nuances of conducting work in a virtual setting, the research team also explored questions related to research approaches to studying virtual-world phenomena. To build on this study's findings and expand opportunities for future research, the researchers are creating a virtual collaboration laboratory, or "Collaboratory," as a research space, exhibition area, and a social science laboratory.

The **Chapter 7** case is "Guides and Visitors: Capturing Stories in Virtual-World and Interactive Web Experiences" by Patricia Wall, Jonas Karlsson, Zahra Langford, Tong Sun, Wei Peng, and Eric Bier (see Figure P.7). This multidisciplinary exploratory ethnographic participant-design case study describes the collaboration between researchers and staff from the Xerox Research Center Webster, Palo Alto Research Center, and the Henry Ford Museum to explore ways to enable museum staff and visitors to interact with artifacts and each other in online environments. Participatory design (also known as co-design) approaches emphasize the inclusion of participants in the design of technology solutions. Building on the premise that stories are an integral part of the museum experience, the team developed prototype technologies to create stories around collection elements (Story Maker) and enable story sharing and collaboration in 3-D immersive environments (Story Garden). In addition to ongoing feedback from the museum staff during early stages of prototype concept development and revisions, several members of the staff participated in evaluations of the prototypes using online technologies.

The Story Maker evaluation took place online via web conferencing and a telephone connection. The Story Garden evaluation took place via OpenSim, an immersive virtual world environment. Open-ended interviews were conducted in each of the evaluations. Participants provided feedback on the usability and applicability of the applications in museum contexts. They made suggestions for improvements to the prototypes and identified opportunities for how the prototypes could be used in museum and educational contexts.

The **Chapter 8** case is "Transitioning from F2F to Online Instruction: Putting the Action Into Online Research" by Wendy L. Kraglund-Gauthier (see Figure P.8). To pursue research interests in education, this action research study used data collected through

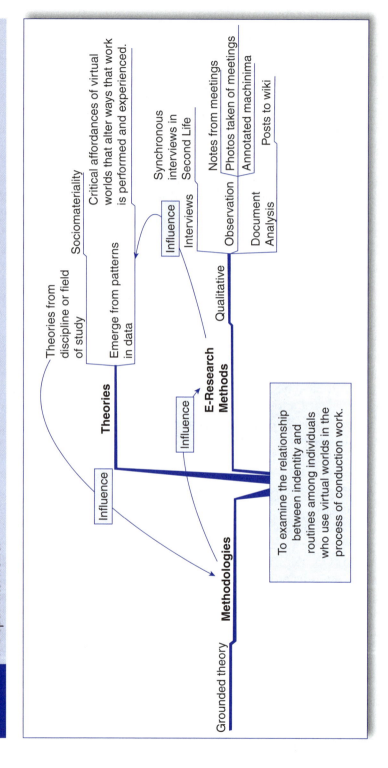

Figure P.6 Research map for "Learning to Work In-World: Conducting Qualitative Research in Virtual Worlds Using In-Depth Interviews."

Figure P.7 Research map for "Guides and Visitors: Capturing Stories in Virtual-World and Interactive Web Experiences."

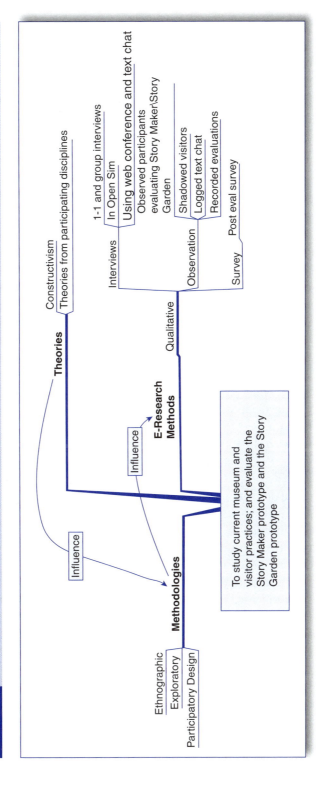

text-based and verbal online interviews conducted in a web meeting space. Data were also collected through observations and surveys. The purpose of the study was to gain an understanding of perspectives and identify teaching styles in relation to the transition Master of Education (MA Ed) professors make from a traditional face-to-face classroom to an online environment that incorporates synchronous and asynchronous teaching tools. In addition to uncovering answers to the research questions, this action research project also moved participants further along their learning journey toward creating community in their virtual Elluminate MA Ed classrooms.

The **Chapter 9** case is "Integrated Interdisciplinary Online Interviews in Science and Health: The Climate and Health Literacy Project" by Lynn Wilson (see Figure P.9). To pursue interdisciplinary research interests in climate science and health literacy, this grounded theory and phenomenological research study used data collected through text-based and verbal online interviews conducted in a web meeting space, via desktop videoconferencing, and through e-mail. Research findings of this ongoing study identify areas of climate information that are of special interest to health professionals across the globe.

The **Chapter 10** case is "Implementing Technology in Blended Learning Courses" by Nellie Deutsch (see Figure P.10). To pursue research interests in education, this phenomenological research study used data collected through verbal online interviews conducted with desktop videoconferencing. Instructors from seven countries participated in this study. The study's purpose was to learn how instructors felt about using technology to complement face-to-face instruction, and what instructional techniques they used to support their students' efforts to bridge the face-to-face live classroom and online learning.

The **Chapter 11** case is "Online Asynchronous and Face-to-Face Interviewing: Comparing Methods for Exploring Women's Experiences of Breastfeeding Long Term" by Sally Dowling (see Figure P.11). To pursue research interests in public health, this grounded theory ethnographic research study used data collected through face-to-face and e-mailed interviews. The purpose of the study was to gain an understanding of the experience of women who continue to breastfeed after most around them have stopped. Findings uncovered influences, such as the attitudes of others, including health care professionals, as well as strategies women used to feel confident about their parenting choices.

Figure P.8 Research map for "Transitioning From F2F to Online Instruction: Putting the Action Into Online Research."

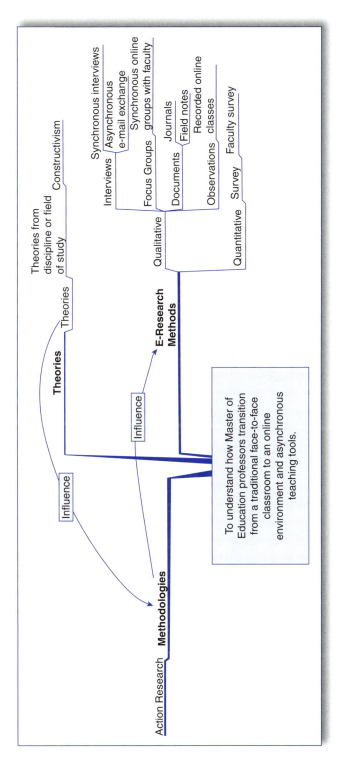

Figure P.9 Research map for "Integrated Interdisciplinary Online Interviews in Science and Health: The Climate and Health Literacy Project"

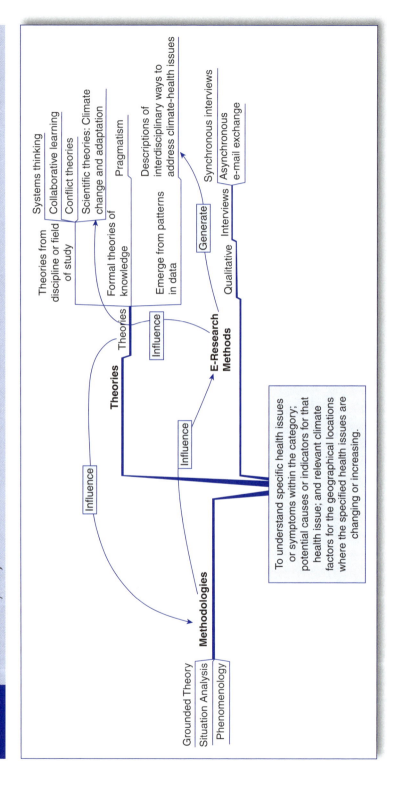

Theories from
discipline or field
of study

Influence

Theories — Theories

Contructivism

Experiential learning

Influence

**E-Research
Methods**

Qualitative

Interviews — Synchronous interviews

Demogaphic and
Questionnaire — background info

Influence

Methodologies

Phenomenological

To explore the experiences
instructors had implementing
technology in blended learning
courses in campus-based
institutions of higher education.

Figure P.11 Research map for "Online Asynchronous and Face-to-Face Interviewing: Comparing Methods for Exploring Women's Experiences of Breastfeeding Long Term."

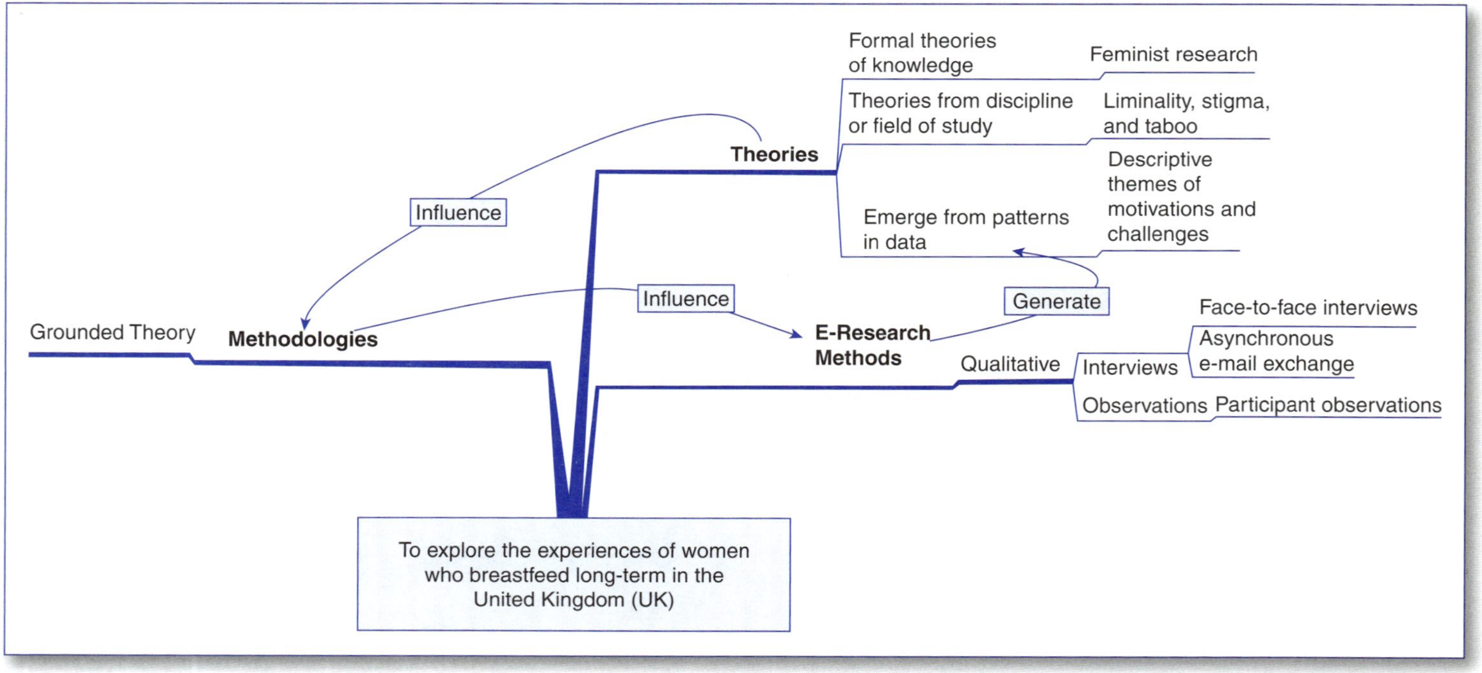

More Resources

See the Appendix and Study Site for additional resources.

IN THE APPENDIX

 An e-interview glossary, suggested resources, and software list are included in the book's Appendix. Throughout the book, this icon will periodically appear to remind you to check the resources you can find in the Appendix.

ON THE STUDY SITE

 Ancillary materials related to the topics of the book are available on the book's companion website. Throughout the book, this icon will periodically appear to remind you to check the resources you can find on the Study Site.

MATERIALS ON THE STUDY SITE

The companion website for the book includes the following types of bonus materials for educators, researchers, doctoral or thesis advisers, and reviewers:

Sample course syllabi. These syllabi for master's- and doctoral-level courses can be used in full for a complete course. Or, units or activities can be drawn from the syllabus to enhance an existing course.

Assignment ideas. Assignments and activities for use in courses, or as research exercises, are available. In addition to assignments on broad themes encompassed by this book and cross-case analyses, case-by-case assignments will encourage discussion and dialogue about each respective study and research approach.

More about the contributors. Links to other published work or materials by contributing researchers.

E-Interview Research Framework Review Guidelines. Practical ideas for guiding student e-researchers; key questions and checklists to use when applying the E-Interview Research Framework.

Research is inquiry in the service of knowledge creation. At this time we see changes in how we seek, find, understand, and use information in everyday, professional as well as academic areas of life. Online researchers have the opportunity to use emerging intellectual and technological approaches to model processes of inquiry and global connection and to discover new insights. I hope this book will inspire you to ask hard questions and to look for answers in whatever corner of the globe where they can be found.

Janet Salmons
Boulder, Colorado

About the Editor

Janet Salmons has served on the graduate faculty of the Capella University School of Business and Technology since 1999. She develops and teaches courses in leadership and team leadership, offers faculty development, serves as dissertation mentor for doctoral learners, and as doctoral Colloquium and Dissertation Writer's Retreat faculty. She is a scholar-practitioner and consultant through her company, Vision2Lead, Inc.

Recent publications include *Online Interviews in Real Time* (2010), and she edited the *Handbook of Research on Electronic Collaboration and Organizational Synergy* with Lynn Wilson (2009). This collection contains 50 peer-reviewed chapters from researchers from 20 countries and diverse disciplines. She has contributed chapters to books, including *Lexicon of Online and Distance Education* (2010), the *Encyclopedia of Information Technology Curriculum Integration* (2007), and *Student Plagiarism in an Online World: Problems and Solutions* (2007). Dr. Salmons is a frequent presenter for face-to-face, online, and virtual-world seminars and conferences.

Dr. Salmons completed her doctorate in interdisciplinary studies at the Union Institute and University with research in online collaboration in leadership education. She earned an MA in social policy studies from Empire State College, State University of New York, and a BS in adult education from Cornell University's College of Human Ecology.

About the Contributors

Eric Bier is a principal scientist in the Knowledge, Language and Interaction area at the Palo Alto Research Center. He is interested in finding new ways to help people get more value from documents and document collections. In his research, he explores software systems that augment the capabilities of people by taking advantage of document content analysis and metadata. Eric has a PhD in computer graphics from the University of California, Berkeley, and master's and bachelor's degrees in computer science from MIT.

Sally Bishai knows more about collectivism, communication, and cultural conflict than she'd care to admit! Born into a family of highly educated, freedom-seeking immigrants from Egypt, she promptly learned the differences between the customs and communication styles in their homeland (which she has been fortunate to visit every year) and their host-land (which was situated in the southern United States). These differences—and the awareness thereof—have informed every aspect of her personal and professional life.

She has written several books, including *Mid-East Meets West: On Being and Becoming a Modern Arab American* and *Date like An Egyptian: The Egyptian American's Guide to Finding a Mate ... or Date.*

Bishai earned her PhD in communication (speech, nonverbal, and intercultural) at Florida State University, where she also focused upon Middle Eastern studies and earned a graduate certificate in digital film production. Other degrees include an MA in communication arts and a BS in psychology. Her next book—*Collectivism, Communication, and Cultural Conflict*—is based upon her doctoral and postdoctoral research on the dialogical acculturation of Egyptians in the diaspora.

Mike Butman, in his role as chief information officer for The Henry Ford Museum, is responsible for the strategic planning, development, and implementation of all technological initiatives to support the institution with emphasis on business information systems including ticketing and accounting, The Henry Ford's website, data center operations, exhibits technology, and desktop technology. During his tenure with The Henry Ford, Butman has successfully reengineered its high-speed Ethernet network to be deployed across multiple buildings in a campuswide environment. He also spearheaded the upgrade of the institution's website and streamlined its ticketing, fund-raising, human resources, retail, food services, and financial data systems.

Dr. Jon Cabiria is currently one of only a small number of people worldwide who holds a doctorate degree in media psychology, and he is on the leading edge of this increasingly important field. Dr. Cabiria's interests and research include online social sites, virtual worlds, and augmented reality technologies, where he specializes in the intersection of psychology and media as they relate to identity exploration and development. He is also a media psychology consultant and public speaker, traveling worldwide to present on topics about the positive benefits of online social engagement, online education, and augmented reality psychology. Dr. Cabiria teaches in the media psychology master's program for Walden University, and in the Media Psychology and Social Change program for Fielding Graduate Institute, where he developed the popular course "Identity in the Virtual Age." He currently serves as a board member for Division 46 (Media Psychology) of the American Psychological Association, and chairs their Website Development Committee and their News Media, Public Education, and Public Policy Committee.

Allison Deegan received an EdD in educational leadership from California State University, Long Beach (CSULB). She also holds an MPA from the Graduate Center for Public Policy and Administration at CSULB, and a BS in marketing from Syracuse University. She is an administrative manager for the Los Angeles County Office of Education, the nation's largest regional educational agency. In addition, she is a founding member and serves as associate director of WriteGirl (www.WriteGirl.org), a Los Angeles-based creative writing and mentoring program for teen girls that publishes award-winning anthologies of its members' work, which are sold nationwide. WriteGirl served as the site of the research described in Chapter 3 of this volume. Now in its 10th year of serving at-risk girls, WriteGirl was recently named 2010–2011 California Non-Profit of the Year by Governor Arnold Schwarzenegger and First Lady Maria Shriver.

Dr. Nellie Deutsch is a Canadian English teacher, founder of Integrating Technology for Active Lifelong Learning (IT4ALL), a nonprofit organization that provides free professional development workshops for educators around the world. She designs and facilitates online workshops for Moodle for Teachers (M4T), which organizes, presents, and moderates online conferences and e-learning classes.

Dr. Deutsch has an MA in education specializing in curriculum and technology from University of Phoenix (2005) online. Her master's research involved an action research project on ESL/EFL students' lack of skills to cope with reading comprehension tests. She has a doctorate of education in educational leadership specializing in curriculum and instruction from the University of Phoenix. For her dissertation, she researched instructor experiences in implementing technology in blended learning courses in higher education in seven countries.

Dr. Deutsch writes, reviews, edits journals, and presents at conferences. She presented in Boston at the International Leadership Association (ILA) in October 2010 and is preparing to lead a panel on using technology for education at the upcoming ILA conference in London in 2011. Dr. Deutsch has organized the annual CO11 free webinar since 2009.

Sally Dowling, in her role as a senior lecturer in the Department of Nursing and Midwifery at the University of the West of England (UWE), Bristol, UK, teaches sociology, psychology, research methods, and evidence-based practice for the adult nursing program and the master's in public health. Trained as a mental health nurse and as a public health specialist, she has worked in various roles in the National Health Service (NHS) for a total of 21 years. She has master's degrees in women's studies and public health and became a member of the faculty of public health in 2006.

Her doctoral research examined the experiences of women who breastfeed "long term." Her research interests include looking at different aspects of experiences of breastfeeding, including breastfeeding in public (see Dowling, S., Naidoo, J., & Pontin, D. [in press]. Breastfeeding in public: Women's bodies, women's milk. In P. L. Smith, B. Hausman, & M. Labbok (Eds.), *Beyond health, beyond choice: Breastfeeding constraints and realities.* New Brunswick, NJ: Rutgers University Press). Dowling is also interested in exploring the use of different methods in qualitative research to understand more about experiences of breastfeeding, particularly after her experience of using online interviews in her doctoral research.

She has spoken at a number of national and international research conferences about aspects of her work, including breastfeeding and feminism (2010 and 2011) at the University of North Carolina (Greensboro and Chapel Hill) and the British Sociological Association (2010 and 2011, in Glasgow and London). Presentations have addressed both topic-related and methodological issues.

Suzanne Fischer, in her role as curator of technology at The Henry Ford Museum, collects, researches, interprets, and provides access to the artifacts of communication technology, including printing presses, telegraphs, telephones, televisions, office equipment, and computers, as well as medical, health and scientific equipment. She develops content for exhibits and web products and connects visitors, staff, and scholars to The Henry Ford's exceptional collections. She also serves as an institutional advocate for digital projects. She has a PhD in the history of science and technology from the University of Minnesota.

Jonas Karlsson is a senior researcher at the Xerox Research Center Webster. His primary research interest is the application of immersive virtual worlds for collaboration, simulation, and visualization. Jonas has a PhD in computer science from the University of Rochester, and a BS in computer science from Stanford University.

Lisa Korzetz is the registrar at The Henry Ford Museum in Dearborn, Michigan. She has a BA in history from Wayne State University and has more than 24 years of experience in the museum field. She is one of the project coordinators for the Document Interactions Project, a collaboration between Xerox Research and The Henry Ford.

Wendy L. Kraglund-Gauthier is the instructional designer for Saint Francis Xavier University's (StFX) Continuing and Distance Education Department and a part-time instructor for its Faculty of Education, in Antigonish, Nova Scotia, Canada. In this role, Kraglund-Gauthier works collaboratively with faculty of undergraduate and graduate courses as they design engaging, student-centered materials for online delivery. Central to her work is achieving and facilitating sound teaching pedagogy and authentic means of assessment and evaluation of online learning.

Kraglund-Gauthier holds a bachelor of arts, a bachelor of education, and a master's in adult education from StFX and a doctorate from the University of South Australia. An award-winning researcher, her doctoral work was a mixed-methods exploration of the ways teachers—who are skilled in face-to-face pedagogy and practice—transition to online modes of teaching and learning. She was awarded a multiyear Social Sciences and Humanities Research Council of Canada (SSHRC) doctoral fellowship for this work, as well as a graduate research stipend from the Canadian Network for Innovations in Education (CNIE).

Kraglund-Gauthier's ongoing research and publications include explorations into ways technology can be used in virtual classrooms to promote collaborative, safe learning for students of differing levels of age and ability. She is also interested in the impacts online technologies have on issues of privacy and on the ethical processes of conducting research online. In addition, as an advocate of the validity of online modalities, Kraglund-Gauthier fosters learning partnerships that have contributed to the construction and dissemination of information between institutions and organizations throughout Canada.

Zahra Langford is an interaction designer in the Computing and Information Services Lab at the Xerox Research Center Webster. She helps connect innovation to people through user research, user interface design, and usability evaluation. Her background in interface, graphic, web, and multimedia design give her the skills to architect intuitive and creative ways for users to interact with Xerox technology. Langford received her master of science in information with a specialization in human–computer interaction from the University of Michigan. She has a bachelor of arts in theater arts from Santa Clara University. Outside of her design career, Langford owns a small business called Hedonist Artisan Chocolates (www.hedonistchocolates.com) with her partner Jennifer in Rochester, New York.

Christian W. Øverland, as vice president of collections and experience design for The Henry Ford Museum, is responsible for leading and managing the strategic planning, national positioning, and visitor experiences both virtual and on-site. In addition, he oversees all historical research, education programs, and experience design and is responsible for the maintenance and growth of the institution's collections. His work focuses on creating quality visitor experiences and building staff excellence, including developing and sustaining a strategic direction for the museum and leading the implementation of annual product and marketing plans. He has also built and maintained a strong vision and common agenda for the core business of the organization, working closely with The Henry Ford's president and Institutional Advancement Team to manage external partnerships and raise funds toward achievement of the institution's goals.

CASES IN ONLINE INTERVIEW RESEARCH

Wei Peng received a BS in computer science from Xi'an Polytechnic University, Xi'an, China, in 2002 and a PhD in computer science from Florida International University, Miami, in 2008. She is currently a member of the research and technical staff at the Xerox Innovation Group of Xerox Corporation, Rochester, New York. Her primary research interests are data mining, information retrieval, and machine learning.

Ann Randall holds MS and EdS degrees from the University of Idaho, where she is earning a PhD in education, with an emphasis in adult and organizational learning. She is a member of the Golden Key Honor Society.

Currently, she is the distance education faculty development coordinator at Boise State University. Her primary achievement there has been to collaborate with the Department of Academic Technologies to establish and develop the eLearning Quality Instruction Program (eQIP), a comprehensive program to train faculty in online teaching pedagogy, as well as to facilitate the development and review of online courses. She currently administers and co-facilitates the program, which, since 2006, has trained more than 100 faculty, developed more than 50 courses, and reviewed 40 course sites based on the Quality Matters rubric.

In addition to her distance education responsibilities, Randall is an affiliate professor in the College of Graduate Studies, where she teaches an online course for the Department of Educational Technology, called "Teaching Adult Learners Online." She has been a presenter at annual conferences of the WICHE Cooperative for Educational Technologies (WCET). She is a charter member of Applied Research in Virtual Environments and Learning (ARVEL), the special interest group in the American Education Research Association (AERA) that focuses on virtual environments.

Prior to working for Boise State, Randall spent 10 years in government regulation and training for the State of Oregon. She also is a certified Quality Matters reviewer and has 11 years experience in standards-compliant web design and coding.

Jonathon Richter's professional interests occupy a spectrum of activity including the creation of future-focused, media-rich learning environments that promote the engagement, persistence, and achievement of diverse learners through the customization and differentiation of media and instruction, and the development of 21st Century Digital Learning and Scholarship capacities and the contexts for organizational and team leaders to enable teachers, students, and learning communities to effectively navigate profound cultural changes corresponding to radically different or transforming learning environments. Richter is a research associate for the University of Oregon's Center for Advanced Technology in Education (CATE) and the director for the Center for Learning in Virtual Environments (CLIVE), where he is cofounder and current chair of the Applied Research in Virtual Environments for Learning (ARVEL) Special Interest Group of the American Educational Research Association (AERA) as well as founder and current leader of the MultiMedia Educational Resources for Learning and Online Teaching (MERLOT) Virtual Environments Taskforce.

Taryn Stanko is an assistant professor of management at the University of Oregon's Lundquist College of Business. Stanko received her PhD from the University of California, Irvine, and an MBA from New York University's Stern School of Business. Her research interests revolve around the use of technology in organizations and the role it plays in virtual work, the management of multiple identities, and collaboration in organizations, and she has been published in outlets such as *Organization Science.* One of Stanko's recently published works, along with Cristina Gibson and other coauthors, focuses on the changing nature of work that communication technology has triggered through the greater use of virtual work arrangements and the impact that working virtually has on psychological states affecting motivation. Her more recent work explores the use of communication technology in the Navy and the implications that more permeable organizational boundaries have for individual identity. Stanko also has ongoing research exploring the nature of work routines and work identity in three-dimensional work environments. Her research has been supported by the National Science Foundation; University of California, Irvine's Center for Organizational Research and Center for Research on Information Technology in Organizations; and the American Association of University Women.

Dr. Tong Sun is a principal scientist at Xerox Research Center Webster. Her research interests include large-scale semantic social network analysis, collaborative document interactions, business intelligence and knowledge management, and enterprise service integration architecture. She has led several cutting-edge and cross-disciplinary research projects and helped to develop the long-term strategic visions and research portfolios in Xerox research labs. During her tenure at Xerox, Sun authored and coauthored more than 20 scientific papers in prestigious conferences and journals and has 4 U.S. patents with 10 more pending. She has also actively served as industry liaison chair, special session chair, guest journal editor, and program committee member at various international conferences. She is a member of the IEEE Computer Society. Sun received her PhD in distributed computing and parallel processing from the University of Rhode Island, and BS and MS degrees in electrical and computer engineering from Huazhong University of Science and Technology in China.

Patricia Wall is a principal scientist and manager of the Work Practice and Technology area in the Computing and Information Services Lab at the Xerox Research Center Webster. She conducts socio-technical studies of customer work to inform the design of new technologies, practices, and services. Her research interests include participatory design-based technology development, tools to support codevelopment, and visual representations of user work practices. She has conducted ethnographic studies in several domains, including K–12 and higher education, digital libraries, custom publishing, health care, and mobile work. She has a bachelor's degree in psychology from the State University of New York, and a master's in psychology and human factors from North Carolina State University.

Lynn Wilson is executive director for SeaTrust Institute, a scientific and educational nonprofit organization in the Pacific Northwest. She is senior analyst for the consulting firm OSSIA, offering research, conflict management, and strategic and policy guidance for over 25 years. Her work appears in books, lectures, workshops, global and regional conferences, and in academic, technical, and trade publications. Recent publications include *Environmental Issues, Policy and Management Collaboration Toolbox* (2011), book chapters in *E-Research Collaboration: Frameworks, Tools and Techniques,* (2010), and *Handbook of Research on Electronic Collaboration and Organizational Synergy* (2009), which she edited with Janet Salmons. Current research as codirector of the Coalition on Health and the Environment: Climate Change Initiative, in collaboration with global climate and health professionals, will be presented through the United Nations climate change negotiations process throughout 2011; both the research data and the process of introducing it within the climate regime will inform the forthcoming book, *Climate and Health Literacy: A Guide to Understanding and Action.*

Dr. Wilson develops and delivers face-to-face and online courses related to science and policy, sustainability, and collaboration and teaches environmental policy graduate courses in the School of Legal Studies at Kaplan University. As director of the 2010 Consortium on Climate Change and Population Health, she leads a 2-year project for research and publications on climate and human health concerns. She serves on advisory and review boards for policy, education, science, and the environment and is Head of Delegation from SeaTrust Institute, NGO Focal Point to Conference of Parties/ UNFCCC to the United Nations Climate Change Conferences in Copenhagen, Denmark, 2009; Cancun, Mexico, 2010; and Durban, South Africa, 2011.

Praise for *Cases in Online Interview Research*

This is foundational and state-of-the-art for online interviewing methods and technologies. I am overwhelmingly impressed by the organization of this text. By including 10 actual studies, we not only learn about the design and organization of the research questions which animate the beginnings of the research project, but we learn what really happened, the problems and difficulties actually encountered (these are inevitable in all research), and how these were handled. The editor provides a common schematic diagram for each chapter. This is really an innovative, ground-breaking organizational format for qualitative methods.

John M. Johnson, *Arizona State University*

I haven't seen any other attempts to present this kind of approach. The case studies are interesting, but it is the editor's commentary and theoretic schema that I find the most useful. I especially like the discussion about the IRB issues.

Judith Sylvester, *Louisiana State University*

The editor has made meticulous efforts to place the various chapters within a useful grid of interpretation, and this will aid readers' understanding and use of the material. It is a very up to date presentation of new technologies that will become increasingly important in all aspects of social research.

S.E. Bennett, *Carleton University*

The information presented reflects the current thinking in the field with regard to alternative interviewing techniques in a technologically driven society.

Nataliya V. Ivankova, *University of Alabama at Birmingham*

The breadth of disciplines and technologies included are key strengths of this book. The editor has done a great job of including cases that represent the full range of e-interviewing sites, and the cases highlight the many issues that arise when using new technologies to conduct qualitative research. In addition, the book is also strong in showcasing how qualitative interviewing is used in conjunction with a variety of other methods. The commentary from the editor at the end of each case with the research map is very helpful for comparing across cases.

Kris M. Markman, *University of Memphis*

First, pick up this book. Second, don't put it down. These case studies provide a wealth of lived experience about the process of doing research in online contexts. Ostensibly focused on online interviewing, the cases reveal much more than a simple set of techniques or strategies and move far beyond interviewing.

Annette N. Markham, *Aarhus University*

Acknowledgments

I would like to acknowledge the inspiration offered by my Capella University School of Business Technology doctoral students and mentees, aspiring researchers who aim to learn about a globally connected world, using globally connected tools.

Cases in Online Interview Research was a collaborative project, with valuable contributions from all of the innovative researchers whose cases appear in this book. This was not the kind of project that allowed them to cut and paste from another piece of work—they had to rethink their work to focus specifically on the e-interview part of it. They were also expected to read, think, and write about another case—and they did so, cheerfully. Even with busy schedules few reminders were needed. Thank you for being a part of this book!

I am grateful for the enthusiastic support of Vicki Knight, acquisitions editor, and the whole team at Sage Publications.

The constructive feedback and insightful observations of the reviewers were appreciated; I am sure your comments resulted in a better final manuscript. Thanks to S. E. Bennett, Carleton University; Judith Sylvester, Louisiana State University; Rachel Kraus, Ball State University; Nataliya V. Ivankova, University of Alabama at Birmingham; John M. Johnson, Arizona State University; and Kris M. Markman, University of Memphis. The *E-Interview Research Framework* was improved based on thought-provoking comments from focus group participants: Cliff Butler, Capella University; Tabitha Hart, University of Washington; Kim Grover Haskin, Texas Woman's University; Julie Jones, University of Oklahoma; Michael Kieley, Loyola Marymount University; Laura Markos, Capella University; Shannon M. Oltmann, Indiana University; Lois Scheidt, Indiana University; DeNel Rehberg Sedo, Mount Saint Vincent University; and Jim Spickard, Fielding Institute.

Finally, my work benefits from ongoing conversations with my husband and life partner, Cole Keirsey, who rarely changes the subject even when he has undoubtedly heard more about online interview research than he ever wanted to know.

Designing and Conducting Research With Online Interviews

Janet Salmons

1

A t its heart, research is research—regardless of methodology and methods. All research begins with a burning question, a sense of curiosity, and an openness to discovery. All research is conducted to serve a purpose, answer questions, or prove a hypothesis, and all use some combination of methods to find and analyze whatever information is needed to answer the question. Researchers have devised numerous ways to carry out these steps.

Qualitative interview research is unique because the researcher is the instrument for data collection. Qualitative interview research contrasts with quantitative approaches such as surveys, where a conscious effort is made to insert a validated and (ideally) objective instrument between the researcher and the research participants. Interview research is unique in its reliance on direct, usually immediate, interaction between the researcher and participant. The successful researcher draws on the best of human qualities when conducting an interview: trust, thoughtful questioning and perceptive probing, empathy and reflective listening.

To understand a piece of research and assess its credibility and potential contribution to knowledge in the field, we need to understand the researcher's motivations, purpose, and designs. We need to understand how the study was conducted so we can grasp the implications of its conclusions. If the study was based on data collected through qualitative interviews, we also need to know who the participants were, and why and how they were chosen. We want to grasp the nature of the interaction between researcher and participant that allowed data to be collected or generated.

Studies using data collected through online interviews follow fundamental steps and thinking involved in any research as well as those involved more specifically with qualitative interview research, then add an important dimension—the technology. When the direct interaction between researcher and participant occurs through computer-mediated communications (CMCs), technology is more than a simple transactional medium. The human qualities so important to interview communications are experienced differently; the technology delimits the form of the communication in ways both subtle and obvious.

Some information and communications technologies (ICTs) allow for a full range of visual and verbal exchange. Some ICTs, such as videoconferencing, allow for an interview that closely resembles the natural back-and-forth of face-to-face communication, including verbal and nonverbal signals.

TYPES OF NONVERBAL COMMUNICATION

Types of nonverbal communication include:

- *Chronemic communication* describes the use of pacing and timing of speech and length of silence before response in conversation.
- *Paralinguistic* or *paralanguage communication* describes variations in volume, pitch, and quality of voice.
- *Kinesic communication* includes eye contact and gaze, facial expressions, body movements, gestures, and postures.
- *Proxemic communication* is the use of interpersonal space to communicate attitudes (Gordon, 1980; Guerrero et al., 1999; Kalman, Ravid, Raban, & Rafaeli, 2006).

Nonverbal signals can be noted during an interview, or categorized as part of the transcription process when reviewing a recorded interview.

Other ICTs allow for written text, with limited visual elements such as colored fonts or graphic emoticons. While text-only studies do not allow researchers to observe participants' nonverbal signals, they allow participants with mobile devices to participate in interviews anytime, anywhere. Indeed, participants could converse with the researcher from the field or report live while experiencing an event related to the research phenomenon.

Still other ICTs allow participants to share real or imagined visual artifacts, images, or environments. Web conferencing tools allow researchers and participants to look at or generate visual images. In immersive multi-user visual environments (MUVEs), researchers and participants can navigate the virtual worlds or environments chosen or created by the researcher or the participant. Four main types of synchronous communications technologies are summarized in Figure 1.1. These communications options are further described in Table 1.1.

How do these varied styles of computer-mediated communication impact the quality or perception of the dialogue between researcher and participant? This is a question researchers are beginning to explore as they experiment with the use of ICTs and CMCs in scholarly research interviews. Each study conducted in this way provides us with an instructive exemplar for the opportunities and challenges this method offers contemporary researchers.

Figure 1.1 Four types of synchronous communication (Salmons, 2010).

Text Based	Videoconference or Video Call
• Communicate through typed words, limited use of images through emoticons or exchange of pictures. • Connect on phone, mobile device, or computer.	• Communicate through audio and video. • Connect in videoconference facility, computer, or mobile device.
Synchronous Communication Types for Online Interviews	
Multichannel Meeting	**Immersive 3-D Environment**
• Communicate through audio, video, text, and/or shared applications. • Connect by computer or mobile device.	• Communicate through audio or text, and visual exchange. • Connect by computer or mobile device.

Table 1.1	Communication Options for Preparation, Interviews, and Follow-Ups With Participants (Salmons, 2010)

	Text	Multichannel
Asynchronous Any Time	**E-mail:** Send and receive questions and answers. **Forum:** Post and respond to questions and answers in a secure online threaded discussion area. **Weblog (Blog):** Personal online journal where entries are posted chronologically. Microblogs allow for very short entries. Blogs can be text only or multichannel, with links to images or media. Viewing may be public or limited to a specified group of subscribers or friends. **Wiki:** Multiple authors add, remove, and edit questions and responses about the research phenomena on a user-generated website.	**Podcast or Vodcast:** Ask and answer questions by sending audio or video files. **Video:** Post, view, and respond to video clips. **Visual Exchange:** Post, view, and respond to photographs, charts and diagrams, and visual maps.
Synchronous Real Time	**Text Message:** Send and receive questions on mobile phone or handheld device. **Instant Message or Chat:** Post and respond to questions and answers on computer through a secure online website.	**Voice-Over Internet Protocol (VOIP):** Ask and answer questions using live audio. **Videoconferencing or Video Call:** See interview participants while conversing.

	Text	Multichannel
		Shared Applications:
		View and discuss documents, media, or examples.
		Log in together and use web-based software applications, research tools, or forms.
		Generate responses by writing, drawing, or diagramming ideas on whiteboard or in shared documents.
		Ask and respond to questions through the physical form and identity of an avatar you create to represent yourself.
		Experience immersive events or phenomena.
		View examples or demonstrations.

For the purpose of this book, *online interviews* or *e-interviews* refer to in-depth interviews conducted with CMCs. While any ICT can be used for online interviews, the focus here is on the kinds of communication technologies that enable real-time dialogue between researchers and participants.

Online interviews are used for primary *Internet-mediated research* (IMR), that is, they are used to gather original data via the Internet with the intention of subjecting them to analysis to provide new evidence in relation to a specific research question (Hewson, 2010). This stands in contrast to secondary Internet research, that is, the use of existing documents or information sources found online (Hewson, 2010). Scholarly online interviews are conducted in accordance with ethical research guidelines; verifiable research participants provide informed consent before participating in any interview.

DISSECTING ROLES IN IN-DEPTH INTERVIEWS

In-depth interviews involve interrelationships among the following (Salmons, 2010):

- The *interviewer*, regardless of interview style, is responsible for ethical, respectful inquiry and accurate collection of data relevant to the research purpose and questions. As a *researcher*, the interviewer places the interview exchange within a scholarly context.
- The *interviewee* responds honestly to questions or participates in discussion with the researcher to provide ideas or answers that offer insight into his or her perceptions, understandings, or experiences of personal, social, or organizational dimensions of the subject of the study. Depending on the nature and expectations of the research, they may also be called *subjects, respondents,* or *research participants.*
- The *research purpose* and *questions* serve as the framework and offer focus and boundaries to the interactions between researcher and interviewee.
- The *research environment* provides a context for the study. Depending on the nature of the study, the environment may be significant to the researcher's understanding of the interviewee. Cyberspace is the research milieu for online interviews.

Understanding E-Interview Research

To understand e-interview research, we need to pose many of the same questions we would ask about any study. Additionally, we need to inquire about the influences of the technology on research design, conduct, and ultimately on the study's conclusions and on generalizations the researcher offers. The use of the term *understand* is intentional here to encompass both evaluative and instructional purposes. We may look at an e-interview study as a prototype for an approach we want to use in our own research. We may examine the approach because we want to teach or learn about—or develop—interview research methods. Or, we may need to take an evaluative position and review a research proposal, thesis or dissertation, or article for potential publication. Working from any of these perspectives, we need to know what questions to ask.

EVALUATING QUALITATIVE RESEARCH

A qualitative research "quality" framework (Spencer, Ritchie, Lewis, & Dillon, 2002) was developed by a team from the National Centre for Social Research. Drawing on a review of the literature and existing frameworks, Spencer et al. identified four central principles (p. 7):

- *Contributory* in advancing wider knowledge or understanding about policy, practice, theory or a particular substantive field;
- *Defensible in design* by providing a research strategy that can address the evaluative questions posed;
- *Rigorous in conduct* through the systematic and transparent collection, analysis and interpretation of qualitative data;
- *Credible in claim* through offering well-founded and plausible arguments about the significance of the evidence generated.

This quality framework includes 18 key questions. Spencer et al. (2002) suggest beginning with assessment of the findings, then moving through different stages of the research process (design, sampling, data collection, analysis, and reporting). They suggest ending the appraisal by looking at research conduct (reflexivity and neutrality, ethics and auditability).

When we look at a study based on data collected with online interviews we want to know why and how the researcher made choices about the ICTs used for the interviews, and how the interviews were carried out. How did the participant respond to the process, as well as to the interview questions? Did the e-interviews proceed as planned or were adjustments needed—why or why not? What would another researcher need to know if choosing a similar approach? What types of data were collected, and were the data adequate and appropriate given the purpose of the study? Ultimately, did the data allow the researcher to construct an analysis and generate conclusions that achieved the purpose of the study?

THINKING ABOUT EMERGENT METHODS

Sharlene Nagy Hesse-Biber and Patricia Leavy observe that research methods exist to

service research questions that advance our understanding of the social world or some aspect of it. Therefore, as the social world and

(Continued)

(Continued)

> our understanding of it have progressed, so too has our repertoire of social research methods.... Sometimes the field of emergent methods is fueled not by new paradigmatic perspectives but through technological innovation that pushes on the boundaries of methodology. (Hesse-Biber & Leavy, 2010, pp. 1–2, 7)

Online interview research is an emergent method, so a widely accepted set of review questions does not currently exist. Jaccard and Jacoby suggest that when creating a new theoretical framework or model, a first step may involve "generating ideas about new explanatory constructs and the relationships between them or generating ideas about the mechanisms underlying the phenomena that you are trying to explain" (Jaccard & Jacoby, 2010, p. 39). The E-Interview Research Framework (see Figure 1.2) offers just such steps by

Figure 1.2 The E-Interview Research Framework for understanding e-interview research.

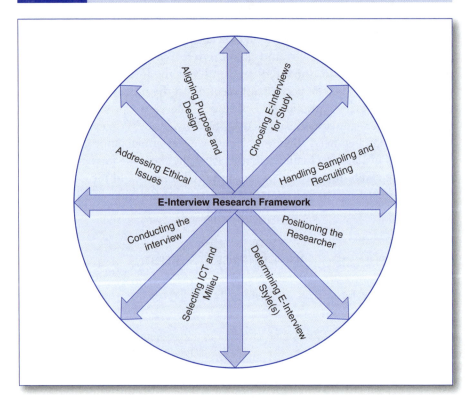

generating ideas and questions about key features of online interviews, relationships between those features, and the underlying mechanisms that make online interviews successful for generating rich, usable data.

The set of model questions proposed here is described as a *multidimensional framework*. The E-Interview Research Framework includes eight interrelated categories of key questions that can help a researcher think through the design of a study that uses data collected with online interviews. It is displayed as a circle to convey the sense that one angle alone will not provide the systems-level view we need to really understand the interrelated mechanisms of online interview research. Taken one by one, the "new" questions suggested here are not in and of themselves significant. But when considered together, they can provide a comprehensive picture of the study at hand, illustrate the context for the online interviews, and provide a springboard for discussion.

Each of the eight categories includes a set of questions and models important to the analysis of a study—whether one is designing original research or analyzing a study proposed or conducted by another researcher. The discussion of these categories begins with "Aligning Purpose and Design." While this may indeed be the first step, the circular nature of the E-Interview Research Framework suggests that once the other categories have been examined it may be necessary to return to the beginning and make sure all pieces of the design fit.

Aligning Purpose and Design

KEY QUESTIONS: ALIGNING PURPOSE & DESIGN

- Are research purpose, theories and epistemologies, methodologies, and methods clearly aligned?
- How will the data collected from e-interviews relate to theories? Does the researcher want to explore, prove, or generate theory?
- Does the researcher offer a compelling rationale for using e-interviews to achieve the research purpose?

Any study is strengthened by coherent discussion of research purpose, theories, methodologies, and methods (see Figure 1.3). By exploring the elements of the research design, we can gain some

Figure 1.3 Diagram of a research design map.

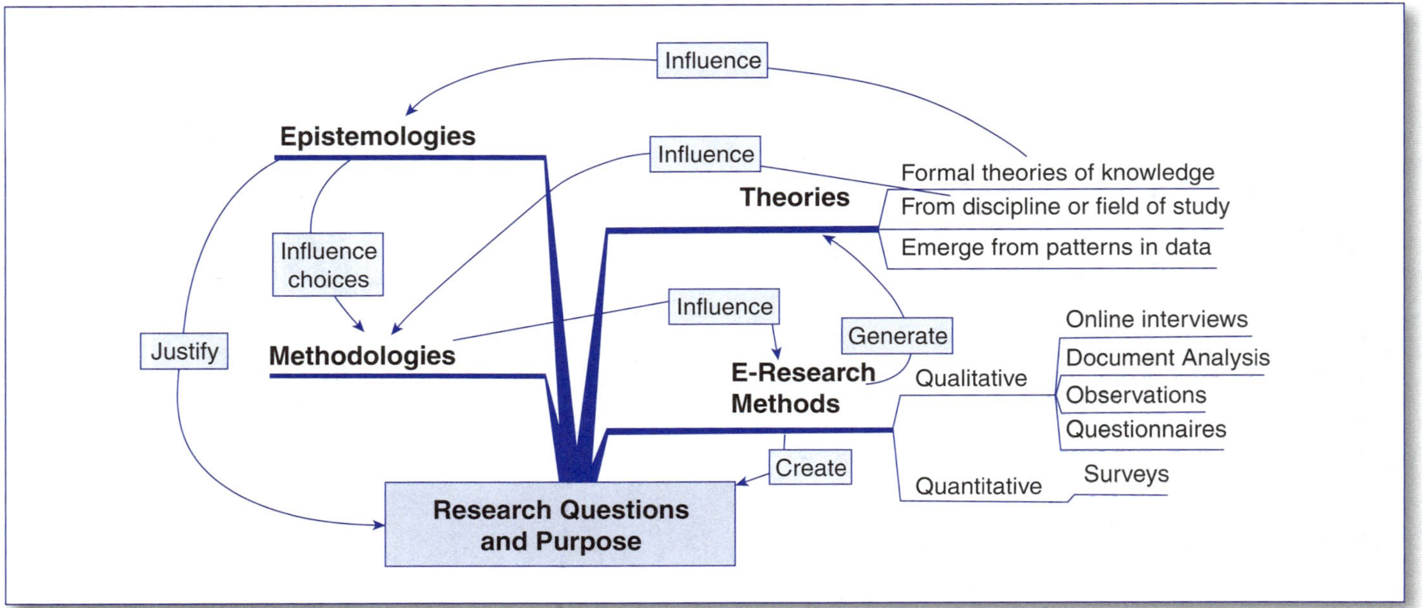

understanding of how the intended use of online data collection methods aligns with the overall purpose and theoretical framework of the study. Importantly, we can learn whether the researcher intends to explore or test extant theories or generate new theory. We can also ascertain whether the researcher is working within, or outside of, disciplinary approaches.

COMPONENTS OF RESEARCH DESIGN

Four interrelated elements of research design—epistemology, theory, methodology, and method are defined for our purposes as follows:

- *Epistemology* refers to the study of the nature of knowledge, or the study of how knowledge is justified;
- *Theory* refers to an explanation that is internally consistent, supportive of other theories, and gives new insights. An important characteristic of theory is that it is predictive.
- *Methodology* refers to the study of, and justification for, the methods used to conduct the research (Gray, 2009). Methodologies emerged from academic disciplines in the social and physical sciences and, although considerable cross-disciplinary exchange occurs, choices generally place the study into a disciplinary context.
- *Method* refers to the practical steps used to conduct the study (Anfara & Mertz, 2006; Carter & Little, 2007).

Understanding the alignment of key research elements—theory, epistemology, methodology, and methods—is important when trying to dissect any research design, and particularly essential for understanding online interview research. When operating online, greater clarity and precision is needed, since the potential for misunderstanding is arguably greater. Researchers and research participants need to know what is expected of them, why, and when. Both need to be sure that when a consent agreement is signed all parties are clear about the purpose of the study, the use of the data—and the parameters of the data collection. As readers or reviewers, we need to know the rationale for using online interview methods to determine whether and how the data collected accomplishes the purpose of the study.

Choosing E-Interviews as a Data Collection Method for the Study

KEY QUESTIONS: CHOOSING E-INTERVIEWS

- Does the researcher provide a compelling reason for using data collected from online interviews? Is the rationale aligned with methodologies, research purpose, and questions?
- Are online interviews chosen to investigate real-world phenomena?
- Are online interviews chosen to investigate online phenomena?

What is the researcher's motivation for conducting the interviews online? Some researchers want to study behaviors or phenomena that take place online by exploring them in the kind of setting where they occur. Patterns of technology use, modes of participation in online communities, or human–computer interaction can best be studied by using ICTs to conduct the interview. In such circumstances, the participant essentially selects the interview technology and the technology itself may be a part of the phenomenon under investigation.

Computer-mediated communication also offers a way to discuss behaviors or phenomena unrelated to the Internet that occur offline. Technology is not part of the phenomenon under investigation. The researcher may decide to conduct interviews online because it is a convenient way to meet participants, because participants are geographically dispersed, or because they want to collect visual data not possible with a telephone interview. Technology may be selected by the researcher based on preferred kinds of data (visual, verbal, text) or by the participant based on familiarity, availability, or access.

Additional questions should be asked about the study, depending on the motivation for choosing e-interviews (see Figure 1.4).

In either use of online interviews—to study on- or offline behaviors—the researcher may prioritize intentions of the study and/or the needs of participants when making choices about whether to interview online and what ICT(s) to use. For example, a researcher who wants to use videoconferencing tools for the interview to enable both verbal and nonverbal communication could choose to screen out participants unwilling or unable to participate in a videoconference. Alternatively, the researcher could agree to meet the participant using a technology the researcher must learn to use, because the value of this participant's data outweighs the extra effort required for the researcher.

In addition to interviewing participants, the researcher may collect other qualitative or quantitative data through online observation

Figure 1.4   Additional questions about the choice of online interviews.

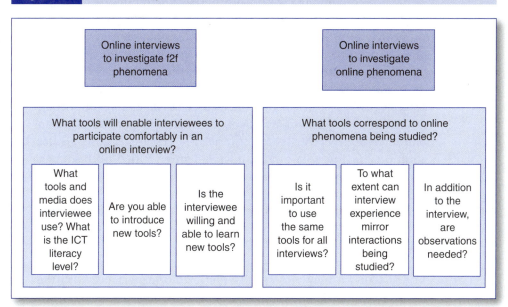

or participant observation, questionnaires, or surveys. If so, does the researcher explain how this data will be collected and how it will complement data collected from interviews?

By understanding the motivations and considerations for the choice of ICT, we can better grasp how the online interview data collection process and the types of data used align with other elements of the research design.

Handling Sampling and Recruiting

KEY QUESTIONS: HANDLING SAMPLING & RECRUITING

- What sampling approaches are appropriate given the purpose of the study and e-interview approach?
- How will the researcher assess whether the target population has access to the interview technology, and the capability and willingness to use it as a research participant?
- How can the researcher locate credible research participants? How will the researcher verify the identity and age (or other relevant criteria) of research participants recruited online?
- How will online recruitment be carried out?

Qualitative researchers often use what is broadly defined as purposive or purposeful sampling when selecting people to interview because the sample is intentionally selected according to the purpose of the study. The online interview researcher customizes purposive sampling depending on the motivations for conducting the interviews online, the selected ICT, and the target study population. Criterion sampling allows the researcher to specify the characteristics that serve as the basis for selection of research participants—important given the additional characteristics needed for a participant in an online interview. By stating criteria, the researcher also creates additional factors that can be independently verified from sources other than the research participant's own statements (Salmons, 2010, p. 106).

For researchers using online interviews to collect data, sampling criteria will to some extent include a reference to technology access and/or the specific ICT being used for the interview. Will participants need webcams? Headsets or microphones for using VOIP? Criteria may also specify the level of experience with the Internet-related phenomenon or behavior under investigation or the technology skills someone would need to participate in the interview.

Two options for locating credible research participants online are *nomination* and *existing sample frames.* The first relies on verification of identity by another person who knows the potential participant; the second relies on verification by membership in a group, organization, or reliable administrative list.

SAMPLE FRAMES IN ONLINE INTERVIEW RESEARCH (SALMONS, 2010)

Fundamental to the recruitment strategy is the choice of a sample frame. The term *sample frame* refers to a list or grouping of people from which the sample is selected.

There are two broad types of frames:

- *Existing Sample Frames.* Existing frames usually consist of records previously constructed for administrative purposes. They could include membership lists for organizations or associations or lists of students or program participants (Ritchie, Lewis, & Elam, 2003; Wilmot, 2008). In mixed methods studies where a quantitative research instrument is administered as the first step, the survey sample can be used as a frame from which interview participants are selected for the qualitative stage of the study.

- *Constructed or Generated Sample Frames.* Where an existing frame or list is not available, researchers may have to create their own. In some cases, researchers can construct a frame from partially adequate or incomplete existing frames. Another way to construct a frame is by working through organizations that provide services to or represent a population of potential participants. Researchers can generate sample frames by approaching people in a particular organization, location, setting, or meeting. This method is best used to identify people who are willing to consider taking part in the study, seeking their permission to contact them privately to discuss the study in detail (Ritchie et al., 2003).

By understanding the sampling and recruiting plans, we can learn more about the individuals who will contribute data and determine whether choices made by the researcher best serve the purpose of the study.

Positioning the Researcher

KEY QUESTIONS: POSITIONING THE RESEARCHER

- Is the researcher positioned as an insider, as one of the actors in the case? Is the researcher looking at *emic* issues, revealed by actors in the case (Stake, 1995)?
- Is the researcher positioned as an outsider who brings questions in from outside the case, looking at *etic* issues (Stake, 1995)?
- Can the researcher's role be described as miner, traveler (Kvale, 2007; Kvale & Brinkman, 2009), or gardener (Salmons, 2010)?

At this point, we should understand the overall purpose and design of the research, the desired study population, and the researcher's motivation for conducting the study online. Now we are ready to explore whether the researcher's motivations are drawn from a need or gap identified by the researcher or whether the motivation originates in a personal connection to the phenomenon of research interest. The distinction between insider versus outsider is not unique to online interview research. It is, however, a useful data point as we build our understanding of the design and conduct of a study. The position of the researcher can also be described in relationship to the data and attitude toward the process of collection.

RESEARCHERS AS INSIDERS OR OUTSIDERS

Linguist and anthropologist Kenneth Pike originated the terms *etic* and *emic* to describe the difference between native speakers' and outside researchers' ways of understanding languages (Franklin, 1996). Researchers from diverse disciplines have interpreted these concepts; Robert Stake (1995) applies them to case study research by describing etic issues as those that are the issues of the researcher or the larger research community outside the case and emic as the issues that emerge from the actors, the insiders within the case. VanDeVen describes the outside researcher as a "detached, impartial onlooker who gathers data" whereas an inside researcher is a "participant immersed in the actions and experiences within the system being studied" (VanDeVen, 2007, pp. 269–270).

Hesse-Biber and Leavy (2010) raise the insider/outsider question in the context of emergent methods and willingness to question disciplinary research techniques, ideas, concepts, and methods:

> How will I negotiate my research position—as an "insider," an "outsider," or both? If I conduct my research as an "outsider," will I be overly identifying with the other's perspective? If I conduct my research as an "insider," will I lose my ability to challenge my disciplinary perspective? (p. 4)

Hesse-Biber and Leavy (2010) also note that "to successfully negotiate insider and outsider status requires a highly reflexive process" (p. 4) since the researcher must balance the value of inserting his or her own insights about the phenomenon with the risk of biasing the study. In an e-interview situation, particularly where the participants were recruited online and are unknown to the researcher in any face-to-face context, the researcher's insider role may overpower the interview or overly influence the direction of the interview. On the other hand, the understanding gained from personal experience with the research phenomenon could make it easier to discuss sensitive issues.

While discussing a very different type of research—field research—Rosalind Edwards raises the issue of "social capital" that may apply to researchers entering an online "field."

> In order to carry out fieldwork especially, but also other aspects of the research process, researchers often need to cultivate and deploy social capital. . . . Social capital is said to work because it involves mutual collaboration and the expectation of reciprocity. . . . People do things for each other in the expectation and trust that, at some time, these actions will be repaid. This is an iterative view of the generation and maintenance of social capital. (Edwards, 2004, p. 4)

Just as insiders can use social capital and social/professional networks to gain entry into rural or ethnic communities and find people willing to participate in interviews, insiders may have an easier entrée into online communities. Within a community, insider status can help to build trust or rapport based on shared experiences or values. Sometimes the researcher may gain the advantages of an insider by partnering with an "insider assistant," a gatekeeper to the community who can negotiate access to the community and assist in recruiting participants. "If the request is coming through a known and trusted colleague, people are more likely to give it proper consideration than if it had arrived from a stranger, where it might be seen as just another form of junk mail (this may be especially likely to happen with 'cold' requests received via email" (King & Horrocks, 2010, p. 32). Insider assistants can also help by establishing credibility for the study and thereby encouraging honesty and commitment on the part of interviewees.

Some methodologies intrinsically rely on researcher as *insider*, such as participant observation or action research, or *outsider*, such as observation or document analysis. Interview research can be conducted from a full range of positions. Some insiders contribute data in the form of reflective journal entries or field notes to complement data collected from participants.

VanDeVen (2007) points out the complementarity of the knowledge gained from insider/outsider research, since the insider perspective may allow the researcher to provide a concrete grounding in the research problem in a particular context or situation. Research from an outside perspective, he notes, can provide empirical evidence of the scope of the problem.

I suggest that while the etic/outsider or emic/insider positions seem to be either/or, in many situations the researcher may have inside knowledge or experience without conducting the study from an exclusively emic stance. Researchers may be inspired to study a topic because they understand the issue or need from a personal, as well as a scholarly perspective. By using what phenomenological researchers call *bracketing* or *epoche*, researchers can take an etic perspective by intentionally clearing their minds of preconceived notions and listening without prejudgment to each respective research participant's responses (Moustakas, 1994).

In online research, some degree of balance between etic and emic perspectives may be needed. At least some knowledge of the situation, culture, and type of experience being studied may help the researcher to develop rapport and trust with the virtual research participant. Insider status may help the researcher gain access to an online environment or community. At the same time, the researcher can bring broader understandings of the research problem into the study and devise thought-provoking or challenging interview questions. Whether inside, outside, or somewhere in the middle, the researcher needs to clearly state a position and provide a rationale for how that position serves the study (see Figure 1.5).

METAPHORICAL DESCRIPTIONS OF THE RESEARCHER'S POSITION

Another way to look at the relationship of the researcher to the study and the participants is through the metaphorical stances of the miner, traveler (Kvale, 2007; Kvale & Brinkman, 2009), or gardener (Salmons, 2010) (see Figure 1.6). The researcher who digs out facts and feelings from research subjects is characterized as a *miner*. The

Figure 1.5   Position of the researcher.

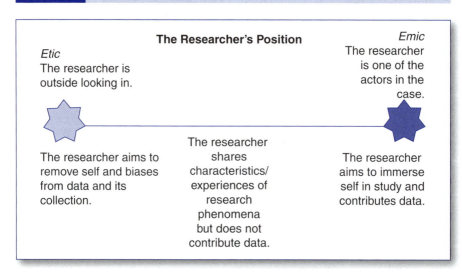

Figure 1.6   Role of the researcher.

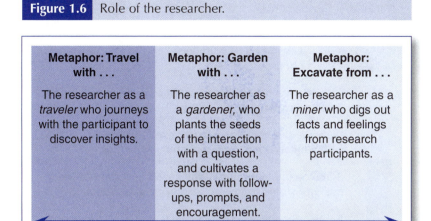

Metaphor: Travel with . . .	Metaphor: Garden with . . .	Metaphor: Excavate from . . .
The researcher as a *traveler* who journeys with the participant to discover insights.	The researcher as a *gardener,* who plants the seeds of the interaction with a question, and cultivates a response with follow-ups, prompts, and encouragement.	The researcher as a *miner* who digs out facts and feelings from research participants.

researcher as a *traveler* is one who journeys with the participant. Most common interview practices lie between these two extremes. The metaphor of the *gardener* describes semi-structured interviews. The interviewer as gardener uses the question to plant a seed and follow-up questions to cultivate the growth of ideas and shared perceptions.

By understanding the etic or emic stance of the researcher and the intention to travel with, garden with, or excavate data from, we can learn more about the way the researcher relates to the phenomenon and potentially to the research participants.

Determining E-Interview Style(s)

KEY QUESTIONS: DETERMINING E-INTERVIEW STYLE(S)

- Does the researcher plan to use *structured, semi-structured, unstructured,* or a combination of styles for the interviews?
- How does the researcher align ICT functions, features, and/or limitations with the selected e-interview style(s)?

Any interview researcher must decide whether a structured, unstructured, or semi-structured interview best achieves the purpose of the study. The e-interview researcher must also consider alignment of interview structure and questioning style with choice of technology (see Figure 1.7).

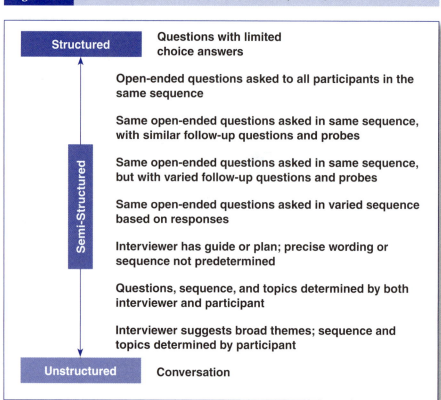

Figure 1.7 Level of interview structure (Salmons, 2010).

Structured interviews usually consist of the same questions posed in the same sequence to all participants. They may include closed-ended or limited-response questions or open-ended questions designed to elicit short narrative answers. Interview respondents do not have the option to redirect questions or embroider on responses. To prepare for structured interviews, the researcher determines the exact wording of all questions in advance. Because the role of the interviewer is meant to be as neutral as possible, the researcher may recruit and train others to implement the interview.

Semi-structured interviews balance the preplanned questions of a structured approach with the spontaneity and flexibility of the unstructured interview. The researcher prepares questions and/or discussion topics in advance and generates follow-up questions during the interview. *Unstructured* interviews are used to collect data through what is essentially a conversation between the researcher and participant.

Every ICT has opportunities and drawbacks for communications effectiveness, and each researcher must weigh how the pros and cons will enable or obstruct the research interview (see Figure 1.1 and Table 1.1). The choice of interview style is closely related to the choice of interview technology. Structured interviews can be conducted with almost any ICT; in general, a rich media technology is not needed since answers may be yes/no or simple statements. Semi-structured and unstructured interviews, however, require more careful thought. For example, text-only interviews may require careful planning to avoid the expectation of long written answers. That means at least some structure—and advance crafting of questions—is needed. If text-only ICTs are used for chatty, conversational unstructured interviews, the researcher will need to be prepared to respond quickly with follow-up or next questions to hold the participant's attention. The free-flowing, conversational characteristic of videoconferencing most closely compares with face-to-face dialogue, so it can be used with semi-structured or unstructured styles. The multichannel meeting space lends itself to semi- or unstructured interviews that use visual communication or collaboration, while immersive environments can offer a rich mix of visual navigation with sometimes limiting aspects of text-based communications (see the Typology of Online Visual Interview Methods in Table 1.2).

By understanding the level(s) of structure the researcher intends to use, we can learn more about the kind of preparation the researcher will need before the interview. We can also discern the kinds of ICTs that might best fit the communication needs of the interview.

Selecting Information and Communication Technology (ICT) and Milieu

KEY QUESTIONS: SELECTING ICT & MILIEU

- Will the interview use text based, audio, and/or visual communication options?
- Where will the interaction fall on the *Time-Response Continuum?*
- Will the interview setting be in a public or private online milieu?
- Is the choice of ICT aligned with research purpose, interview style, and access/preference of the research participants?

TIME RESPONSE AND COMMUNICATIONS

Researchers choose the interview technology and setting for a variety of reasons, including personal preferences, skills, or access by participants. Some researchers are looking at use or function of an ICT, so in essence the technology is itself the research phenomenon. The interview style and level of structure influence the choice of ICT for the interview. Key questions for understanding researchers' ICT choices relate to the alignment of research purpose with availability of visual, verbal, or text forms of exchange (see Table 1.1), the degree of immediacy possible between question and response, and/or the potential for visual communication or collaboration.

The terms *synchronous* and *asynchronous* have until recently seemed mutually exclusive. Either the technology allowed communication partners to converse in real time, or it did not. Now, many ICTs and patterns of usage allow for what we will call *near-synchronous* conversations. One party may post, text, or send a comment, update, or question and the receiving party may respond immediately, or soon. The message is typically brief and conversational. The sender expects the recipient to respond quickly, and engage in an extended kind of interchange.

On the other hand, technologies that are seemingly synchronous may indeed offer real-time exchange but not result in a focused dialogue. When we can see the other person face-to-face, it is obvious whether the other person is pondering the question, gathering his or her thoughts, or is distracted by household chores, children, mail, or other conversations. Online, we may not be able to see the other person, so we do not know whether he or she is contemplating an answer to our question, or is off doing other things and will return to the conversation at some point. Media Richness Theory (Daft & Lengel, 1986) prioritized the "rich" exchange across multiple channels with immediate back-and-forth responses between communication partners. Media Synchronicity Theory (MST) refined that concept by offering a definition for *synchronicity* that distinguishes high-quality, real-time communications from those exchanges that, while ostensibly synchronous, do not entail attentive participation in an in-depth, focused exchange or productive dialogue (Carlson & George, 2004; Dennis, Fuller, & Valacich, 2008). Dennis et al. observed that it is not simply the choice of ICT, but

> the *manner* in which individuals use media influences their communication performance (the development of shared understanding). Generally speaking, convergence processes benefit from the use of

media that facilitate *synchronicity*, the ability to support individuals working together at the same time with a shared pattern of coordinated behavior (p. 576).

Synchronicity refers to the successful convergence that, it can be argued, is beneficial to an interview process.

Researchers who select asynchronous methods (such as e-mail or posts to a discussion forum) report high-quality exchanges that result when participants have a chance to think about the response, or gain new experiences with the topic of the research, between questions (Hunt & McHale, 2007).

The Time-Response Continuum offers a way to categorize the level of immediacy and timing of response in a way that offers more subtle gradations than the prior synchronous/asynchronous dichotomy (see Figure 1.8).

Figure 1.8   Time-Response Continuum.

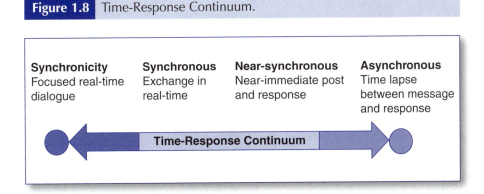

Synchronicity	Synchronous	Near-synchronous	Asynchronous
Focused real-time dialogue	Exchange in real-time	Near-immediate post and response	Time lapse between message and response

Time-Response Continuum

VISUAL NATURE OF ONLINE COMMUNICATION

KEY QUESTIONS: USING VISUAL METHODS & DATA

- If the interview technology has capacity for visual exchange, has the researcher acknowledged the visual nature of interview in the research design and planned for collection and analysis of visual data?
- Does the interview entail visual communication, elicitation, and/or collaboration? Will researcher and/or participant provide or generate visual images?
- Have permissions for use of visual data been included in the consent agreement?

The visual communication potential of a selected ICT is another consideration for researchers. Increasingly, technologies enable the researcher and participant to see each other, view, share, or create images. These possibilities add to the media richness of the interview, while raising a new set of questions.

Visual research methods can make use of these four types of enabling technologies to accomplish various tasks in the interview (see Table 1.2). Researchers and participants may use *visual communication* techniques to convey the question or represent the response. Visual communication describes the use of images to communicate abstract concepts, relationships between concepts or data, or examples of research phenomena. Using *visual elicitation,* the researcher

Table 1.2   Typology of Online Visual Interview Methods (Salmons, 2010)

Researchers can do the following. . .	. . . to achieve the following interactions with research participants:
Transmit visual images. Image or media files, links to images posted on a server or website, or images captured in the moment are sent to the other party during the interview.	*Visual communication* describes the use of images to communicate abstract concepts, relationships between concepts or data, or examples of research phenomena.
View visual representation of phenomena together: Researchers can view photos, graphics, artifacts, or media during the interview.	*Visual elicitation* refers specifically to the process of using visual stimuli to draw out a verbal or a visual response. The scenery or events in an immersive virtual environment navigated by researcher and participant, the images or media viewed together, or the graphic generated during the interview may stimulate response.
Navigate in a visual virtual environment. Observe and experience websites, software applications, or 3-D virtual environments.	
Generate visual images. Access shared tools that allow researchers and/or participants to create drawings, diagrams or visual maps, snapshots or videos.	*Visual collaboration* refers to a collaborative approach to either stimulate new thinking or create responses in relation to visual representations of the research phenomena. Researchers and participants can create, edit, or embellish images together during the interview.

can use visual stimulus to draw out a verbal or a visual response. Researcher and/or participant can generate new visual representations of the research phenomenon using *visual collaboration,* which refers to a collaborative approach to either stimulate new thinking or create responses in relation to visual representations of the research phenomena.

PUBLIC–PRIVATE SETTING

Finally, the decision about ICT may also relate to a choice of interview setting because the online interview must occur in some milieu. Each type of setting offers its own mix of visual communication, navigation, or collaboration and voice or text dialogue options the researcher can select or mix and match. At the same time, the virtual world, online platform, or community where researchers and participants communicate may be considered public, open to all, or private, accessible to owners or members. While the distinction between "public" and "private" is not universally agreed upon, the continuum illustrated in Figure 1.9 can provide a guideline: If participants register and pay to be involved in the activities occurring in the setting, they can be considered "private," while the open web

Figure 1.9   Consent in public or private online milieu.

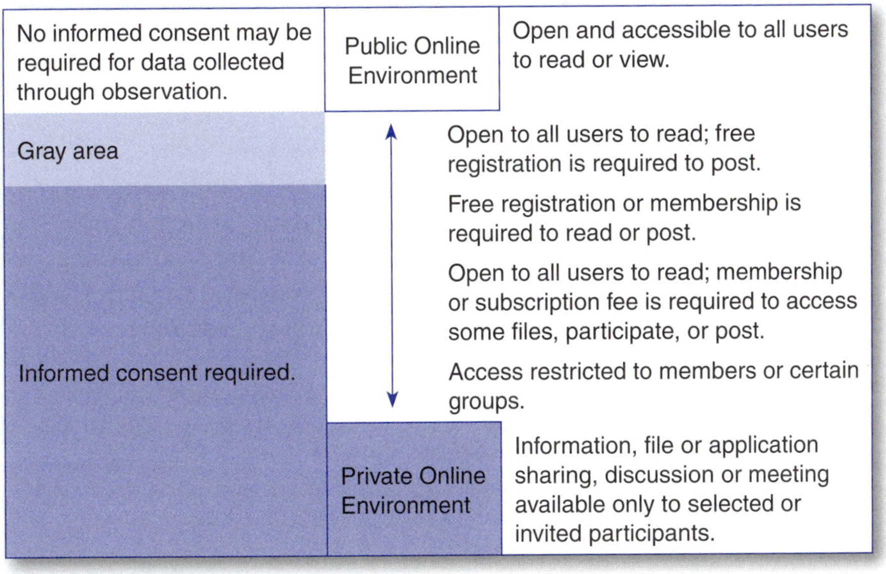

No informed consent may be required for data collected through observation.	Public Online Environment	Open and accessible to all users to read or view.
Gray area	↑	Open to all users to read; free registration is required to post.
		Free registration or membership is required to read or post.
		Open to all users to read; membership or subscription fee is required to access some files, participate, or post.
Informed consent required.	↓	Access restricted to members or certain groups.
	Private Online Environment	Information, file or application sharing, discussion or meeting available only to selected or invited participants.

accessible to all can be considered "public." Another way to look at the question is through the expectations of participants: when they post or converse, do they expect that they have shared privately with selected friends or publicly with everyone?

In public, or generally open spaces, researchers need to consider a number of factors such as potential interruptions and intellectual property or copyright issues. Additionally, if observations of the environment, artifacts, or images posted by participants; information included in profiles; and so on are to be used as data, informed consent or permissions will be required.

By understanding the features of possible ICTs and environments where they are used, we can determine which will enable the researcher to collect the visual, verbal, or text data needed from interviews. We can also discern potential ethical or informed consent issues related to the public or private virtual milieu.

Conducting the Interview

KEY QUESTIONS: CONDUCTING THE INTERVIEW

- Does the researcher have a plan for conducting the interview with either prepared questions or an interview guide?
- Does the researcher have a plan for the 4 interview stages: opening, questioning and guiding, closing, and following up?
- Does the researcher have a contingency plan in case there are technical difficulties?

How will the researcher bring together purpose and process when faced with the research participant? In this area of the framework, we are interested in whether the researcher has the skills and abilities to carry out the interview as planned. We also want to know what the researcher will do if the interview does not proceed as planned. With emergent methods generally, flexibility is of utmost importance.

> Emergent methods typically require the researcher to remain flexible and open to modifications. In fact, emergent methods are often discovered as a result of modifying more conventional research projects when traditional projects fail to "get at" the aspect of social life the researcher is interested in. (Hesse-Biber & Leavy, 2010, p. 3)

With any kind of CMC, the possibility for problems with connectivity, access, and software are present. The e-interview researcher needs a contingency plan that is understood by the research participant.

By understanding the researcher's rationale for the interview approach and plans for conducting the interview as well as back-up options, we can acquire experience and develop new knowledge and success strategies for e-interview methods. After the online interview research, we are interested in the reflexive process by which the researcher considers or reconsiders choices made.

Addressing Ethical Issues

KEY QUESTIONS: ADDRESSING ETHICAL ISSUES

- Has the researcher taken appropriate steps to protect human subjects, and where appropriate, their avatars or online representations?
- Has the researcher obtained proper informed consent?

Ethical issues abound in any interview research. In the case of online interview research, there are some particular considerations. Some are related to the possibility that the interview participant may unwittingly reveal more than was intended because online profiles or environments contain information not noted in the consent agreement.

Questions to ask about potential ethical risks in an e-interview study include the following (Salmons, 2010):

- Does the research involve observation or intrusion in situations where the subjects have a reasonable expectation of privacy? Would reasonable people be offended by such an intrusion? Can the research be redesigned to avoid the intrusion?
- Will the investigator(s) be collecting sensitive information about individuals? If so, have they made adequate provisions for protecting the confidentiality of the data through coding, destruction of identifying information, limiting access to the data, or whatever methods that may be appropriate to the study?
- Are the investigator's disclosures to subjects about confidentiality adequate? Should documentation of consent be waived to protect confidentiality? (Porter, 1993)

- Is it clear to the participant that there is no penalty for withdrawing from the research?
- Are safeguards in place to protect confidentiality of the participant?
- Can the researcher protect the data and ensure that it is not used for purposes other than those the participant consented to in the agreement?

Closing Thoughts

The E-Interview Research Framework can be used as a tool for planning and designing as well as dissecting and analyzing research that utilizes online interview data collection methods. This framework informs the editor's commentaries on each chapter throughout the book and serves as the basis for a metasynthesis of all 10 cases, presented in Chapter 12.

See the **Appendix** for suggested readings and resources on the software, methodologies, and methods discussed in this chapter.

Find More Materials on the Study Site! See the book website for additional ideas about understanding and assessing research designs, and resources for dissertation/thesis or review board committee members who need to evaluate student research proposals and theses or dissertations. Also on the book website, educators and instructional designers can find discussion and assignment ideas and sample syllabi.

References

Anfara, V. A., & Mertz, N. T. (Eds.). (2006). *Theoretical frameworks in qualitative research.* Thousand Oaks, CA: Sage.

Carlson, J. R., & George, J. F. (2004). Media appropriateness in the conduct and discovery of deceptive communication: The relative influence of richness and synchronicity. *Group Decision and Negotiation, 13*(2), 191–210.

Carter, S. M., & Little, M. (2007). Justifying knowledge, justifying method, taking action: Epistemologies, methodologies, and methods in qualitative research. *Qualitative Health Research, 17*(10), 1316–1328.

Daft, R. L., & Lengel, R. H. (1986). Organizational information requirements, media richness and structural design. *Management Science, 32*(5), 554–571.

Dennis, A. R., Fuller, R. M., & Valacich, J. S. (2008). Media, tasks, and communication processes: A theory of media synchronicity. *Management Information Systems Quarterly, 32*(4), 575–600.

Edwards, R. (2004). *Social capital in the field: Researchers' tales.* Retrieved from http://www.lsbu.ac.uk/families/workingpapers/familieswp10.pdf

Franklin, K. J. (1996). *K. L. Pike on etic vs. emic: A review and interview.* Retrieved February 25, 2011, from http://www.sil.org/klp/karlintv.htm

Gordon, R. L. (1980). *Interviewing: Strategy, techniques and tactics.* Homewood, IL: Dorsey.

Gray, D. (2009). *Doing research in the real world* (2nd ed.). London: Sage.

Guerrero, L. K., DeVito, J. A., & Hecht, M. L. (Eds.). (1999). The nonverbal communication reader: Classic and contemporary readings. Prospect Hills, IL: Waveland.

Hesse-Biber, S. N., & Leavy, P. (2010). Pushing on the methodological boundaries: The growing need for emergent methods within and across the disciplines. In S. N. Hesse-Biber & P. Leavy (Eds.), *Handbook of emergent methods* (pp. 1–15). New York: Guilford.

Hewson, C. (2010). Internet-mediated research and its potential role in facilitating mixed methods research. In S. N. Hesse-Biber & P. Leavy (Eds.), *Handbook of emergent methods* (pp. 543–570). New York: Guilford.

Hunt, N., & McHale, S. (2007). A practical guide to the email interview. *Qualitative Health Research, 17*(10), 1415–1421.

Jaccard, J., & Jacoby, J. (2010). *Theory construction and model-building skills: A practical guide for social scientists.* New York: Guilford.

Kalman, Y. M., Ravid, G., Raban, D. R., & Rafaeli, S. (2006). Pauses and response latencies: A chronemic analysis of asynchronous CMC. *Journal of Computer-Mediated Communication 12*(1), 1-23.

King, N., & Horrocks, C. (2010). *Interviews in qualitative research.* London: Sage.

Kvale, S. (2007). *Doing interviews.* Thousand Oaks, CA: Sage.

Kvale, S., & Brinkman, S. (2009). *InterViews: Learning the craft of qualitative research interviewing* (2nd ed.). Thousand Oaks, CA: Sage.

Moustakas, C. (1994). *Phenomenological research methods.* Thousand Oaks, CA: Sage.

Porter, J. P. (1993). *Institutional Review Board guidebook.* Washington DC: U.S. Department of Health and Human Services, Office for Human Research Protections.

Ritchie, J., Lewis, J., & Elam, G. (2003). Designing and selecting samples. In J. Ritchie & J. Lewis (Eds.), *Qualitative research practice: A guide for social science students and researchers* (pp. 77–109). London: Sage.

Salmons, J. E. (2010). *Online interviews in real time.* Thousand Oaks, CA: Sage.

Spencer, L., Ritchie, J., Lewis, J., & Dillon, L. (2002). Quality in qualitative evaluation: a framework for assessing research evidence. Retrieved March 17, 2004, from http://www.strategy.gov.uk/files/pdf/Quality_framework.pdf

Stake, R. E. (1995). *The art of case study research.* Thousand Oaks, CA: Sage.

VanDeVen, A. H. (2007). *Engaged scholarship.* Oxford, UK: Oxford University Press.

Wilmot, A. (2008). *Designing sampling strategies for qualitative social research.* Newport, UK: Office for National Statistics.

PART I

INTERVIEW RESEARCH WITH SOCIAL MEDIA TOOLS

The terms *social media* or *social networking* describe a number of communications technologies that allow for various options and combinations of one-to-one, one-to-many, and many-to-many communication. There is usually an option to create affiliate networks of friends or members. A social networking community may offer its own unique mix of communication options, targeted to attract a particular set of members who join for social or professional reasons. Such communities are designed to be accessed from computers as well as mobile devices and smartphones for the purpose of reading or for contributing content.

Social media can include chat communications tools that allow for one-to-one, text-based conversations or a conference option for many-to-many chat. The private chat functions can be used for text-based interviews.

Social networking communities also include features that can help researchers and participants to become acquainted. They allow a member of the community to post messages that can contain text, images, and/or media on a personal wall, a user-customized page that can be read by all of the individuals who subscribe or "friend" the member. Members can stratify their groups and choose whether posted messages can be viewed by some or all of their friends, offering options for degrees of public and private communication.

TEXT MESSAGING, INSTANT MESSAGING, AND CHAT

- People can communicate online in real time by exchanging short written messages. Typically, the term "text message" is used when people write back and forth over mobile phones or devices, while "instant messaging" or "chat" refers to the same kind of communication on computers. Chat or messaging may require registration and/or log in to enter and post; it may be private or open to the public. One-to-one, one-to-many, or many-to-many individuals can converse in writing. When the interview is in writing, an accurate transcript is immediately available with no loss or inaccuracy in transcription.

Blogs not associated with a specific social networking community operate much the same way. While typically public and freely accessible, they allow varying degrees of commenting and exchange among readers. Some allow anyone to post; others require that the blogger or a moderator approve the message. While such comments are usually public for viewing by all readers, it is possible for more private dialogue to occur.

WEBLOGS, OR BLOGS

A blog (short for weblog) is a personal online journal where entries are posted chronologically. Users create their own blogs as a way to share thoughts and ideas, and link to other websites and blogs to create families of sites with common interests. Microblogs use the same principle but limit the posts to very short entries.

Styles of Online Communication and Timing of Response

Changes in information and communications technologies, access, and usage patterns cause researchers and observers to note that the distinction between communication that is synchronous (communication in the same time with minimal gap of time between message and response) and asynchronous (communication any time, with a gap of time between message and response) needs to be rethought. The boundary between the two is less of a black-and-white line and more of a gradient pattern of gray. Social media tools inhabit the emerging gray area between synchronous and asynchronous.

A seemingly synchronous tool like chat can be used for conversations that span some period of time, because one party may step away then come back and respond. A seemingly asynchronous tool like a blog may be close to synchronous when readers respond right away and comments flow back and forth.

Media Richness Theory (MRT) provides one way to classify different kinds of Internet communication by distinguishing between "lean" and "rich" media based on "the capacity for immediate feedback, the number of cues and channels utilized, personalization, and language variety" (Daft & Lengel, 1986, p. 580). Media Richness Theory (MRT) claims that immediate feedback is one indicator of "richness," a desirable quality in communication. Effective communication, of course, is about more than timing of response. Some argue that, especially for research purposes, the pause between question and response allows participants to think carefully and formulate an answer (Bampton & Cowton, 2002; Hunt & McHale, 2007).

However, the pause between question and response can also mean the participant is engaged in some other on- or offline activity. Multitasking participants may participate in several synchronous events, without truly focusing attention on any one conversation. Media Synchronicity Theory offers a definition for *synchronicity* that distinguishes high-quality real-time communications from those interchanges that while ostensibly synchronous, do not entail an in-depth exchange or productive dialogue (Dennis, Fuller, & Valacich, 2008). Dennis et al. observe that while the medium may allow for immediate feedback, it may also allow for multiple activities and distractions that can detract from the communication partners' potential to really collaborate or solve problems. Social networking environments, with their options for shared visual posts, alerts for new posts, games, and other distractions, may have the potential for rich synchronous exchanges but actually miss the potential for real synchronicity. At the same time, seemingly lean asynchronous communication styles may allow for fruitful exchange with time to think between message and response.

We may need to think in terms of a continuum (see Figure 1) that acknowledges the gradations of time between message and

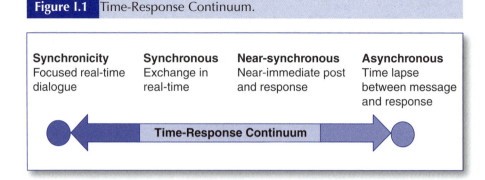

Figure I.1   Time-Response Continuum.

response—and their significance to the kind of communication between researcher and participant essential for a successful interview. Deeper dialogue through real-time synchronicity, the synchronous exchange that may be one of several simultaneous activities, the near-synchronous post and response, and the truly asynchronous communication where hours or days may pass between message and response are all now possible with social media.

Communication issues as they relate to quality and focus on a coherent, fluid interplay of questions and responses, perhaps not a priority for social users, are critical for researchers who choose to use social networking communities as settings for research interviews. Social networking communities and social media more broadly are attracting the interest of interview researchers, who are exploring new ways to engage research participants.

SUGGESTIONS FOR PLANNING A TEXT-BASED INTERVIEW (SALMONS, 2010)

- Select a text interview technology with which participants are familiar; discuss platform choice as part of consent agreement.
- Familiarize yourself with communications options in that setting; review archiving function for saving transcript.
- Familiarize yourself with electronic paralinguistic expressions, emoticons, or other communication shortcuts or slang used by the target population. Decide how you will use these shortcuts to save time and keep the conversation moving.
- Articulate a greater number of questions that elicit shorter responses; break big questions into a series of subquestions.

- Write out questions or key phrases in advance so you can cut and paste them into the text window to save time and keep the interview flowing.
- Provide any background information in advance so you can move quickly into a dynamic exchange.

Social Media and Interview Research

The two cases presented in Part I: Interview Research With Social Media Tools demonstrate the potential, and some of the challenges, associated with a study that is based on data collected through interviews with social media. Both used a variety of communication tools and approaches from synchronous, and near-synchronous to asynchronous.

The two emerging researchers who conducted these studies both encountered obstacles that caused them to use approaches other than the ones they initially selected. One found it necessary to use an asynchronous approach when the synchronous option did not work for some participants. The other found that the proprietary nature of a privately owned social network resulted in unpredictable barriers that cut her off from the participants—and contact information needed to reach them through another channel. Clearly, creativity and flexibility are essential when a researcher enters largely uncharted territory. They both ultimately succeeded in collecting data for their respective studies, and their experiences may well be instructive to other researchers who intend to collect data using social media tools.

References

Bampton, R., & Cowton, C. J. (2002). The e-interview. *Forum: Qualitative Social Research, 3*(2).

Daft, R. L., & Lengel, R. H. (1986). Organizational information requirements, media richness and structural design. *Management Science, 32*(5), 554–571.

Dennis, A. R., Fuller, R. M., & Valacich, J. S. (2008). Media, tasks, and communication processes: A theory of media synchronicity. *Management Information Systems Quarterly, 32*(4), 575–600.

Hunt, N., & McHale, S. (2007). A practical guide to the email interview. *Qualitative Health Research, 17*(10), 1415–1421.

Salmons, J. (2010). *Online interviews in real time.* Thousand Oaks, CA: Sage.

Blog Like an Egyptian

2

Sally Bishai
Keiser University, Fort Lauderdale, USA

I'm not sure about you, but I have always loved stories. Regardless of my role in one—reader, writer, observer, experiencer, or inspirer—the mere notion of a narrative has never failed to brighten my eyes and put a smile of remarkable goofiness on my face. Therefore, it should come as no surprise that I have spun this study into a bit of a story, because it is, in the end, just that. A true tale to be sure, but an interesting one; a tragic tale at times, but there's hope for a happy ending.

This is a story about moving—moving to another place, or standing still while the world moves around you. It is a story about changes—those you do not want, those you cannot help, and those you cannot help wanting with all your heart.

It is also a story of twos and ones—two viewpoints you try to squash together, two sides you are torn between, two brothers battling over a single birthright. Two groups, one wall; one winner, one end result, one final product.

The thing about twos and ones, though, is that they each—or both—take on different meanings at different times. Finding "just" two cans of Classic Coke in the refrigerator may horrify you beyond belief when seven snobbish sisters-in-law fill your living room, but if you're house-sitting for your brother's family and hanging out with their dogs and a good book, the second carb-filled can may seem like a bonus. And while it is often said that "one is the loneliest number," it doesn't have to be, for it can also represent unity or strength.

So it would seem that this is a tale of multiplicities—in the form of mixed emotions, divided loyalties, double- and triple-standards, have-nots and have-a-lots. Normal, everyday stuff to be sure, and not uncommon in the least. Cultures do often shift to embrace—or at least accommodate—technological advances, don't they? Naturally, those things considered to be cutting edge (or just plain edgy) by previous generations might seem commonplace, even outdated by today's young people; and generational conflicts notwithstanding, clashes will undoubtedly arise as some push for even more change—while others struggle to keep up with (or battle) the shifting cultural climate.

But now let us add the element of geographical shift to this tale. The plot thickens, because it's not just a question of how one *culture* will shift anymore. Rather, it's a question of how a person's way of *life* will shift—or not—in a new location that has its own culture (and cultural issues) to deal with. The individual who has relocated to a new home that does not feel like home might grapple with identity issues, unfamiliar boundaries, and communication barriers with native and nonnative host-landers.

KEY DEFINITIONS

Acculturation: Often called "second-culture learning," acculturation involves the changes that occur to a group based upon their prolonged contact with members of other cultures.

Home-land: The land in which a person was born.

Host-land: The land that a person has moved to.

The subject of acculturation is, therefore, a significant one with potentially far-reaching implications for individuals—and the surrounding communities in their new homes (which still may not feel like home). Furthermore, while the particulars of acculturation struggles may vary from one culture to another (and one person to another), acculturation itself can (and does) somehow affect many or most immigrants—regardless of their home-land and particular circumstances.

As a budding scholar, I was intrigued by the implications of communication, culture, and psychology for acculturation and decided to build my doctoral research (at Florida State University in 2008 and 2009) around them all (Bishai, 2010).

Research Purpose

I have a confession to make: The real reason I chose to study acculturation had nothing to do with the scholarly implications and
everything to do with the fact that my parents immigrated to Florida
in the 1970s, and raised me in the Egypt of 1955 or so (I'm not com-
plaining, by the way). It would appear that mine were not the only
Arabic-speaking parents who accomplished this bit of amateur time
travel in their child rearing, as evidenced by the relatively recent glut
of television programs made for and by Arabic speakers in the
Middle East and the diaspora.

KEY DEFINITIONS

Diaspora: Any place on the globe that (1) houses people from another
country, and (2) is not the country in question. For example, the Egyptian
diaspora could, theoretically, be located in every country but Egypt.

Hyphenated: Term used to refer to a person representing more than one
culture in her/his identity, though there is no standard formula for the
blend denoted by that label, and the hyphen isn't always written. For
example, the labels of Egyptian American, Egyptian-American, and
American Egyptian might be used to denote immigrants from Egypt living in America, American-born children of Egyptian immigrants, or bicultural individuals with one Egyptian parent and one American parent.
Egyptians that have never lived anywhere but Egypt would not be considered hyphenated, however, unless they are also bicultural.

Dialogical model: A model that uses, allows, or emphasizes dialogue
between voices or elements.

Copt: A highly contested term that is rarely used to mean "Egyptian," but
usually refers to a Christian Egyptian, and nearly always refers to a member of the Coptic Orthodox Church. For example, most would consider me
a Copt, but since I'm Presbyterian and not Orthodox, some might argue
with my Coptic status.

These programs—which appear on satellite television and the
Internet—often feature Egyptians and other Arabic speakers (hyphenated and not) who are using such technologies to publicly articulate

their struggles with identity confusion, collectivist clash, and communication incapability, among other things. The always-rich discourses on culture tend to splinter in many directions—including religion, mate selection, and psychological health. These natural categories lent shape to the early stages of my dissertation, and I was compelled to use the dialogical model for my study's theoretical underpinning. From that grew three goals of research, which were attained through the investigation of four main research questions.

THREE GOALS OF RESEARCH

1. An exploration of the acculturation strategies of Egyptians in the diaspora

2. An understanding of current attitudes, anxieties, and/or "dreams" held by Egyptians (living in Egypt or the diaspora)

3. A discovery of participants' manifestations of the dialogical model of acculturation through an examination of three communication dimensions (Identification, Cultural Orientation, and Communication Style)

Research Questions

The four main research questions that guided my study were as follows:

1. What are the acculturation strategies that Egyptian Christians in Egypt and the diaspora use to negotiate their identities?

2. What are some of the positive (goals, wishes, desires, "dreams"), negative ("cultural anxieties," conflicts, tensions), and/or neutral issues in the lives of Christian Egyptians in Egypt and the diaspora?

3. How do Christian Egyptians in Egypt and the diaspora negotiate any tensions or conflicts associated with their own desires and/or cultural anxieties?

4. How is the dialogical model of acculturation manifested in Christian Egyptians in Egypt and the diaspora with respect to the "three communication dimensions" (Identification, Cultural Orientation, and Communication Style)?

Investigations included descriptive questionnaires administered online, and qualitative interviews that were either administered online (synchronously and/or asynchronously) or conducted face-to-face and videotaped. In addition, the review of online blogs from eight bloggers (one Coptic Orthodox, seven Egyptian Muslim) provided additional insights, achieving validity through corroboration and triangulation.

Despite my reliance upon several technological tools during the stage of data collection, I will only be mentioning those relevant to this qualitative case study. They included Yahoo! Messenger (for synchronous online interviews), Surveymonkey (for descriptive questionnaires that preceded the interviews), and Blogspot (which revealed other facets of certain participants).

With regard to data analysis, the method used was grounded theory, which yielded an almost-unnatural number of theories and/or significant findings. Due to the nature of this chapter, however, I will only be discussing those obtained through the use of real-time online interviews (and the aforementioned other two methods, where appropriate).

Research Design Overview

GUIDING THEORIES

While the notion of acculturation has been in circulation since Plato's decrial of cultural contamination in *Laws* (Rudmin, 2003), the definition of what acculturation (and particularly "successful" acculturation) is has changed several times. To Redfield, Linton, and Herskovits (1936), acculturation happened when people or groups from one culture had firsthand and prolonged contact with those from other cultures, resulting in changes to the customs of one or both groups. To Gordon (1964), acculturation was a one-way process, a unidirectional model (UDM), where the immigrant simply had to give up the old culture to take on the new one. To Berry (1980), the UDM became "assimilation," while the concept of shunning one's new culture in favor of old was called "separation." Berry's fourfold model, also called the bidimensional model (BDM), further stipulated that a person who balanced both cultures well was in a position of "integration," while the person who shunned home and host culture equally was displaying the position of "marginalization."

Both uni- and bidimensional models have drawn some criticism in the years since their respective debuts, leading to the reworking of previous models and the introduction of completely different ones.

KEY DEFINITIONS

Dialogical self theory: Identity is made up of the dialogue between multiple strands.

Polychronic culture: Relationships are emphasized, time is elastic, and multitasking is a way of life.

Monochronic culture: The opposite of a polychronic one. This culture is rooted in efficiency, focusing on one goal or task, and getting the job done.

Collectivist culture: Emphasizes interdependence.

Individualist culture: Emphasizes independence.

One model in particular has begun to gain support from the varied fields of psychology and literary criticism, in which this model is rooted. The dialogical model of acculturation (DM), adapted from Hermans' (Hermans, Kempen, & van Loon, 1992; Hermans, Rijks, & Kempen, 1993) dialogical self theory, reflects the multiplicity of incompatible cultural positions within a single person (Bhatia, 2002), and also allows for the concurrent existence of multiple strands (Bakhtin, 1930s/1981; Said, 1999) of language, thought, and self. This is accomplished when some or many of these cultural strands dialogue with one another.

The dialogical models (of acculturation as well as self, for that matter) may seem counterintuitive to the Western notions of a "solid" or "core" identity (Raggatt, 2000), though they do generously lend themselves to the already-polyphonous lifestyle of polychronic collectivists.

For example, as Chaudhary and Sriram (2001) explain,

> For the Indian psyche, the dialogical self is a reality. . . . The notion of a dialogical self is inherent in the social milieu in which Indians grow up, are socialized and live, and on which they depend for physical, social, and spiritual sustenance. (p. 380)

In other words, their culture is already operating under the dialogical model, by virtue of the fact that it is already multistranded and multitasking.

An example of the way the DM would work within an acculturation setting might go something like the story of Miriam.

MIRIAM'S STORY OF ACCULTURATION

Miriam and her family moved to California from Cairo when she was 2. English is her stronger language, but she prefers Arabic food and follows the traditional-but-unwritten guidelines of a "proper" Egyptian girl (i.e., no dating, no slumber parties, lives at home while attending a college in the same city her parents live in). One day, she meets her very own Prince Charming at the hospital where she has now secured a residency in nephrology. He, too, is an Egyptian American physician, and they discover much in common. It turns out, however, that he is a committed Protestant while she is Coptic, Orthodox-born but currently a nondenominational Christian. Her devoutly Orthodox parents would not allow this marriage to happen, since the Coptic Orthodox Church does not recognize marriages to members of other denominations. Because Miriam is torn between her various loyalties—to herself, to her family, to the faith she was born into, to the faith she actually practices, and to Prince Charming himself—she unwittingly uses a dialogical approach to think through this sociocultural and ethno-religious issue. "If I marry him, I get shunned from the church, and the parents might disown me for shaming them. If I don't marry him, the boat isn't rocked ... but I'm gonna be pretty bummed! If I marry him and get disowned, then maybe the parents won't want to meet or become involved with my children, which would be sad and horrible, but also inconvenient while I'm building up my career. And I'd never ask him to convert—not because he would refuse it, which he would, but because then his family would disown him and then we'd be back at square one! Hmm ..."

The Eastern version of the dialogical model is not so much about the various options one may select from, but the fact that many or most of the options presented to Arabic speakers and people from similarly collectivist cultures (such as India, Pakistan, South Korea, and Iran) are "loaded." In other words, deciding to go with a college major or potential spouse that the family does not approve of may result in long-lasting conflicts (or shunnage).

All in all, many elements are represented within past and current models of acculturation, but the DM's emphasis on polyphony made it a natural choice for examinations of a polyphonous culture like the Egyptian one. The only problem was that the DM brilliantly explained or depicted the cultural conflicts we Egyptians often face—but then stopped short of making an actual difference. The solution soon presented itself to me: "Ground the theory tweaking in the collected data!" So I did just that.

METHODOLOGY

To refine the dialogical model of acculturation, I relied upon grounded theory (GT) to approach data analysis (Glaser & Strauss, 1967; Jorgensen, 1989; Scott, 1995). GT stresses "the discovery of theory from data—systematically obtained and analyzed" (Glaser & Strauss, 1967, p. 1).

Very basically, a researcher using GT first collects all sorts of data and then does a great deal of staring. The idea is that notions will emerge from the data, suggesting themselves as theories or bits of theory. Much testing, tweaking, and retesting occur, followed by the birth of a shiny new theory.

In my study, the data included more than 10,000 pages of qualitative interviews, blog postings, and results from the aforementioned descriptive questionnaires. Not surprisingly, dozens of notions emerged from my data (but more on that in the research findings section).

SAMPLING APPROACH

While the overall population of Christians in Egypt has dwindled over the centuries, the people themselves have persevered, whether in Egypt—where they live with or battle against the religious persecution they are often subjected to—or in the diaspora. Despite our tenacity and ubiquity, we are grossly underrepresented in the literature on acculturation, Arab Americans, arranged marriages (which are not uncommon in the Egypt of today, though we tend to call them salon marriages), and "Middle Easterners" in general—hence, my intention of focusing upon Christian Egyptians.

Recruiting was done either face-to-face, online, or by phone. The physical "hunting grounds" included churches, religious conferences, and the homes of social contacts where my associates (parents, sisters, cousins, and friends in Egypt; relatives throughout America) and I happened to be. Once leads had been generated, we followed up via e-mail, Myspace/Facebook postings, and messages targeted to fellow Egyptians.

DATA COLLECTION

Qualitative data has long been revered for its "thickness" and "richness" (Bryman & Bell, 2007, p. 313). To this end, a number of data collection methods have become available to the qualitative researcher. These methods include observation, descriptive questionnaire, textual analysis, and qualitative interview.

These and other methods have been devised because qualitative studies generally have an even greater need for corroboration and validation than do quantitative studies (Bryman & Bell, 2007; Denzin & Lincoln, 1978). For this reason, I was intent upon triangulating my data and devised a three-pronged approach to meet the goal. The first prong consisted of a descriptive questionnaire, the second involved the review of publicly available blogs found online, and the third and final prong was the real-time, qualitative online interview.

Some triangulation came from the fact that each participant had to complete both questionnaire and interview; another method of achieving triangulation involved the document review and textual analyses of English-language blogs maintained by Christian and Muslim Egyptians in Egypt and in the diaspora, only two of whom actively participated in the study (through the questionnaire and interview).

With regard to the first prong, I used a questionnaire because it allowed me to collect qualitative responses and demographic information straight from the primary source, but did not require my direct involvement in the process. While questionnaires are the most frequently used method in quantitative research (Frey, Botan, & Kreps, 1999, p. 99), they are sometimes used to collect information— such as self-reports and others' reports—that can be qualitatively and/or textually analyzed (Frey et al., p. 96).

The questionnaires were asynchronously administered online via Surveymonkey.com, and were completely anonymous in nature— though participants did have to create a distinct username that later functioned as a password. Preceding the username-creation page, however, was an electronic consent form. During the first few days of the study, would-be participants were required to click "Yes, I agree and am ready to begin!" to view the questionnaire at all; but after 50 people gave me the slip (clicked "yes" and then failed to complete any questions), I decided to make the questionnaire available for review (as a pdf) and added a "not at this time" choice to the consent form.

With regard to the questionnaire's contents, items were both direct and indirect, involving scenarios as well as straightforward questions. Response types included multiple choice-multiple response, multiple choice-single response, and short answer.

All told, more than 70 participants identifying as Christian Egyptians completed my descriptive questionnaire. This format increased the efficiency of data collection and management, while the anonymity of the questionnaire's inquiry into sensitive topics yielded particularly insightful results that may have been difficult or impossible to capture during an interview. I should note, however, that 7 would-be questionnaire takers were unable to physically fill out the form (due to issues of language, literacy, and/or technology). In each of those cases, I filled out the questionnaire while an audio or audio-visual recorder captured the speech of the participant, who was sitting beside me.

Shifting to the next form, the document review, I read and dissected 8 publicly available blogs maintained by Egyptians in various parts of the world. In 2 cases, I had the opportunity to chat online with the bloggers, hence my mention of this largely asynchronous data collection method.

Finally, the synchronous online qualitative interview only worked for about 20 people, due to scheduling conflicts, alleged unfamiliarity with the Yahoo! Messenger chatting interface, and various other reasons. Additionally, close to 30 participants (from the more than 70 questionnaire completers) responded to my last-minute idea of transforming the questions originally intended for my semi-structured qualitative interviews into a sort of asynchronous "short essay" type of "questionnaire" (complete with electronic consent form), which was also posted on surveymonkey.com.

DATA ANALYSIS

Before I could immerse myself in the fascinating sea of collected data, I first had to do some tidying up. This included the transcription of any audio or audiovisual conversations, and the verification of my own translations of spoken, written, or transliterated Arabic.

> ## TRANSLITERATED ARABIC
>
> Transliterated Arabic is the use of another alphabet to write Arabic. For example, writing the greeting *Ahlan 7abibi* ("hello, darling/dear" in English) is considered transliteration due to (1) the use of the English alphabet to write an Arabic word, and (2) the use of "7" to replace the Arabic letter *'ha* (which has no accurate equivalent in English).

Once transcription of conversations was complete I was able to begin my transcript-based analysis. To accomplish this, I first read and reread each interview, all while consulting a list containing the questions I needed answered. These questions—one representing each topic of interest—included the following:

1. What cultures, media preferences/likes/dislikes were mentioned? (IDENTITY)

2. What were their feelings about biculturality and/or changing cultures of residence? (CONFLICTED IDENTITY)

3. From their comments, did their communication seem more "high context" or "low context" or both? (COMMUNICATION STYLE)

4. From their comments, did they seem individualistic or collectivistic, both, or neither? (CULTURAL ORIENTATION)

5. What were some examples/stories they shared about these things (i.e., culture, cultural orientation, communication style, identity, biculturalism, etc.)?

After using up well over 100 fluorescent yellow markers during several go-rounds with the dizzying number of words, a sixth question arose, and I revisited the transcripts once more. The question was

6. Did they make any mention of experiencing confusion, closeting, conflicts, or any other sort of distress tied to cultural things? Have they ever sought or received professional help and/or medication for any of these things? If so, did such strategies work? (NEGATIVE DIALOGICAL STATE)

At this point, the maddening stacks of paper were only sorted (alphabetically) by participant; that is, if Mr. X had given me a five-minute interview on Yahoo! Messenger, its meager transcript was secured with a cheery metallic binder clip, while Ms. J's section of my living-room floor held a towering stack of hard copies including her descriptive questionnaire, e-mails to me, the transcripts of all 15 of our chats on Yahoo! Messenger, and a printout of her entire blog (each entry secured separately). As the number of relevant snippets (concerning one or more of the above-mentioned themes—Identity, Communication Style, etc.) kept mushrooming, I was struck by the need for two types of organization. The first type involved the themes themselves, and the management of those relevant snippets. The second type of organization was to do with emerging themes, associations, demographics, and identifications.

Eventually, I created several experimental forms on surveymonkey. com, each one aimed at streamlining everything. The first form was 37 pages long, and consolidated all the themes I'd been looking for. It also provided me a place to paste in all of the snippets supporting my claims about those themes. The behemoth also had checkboxes of every theme and subtheme that had appeared in any blog, interview, conversation, or questionnaire. In this way, I could easily create graphic representations of trends shared between all participants, certain groups of them, or a single one. As I began to use the form, the unneeded features stood out very clearly, and I was able to make necessary alterations.

Once I had every last scenario-based question memorized and dissected, I created yet another form using my new or updated categories for each theme. Upon the completion of my data entry for every participant's response to a particular question, I was able to create various charts that displayed any overlaps or grey areas. This allowed me to (again) tweak my models and (yet again) adjust the form to reflect any changed categories.

Following this process, I created new scenario-based questions (corresponding to the final categories) and released two versions (open- and closed-ended) of the new questionnaire. So far, I've had close to a hundred (mostly new) participants complete them.

Technology Choices and Rationale

INTERNET-BASED SYNCHRONOUS COMMUNICATION: ONLINE CHATS

This study's qualitative, in-depth interviews were conducted through Internet chats via Yahoo! Messenger (Gaiser & Schreiner, 2009).

Participants had been asked to add me to their contact list using a non-identifying Yahoo! screen name. They also had a schedule of times I would be online and were told to message me whenever they had 15 minutes to chat. I would inform them that they could pass on any question, and that they should signal the end of their responses with "And that's all." I would then begin with the first question and wait for their signal. In some cases, I asked follow-ups, while in others, I would move to another main question that flowed well with the previous one, and then return at a more appropriate time to any questions that had been missed.

The greatest strengths of this method included participants (ostensibly) feeling freer to share the personal details of some scandalous tales, the convenience of having ready-made transcripts of some rather lengthy conversations, and synchronous chatting seeming to aid the process of building rapport. Chatting in real time, participants could make jokes or respond to mine. The speed with which a person answered (or didn't) sometimes gave me a sign that I had touched upon a topic of great interest (or ire, as was often the case).

Shifting to the other side, the weaknesses of real-time chatting without audio or video included the inability to conclusively verify that participants were actually the ages, genders, and/or at the language proficiencies they claimed to be, and the inability to witness and/or record their nonverbal communications.

INTERNET-BASED ASYNCHRONOUS COMMUNICATION: SURVEYMONKEY.COM

In cases where a synchronous meeting proved impossible, I used an online questionnaire containing the same interview questions I had been asking the synchronous interviewees. I called this the "alternate form" of the qualitative interview and set up a link and advertisement for it on my website and Facebook/Myspace pages. Participants would click on the link, sign the consent form, and create a username (or provide the one they had created for the questionnaire).

As before, the strengths included freedom of speech and lack of transcription time, while weaknesses included lack of verifiability and the inability to note nonverbal communications. Another weakness of this method was the inability to ask targeted follow-up questions. A final weakness was the total inability to build rapport using this method (despite the jaunty comments made by a handful of participants).

Ethical Issues

ESTABLISHING IDENTITY

As previously mentioned, the fact that I could not actually see my interviewees most of the time presented me with an ethical dilemma: How much trust could I (or should I) place in what they were telling me? After all, it could be the same two people sitting in a computer lab somewhere. But to what end would such skullduggery be committed? If they were doing it to sabotage the numbers or findings of my study, they would fail, for other people had participated in front of me, and I did have access to a log of Internet protocol addresses. If they were doing it to help me out, then they need not have bothered, for I was interested in accuracy, not a convenient and insignificant finding.

In the end, I decided two things: First, it did not matter to me if they had changed some details about themselves, because in this study, I sought the absence or presence of a particular something—a process, actually—and not the precise circumstances that brought it about. Second, even if one or two or ten people had falsified some actual instances that seemed to support that particular something I was looking for, I know and have known dozens of people (in real life and online) who have shared stories similar to the possibly falsified ones, so even if some fabrication snuck into my data, it was based on a grain of truth somewhere.

This may seem a bit sketchy, since I was (and am) interested in empirically supporting a brand new theory. But the truth is that (1) at such an early stage, even one bona fide case would have been significant to me (meaning the difference between 8 and 18 bona fide cases wouldn't be completely disastrous), and (2) anything at all can be falsified—from Attention Deficit Hyperactivity Disorder (ADHD) to criminal insanity to love.

On the flip side of this issue were individuals who seemed intent upon letting me know who they were (a few even said their own names, though I suppose someone could have used someone else's name as a joke). In these cases, said participants sent me all sorts of messages about their lives, their families, and their reputations—among other things.

Research Findings

The study provided a veritable bonanza of significant findings. The hardest-hitting findings had to do with identity, namely, the *confusion* and *closeting* of research participants. *Confusion* in this context refers to the person who is unable to resolve the question of "who am I?" *Closeting* in this context refers to the person who knows very well who she/he is, but is unable to *live* that self—in front of relatives and/or other Egyptians anyway. People in both groups reported and hinted at stress galore—though the closeted ones seemed to have less.

The confused individuals displayed a phenomenon I termed the *Negative Dialogical State* (NDS), which often (but erroneously) resembles clinical depression. In the regular or normal dialogical model, voices representing conflicting cultural, demographic, and/or psychological positions might be at odds with one another; but a winner finally emerges, and the person goes with the decision of the winning voice. This is not to say that the person is necessarily happy with the result, or that negative things do not occur as a result of whatever decision is made—only that the particular dialogue in question does not hinder further dialogue.

In this Negative Dialogical State, however, the individuals do not merely ask "who am I, anyway?" and then feel sorrow over the inability to answer that question conclusively, or perhaps stress out over the fact that they are unable to be who they "really" are; rather, the dialogue ends. To put it another way, if the dialogical model of acculturation is based upon an internal dialogue between two or more perspectives, the voices in a person with NDS might never shut up, or they might stop talking altogether—effectively ending the discussion for some time.

Some might argue that *no* particular discussions (between various facets within a person) deserve special distinction or categorization, since the notions of "positive" and "negative" are subjective ones. My justification for proposing a negative category is a diagnostic one. In other words, the dialogical model's inherent lack of valence makes it unhelpful to the ordinary, everyday, garden-variety immigrant or bicultural individual, whereas a "diagnosis" of NDS could at least offer a direction—in the form of strategies, resources, and hope—to that person.

Thirteen participants' responses suggested that they were afflicted with NDS, and every one of the 13 had been diagnosed with depression at some point. Each had also embarked upon some form of regimen (therapy, medication, "self-medication," etc.) to beat the condition—which they were unable to do.

Some other points of interest that I look forward to investigating further include the fact that every single one of the 13 either stated or hinted at another something that seemed to appear quite frequently. I dubbed this phenomenon *cultural fluctuation syndrome* (CFS) because such individuals did, indeed, seem to go through orthogonal phases of preoccupation and disenchantment with one or more of the cultures they identified with. In almost all of the cases, participants seemed to have their acceptance and/or identity as a "true" Egyptian withheld by someone else, usually a parent or older relative that set him- or herself up as the Grand Arbiter of All Things Egyptian.

An interesting observation about NDS and the form of contact with the participant is that each of the 13 in question had conversed with me synchronously (on Yahoo) or else "spilled their guts" on a blog. The reason I find this interesting is that both forms seemed to encourage—or at least permit—a tidal wave of emotion, while the other forms (descriptive questionnaires and asynchronous interviews) did not reveal any cases of NDS—even among the "afflicted" participants. This may have been due to people wanting to hurry up and complete the instruments, but it may also have been because I wasn't there to gently nudge (aka shove) them in a direction that had intrigued me; perhaps my interest ignited their desire to vent to someone, anyone. Or maybe they wanted to get the advice and/or feedback of an Egyptian sister who'd not only been there herself, but who'd been researching and writing about the topic for almost a decade.

Another major finding involved communication style. This style was actually a particular form of venting that was revealed to be a common strategy for dealing with cultural and noncultural woes. This particular form was broken down into five different (but non-mutually-exclusive) styles that accomplished five communication acts or purposes.

An example of this was found in the fact that every single non-blogger participant afflicted with my proposed NDS not only stayed far longer than the 15 minutes I originally advertised (several interviews went on for 3 hours or more), but also made some comment about our conversation being "better than therapy" or helping them to "feel a whole lot better."

Whether those participants' improved states resulted from the catharsis that often accompanies a venting session, from hope renewed by my suggestions and/or advice, or from the mere fact that I did fully understand, sympathize, and in some cases, empathize with their cultural woes, I cannot say. What I can say, however, is that I am grateful for their trust and hopeful that their situations improve.

Limitations, Lessons Learned, and Recommendations

The first main category of limitations was that of the sample; very simply, additional cases of similar data may have yielded further theoretical output, or at least more support for those theories arising from the current data. Apart from a less-than-optimal sample size were the twin issues of participant quality and commitment. One main contributor to these issues may have been the lack of tangible incentive.

With respect to the "quality" of participants, I must confess to having initially feared that the opinions voiced might represent a somewhat biased population—due both to self-selection and the snowball sample—but it turned out that most of the bloggers and several of the face-to-face interviewees actually were far enough removed from me that my fears of self-selection and "the snowball effect" were put to rest.

The second main category of limitations involved the questionnaires and interviews. More specifically, I should have streamlined the process, avoided too much duplication, and provided details without worrying about putting words in participants' mouths. Both questions and directions could have been more concise and much less confusing.

The reason I had originally disallowed free movement within the questionnaire involved a fear that people would get scared off when they saw the nature of the questions. Interestingly, after de-requiring that would-be participants fill in every single answer, I noted that some people who came across as "respectable" by Egyptian standards—church-going, advanced degrees, relatively conservative—left the saucier questions blank, while others took the opportunity to lecture me on Egyptian culture, and/or about why the question was offensive. Just as interesting, those in the former category (the "respectable" ones) indicated that they were over 50 years of age, while those in the latter category (the "lecturers") tended to be in their forties or late thirties.

Some people had issues with the instructions, as well. For example, my original usage of the term "meaningful password" suggested to some that I was asking for their e-mail password, rather than a unique identifier that would be used to link their questionnaire and interview together. This necessitated a modification early on, and "meaningful password" then became "UNIQUE USERNAME," with the additional instructions that names be "nonidentifying, easy-to-remember," and difficult for someone else to come up with or guess.

With respect to the questionnaire's checkbox-based questions ("check all that apply"), these worked quite well, though in some cases, I regretted allowing participants to check more than one response. For example, in the demographic question, two participants did not specify a gender, one checked male and female (!), and another indicated both single and married (!!), resulting in a range of response counts.

In terms of the actual questions asked, I had 17 participants make statements or express frustration regarding what I was "really asking." For example, some complained that "I don't understand what is it that you want to know" or asked me to "hold on . . . I'm trying to understand what you're asking," while others commented that "the questions are a bit vague, would like some more details, please," and one very clever participant quoted my favorite play, *Madrassat el Moshaghbeen* ("School of the Troublemakers"), asking "*Fein el so2al? FEEEEIN EL so2AAAL???*" ("Where is the question?").

With regard to the scenario-based questions in the qualitative interview section, I believe that my wording confounded the results. In the "traitorous brother" question, for example, I should not have asked, "What would you *say* . . ." (emphasis added) but "How would you *feel* if your brother walked in and announced that he had just gotten engaged to someone you've never heard of from him before? And what would you *say* to him?" Happily, a majority of those answering the question denoted what they would say and what they would think.

Conclusions

I have learned many things during this study. A majority had to do with the execution of effective qualitative and online research, though I did gain a few insights into acculturation, as well as a handful of findings about cultural shift, and a few factoids regarding the New Egyptians. And while my fumblings with the DM have not yet resulted in a fully baked model that actually makes a difference, I am nowhere near giving up on my self-appointed task.

The strongest advice I would send back to the Sally of 2008 and 2009 includes the following tidbits:

1. One size does NOT fit all potential participants (in terms of best data collection method).

2. It's far, far better to have rich data from anonymous participants than thin, watery, and sanitized data from people you (might) know.

3. Sometimes it is better to let participants lead the discussion.

4. A lot of times it is better to have several sessions—each devoted to a topic of their choice—instead of attempting to stuff a dozen subjects into one monstrous session that could jeopardize the relationship.

5. A synchronous online interview will net better results if you make the chat take center stage and use data from blogs and questionnaires as sources of supporting information.

6. Finally, remember that triangulation will ALWAYS help you, so do not be afraid to bring in those supporting players and collect sheaves of great data!

 See the Appendix for suggested readings and resources on the software, methodologies, and methods discussed in this case.

 Find More Materials on the Study Site! See the book website for related resources, materials, discussion, and assignment ideas.

References

Bakhtin, M. M. (1981). Discourse in the novel (M. Holquist & C. Emerson, Trans.). In M. Holquist (Ed.), *The dialogic imagination: Four essays by M. M. Bakhtin* (pp. 259–422). Austin: University of Texas Press. (Original work published 1930s).

Berry, J. W. (1980). Acculturation as varieties of adaptation. In A. M. Padilla (Ed.), *Acculturation: Theory, models and some new findings* (pp. 9–25). Boulder, CO: Westview.

Bhatia, S. (2002). Acculturation, dialogical voices, and the construction of the diasporic self. *Theory & Psychology, 12,* 55–77.

Bishai, S. (2010). *Collectivism, communication, and cultural conflict: The dialogical acculturation of Christian Egyptians in the diaspora.* Unpublished doctoral dissertation, Florida State University, Tallahassee.

Bryman, A., & Bell, E. (2007). Business research methods. London: Oxford University Press.

Chaudhary, N., & Sriram, S. (2001). Dialogues of the self. *Culture & Psychology, 7,* 379–392.

Denzin, N. K., & Lincoln, Y. S. (Eds.). (1978). *Collecting and interpreting qualitative materials.* Beverly Hills, CA: Sage.

Frey, L. R., Botan, C. H., & Kreps, G. L. (1999). *Investigating communication: An introduction to research methods* (2nd ed.). Boston: Allyn & Bacon.

Gaiser, T. J., & Schreiner, A. E. (2009). *A guide to conducting online research.* Thousand Oaks, CA: Sage.

Glaser, B., & Strauss, A. (1967). *The discovery of grounded theory: Strategies for qualitative research.* Chicago: Aldine.

Gordon, M. M. (1964). *Assimilation in American life.* New York: Oxford University Press.

Hermans, H. J. M., Kempen, H. J. G., & van Loon, R. J. P. (1992). The dialogical self: Beyond individualism and rationalism. *American Psychologist, 47,* 23–33.

Hermans, H. J. M., Rijks, T. I., & Kempen, H. J. G. (1993). Imaginal dialogues in the self: Theory and method. *Journal of Personality, 61,* 206–236.

Jorgensen, D. L. (1989). *Participant observation: Methodology for human studies.* Newbury Park, CA: Sage.

Raggatt, P. F. (2000). Mapping the dialogical self: Towards a rationale and method of assessment. *European Journal of Personality, 14*(1), 65–90.

Redfield, R., Linton, R., & Herskovits, M. J. (1936). Memorandum for the study of acculturation. *American Anthropologist, 38,* 149–152.

Rudmin, F. W. (2003). Critical history of the acculturation psychology of assimilation, separation, integration, and marginalization. *Review of General Psychology, 7*(1), 3–37.

Said, E. W. (1999). *Out of place: A memoir.* New York: Vintage.

Scott, W. R. (1995). *Institutions and organizations.* Thousand Oaks, CA: Sage.

The Reality of Online Reality

AN ONLINE VETERAN

This is a very interesting chapter, and a number of aspects of the underlying study parallel the one I conducted (see Chapter 3). One key difference, however, is the vast online expertise of Sally Bishai. I did a little research on her (using Google, of course), and she has a wealth of experience over many years, in *virtually* all sectors of the online world (pun intended!). Being a neophyte in online research (and even in some basic facets of modern online life, like chatting and navigating social media networks), I learned much from reading her work and discussing it with her.

I was fortunate to have the chance to chat in real time with Sally using Yahoo! Chat. Because she is such a veteran chatter, I did get the feeling that I was speaking directly with her, even in a discussion of weighty research topics. Her humor, interest, and energy came through loud and clear and I suspect that is how her research participants perceived her as well. I can see how she gained their trust and how her experience online was a key asset in her study.

Why Research Online?

Among the topics we discussed was her decision to gather data online.

> **Allison Deegan** (5:41 PM): A. Did you ever think of *not* using an online facet to gather data, given your experience with the technology? And how do you think your study would have been different if you had?
>
> * * *
>
> *(Continued)*

(Continued)

Sally Bishai	(5:41 PM): hmmmm....
Sally Bishai	(5:42 PM): shall i give the briefest answer that's coherent
Sally Bishai	(5:42 PM): OR
Sally Bishai	(5:42 PM): "the real answer" ?
Allison Deegan	(5:43 PM): Real, please – I am verbose and don't know what brief is. That's why I'm such a bad chatter.
Sally Bishai	(5:43 PM): yay, glad to hear it! that's why we're qualitative, and why qualitative *rocks*! ☺
Sally Bishai	(5:43 PM): so ...
Sally Bishai	(5:44 PM): if you looked me up online, you may have seen a book i wrote many years ago...
Sally Bishai	(5:44 PM): Mideast Meets West:
Sally Bishai	(5:44 PM): On Being and Becoming a Modern Arab American
Sally Bishai	(5:44 PM): that was my master's thesis
Sally Bishai	(5:44 PM): I did it almost completely face-to-face, with some phone interviews as well
Sally Bishai	(5:44 PM): but i learned so much from the experience...
Sally Bishai	(5:44 PM): both in terms of interviewing (in general)
Sally Bishai	(5:45 PM): and in terms of Egyptians, Egyptian culture, and Egyptian fears/paranoias
Sally Bishai	(5:46 PM): (which I'm subject to, by the way, hence my sensitivity to it now... and the resourcefulness I had to obtain and use when dealing with this tricky population)
Sally Bishai	(5:46 PM): anywhoodle, that book, like the dissertation of doom, was based on identity.
Sally Bishai	(5:47 PM): but the biggest mistake I made all those years ago (let's call it "2003") was that I actually thought people would answer me correctly
Sally Bishai	(5:47 PM): i don't mean just accurately
Sally Bishai	(5:48 PM): in terms of scrambling the details in order to protect their reputations
Sally Bishai	(5:49 PM): online, however, they didn't feel like a person who could identify them would automatically know what they were trying to hide...though they (in some cases) didn't get my questions, or didn't think something applied to them when it *so* did...
Sally Bishai	(5:49 PM): by the way, feel free to interrupt with any follow-up or clarification questions at any moment, we

egyptians love to pursue several slightly connected convos at once . . . ☺

Allison Deegan (5:50 PM): I think that kind of sensitivity is real for a lot of research participants, but the research forum doesn't always allow for it – in that way, online research can provide a bigger window to speak the truth.

Sally Bishai (5:50 PM): agreed!

Sally Bishai (5:50 PM): but with egyptians...

Sally Bishai (5:50 PM): (and this is one thing i don't think i was able to stress enough, because in the west, people aren't prone to our kind of insanity . . . ☺

Sally Bishai (5:51 PM): it's like, if mrs. x told me that she held hands with a guy she wasn't married to, she could be dumped (divorced) or disowned over it

Sally Bishai (5:51 PM): a seemingly-tiny thing can not only haunt the person in question, but her or his whole family and all the people "unfortunate" enough to be their friends...

Sally Bishai (5:52 PM): so in a way, online research was literally the ONLY way i could have asked certain things

Allison Deegan (5:53 PM): And maybe having that removed from in-person scrutiny can help them change. Who knows. Can the internet save the world (moments before it destroys it)?

Sally Bishai (5:54 PM): so, i guess the 'one-line' answer is, "Having experienced certain difficulties with the same general population in my previous studies, I realised that the anonymity "promised" to participants would have made a big difference in those earlier studies; furthermore, I believe that the current study was—in many cases—greatly aided by the online format."

Sally Bishai (5:54 PM): maybe!

Sally Bishai (5:54 PM): hmm, i think it already destroyed it!

Sally Bishai (5:54 PM): but mayhap there's still hope ☺

In her study, Sally was committed to triangulation of data and thus used multiple online data gathering methods. This added a lot of depth to her study. She was also very flexible and even nimble, as one needs to be when using online methods, so she could respond when things changed, participants were not available in the originally planned setting, when survey participants needed extra clarification, and even when online texts or in-person interviews needed to be translated. Things change in these kinds of studies as the data-gathering process is very dynamic online, and researchers need to be responsive if they do not want to miss valuable opportunities.

Blogs as Data

Another key aspect of Sally's study was the utilization of reviews of blog sites as part of her data-gathering strategy. She developed a collection of very insightful tools and review templates to use in sifting through tens of thousands of pages of blog entries. Given the proliferation of online identity invention, we discussed whether or not blogs could provide more "real" insights into participants than interviews could.

Allison Deegan (6:28 PM): I love the idea of blogs as data sources – do you think they provide a more free discourse or even a different approach to revealing personal details than you could gather through a survey – are bloggers more "themselves" when they blog (and self-direct the content) or when they are asked deeply provocative questions (like the ones you seemed to ask)?

Sally Bishai (6:29 PM): i love this question! ☺

Allison Deegan (6:29 PM): I wish you had been on my committee!

Sally Bishai (6:29 PM): well, i did like the self-directing aspect of it, coz in that case, it meant that it was something that was affecting THEM, and not something i had pushed on them

✳ ✳ ✳

Allison Deegan (6:31 PM): Still recovering. Do you have a blog, and do you feel free when you write it?

Sally Bishai (6:32 PM): but you know, my provocative and hellish questions DID provide me with something [of] interest, and that is the reaction of the person

Sally Bishai (6:32 PM): i have several blogs, actually

Sally Bishai (6:32 PM): and i only feel truly free when i write under a pseudonym

Sally Bishai	(6:32 PM): ☺
Sally Bishai	(6:32 PM): but then, i've gotten death threats and junk
Sally Bishai	(6:32 PM): coz i used to write about religion (i'm Christian but most Egyptians are Moslem)
Allison Deegan	(6:32 PM): Would you rather a researcher just read your blog or interview to find out your true feelings?
Sally Bishai	(6:33 PM): it depends on what their intention was
Sally Bishai	(6:33 PM): because i might not be inclined to lecture and/or provide background/cultural whatnot to an audience, whereas the researcher might need to know stuff to make sense of it
Sally Bishai	(6:34 PM): and it also depends on what they were trying to find out
Allison Deegan	(6:34 PM): It is a unique format – a public diary – that may provide a unique kind of data
Sally Bishai	(6:34 PM): i agree
Sally Bishai	(6:34 PM): but i also think that some bloggers create a persona
Sally Bishai	(6:34 PM): and use their popularity as that persona
Sally Bishai	(6:34 PM): to gain confidence in the real world
Sally Bishai	(6:34 PM): like they might be unpopular in real life
Sally Bishai	(6:35 PM): but wow, they got 10000 hits this month!
Sally Bishai	(6:35 PM): i started to do a study on gamers who used their prowess at a game to build their confidence levels IRL

* * *

Sally Bishai	(6:37 PM): but re: blogging, it's easy to throw words into a vortex you may never see... but saying words to some people, you have to see their face/reaction
Sally Bishai	(6:37 PM): hear their disapproval (if it is "dis")
Sally Bishai	(6:38 PM): with a blog, you slap the words on the "paper" and if someone reads it, you know they "cared" enough to read it
Sally Bishai	(6:38 PM): it's not like someone will read a blog and then say "why did you tell us that? what a waste of space!"
Sally Bishai	(6:38 PM): coz the blogger can come back and say "well, why did you READ it then, genius?!"

The Concept of Diaspora

There were many other very significant points in Sally's chapter. Among them was the notion of defining the diaspora as a place rather than a movement or a phenomenon. I think this is a great analogy for the online world and the way it defines itself, in part, even though it lacks a physical place. We discussed whether it was even possible to sustain the notion of diaspora since we are all moving everywhere and can be in contact with anyone nearly anywhere.

Knowing Your Population

Sally's experience with this population (Egyptians, Egyptian immigrants to the United States, and Egyptian Americans) provides a great foundation from which to understand and ultimately interpret what the study participants are saying. Although she did not know her participants personally, she knows their culture and has shared many of their experiences. This makes her a highly credible analyst of the data they provided and one who could effectively and quickly bridge the distance between an online research subject and a participant. Her interactions with research participants online provided very rich data. A researcher can gain insight from being a new, objective observer in an online world, but there is also much to gain by interacting and studying a population that you are a member of in some way. Although she expresses concern about the veracity of the responses or the true identity of some of the participants, she seems fully able to ferret out anything that does not ring true for this population.

We also discussed the idea that the Internet can foster great connections and how, for some who are critically at risk or truly isolated, it can be a lifeline. But it can also keep us apart, if we are not presenting who we really are to a world of "friends" we do not really know (meaning we do not ever or hardly ever see them). I have mixed feelings about this. I want to maintain my appreciation for everything that is good about online communication while clinging to my concerns about all the ways in which it seems to keep us apart. Sally also expressed her belief that there are hugely beneficial and very worrisome aspects of living online.

Connectedness

Other themes, such as comparing acculturation to marginalization, and describing that process as being akin to depression, provide critical insights into the immigrant experience and how it is being expressed in online forums. In addition, Sally describes modern life as a "concurrent existence of multiple strands," and that resonated deeply with me. Multitasking, always being connected—the more these stresses impact our actual lives, they will wend their way into online research and may prove to have a significant impact on research data gathered in that arena. I believe, as a research setting, the online world is free of many of the constraints that all researchers face. In that way, the logistical benefits are huge. However, it is likely also the cause of a whole host of other concerns that are unique to online discourse. I believe that online research methods can become part of the study, beyond just vehicles we use to gather data.

There is so much more that I could say about this chapter, which mirrors some of the challenges Sally faced and probably a cause for concern for all online researchers—there can be a ton of data and we must locate and even develop methods to manage it all.

CHAPTER 2
FRAMEWORK COMMENTARY:
"BLOG LIKE AN EGYPTIAN"

Janet Salmons

In this qualitative, grounded theory study, Dr. Sally Bishai successfully generated new theory based on her analysis of data collected online. She used multiple approaches—all text based—to interact with and learn from the research participants. This flexibility allowed her to accommodate participants' schedules and preferences, and provided triangulation needed to substantiate the data.

Bishai chose to use online interviews because her study population is geographically dispersed. The behaviors and attitudes central to her study—cultural adaptation—are not behaviors that necessarily occur online. In other words, the purpose of the study was not to explore acculturation issues in online environments, rather to study the attitudes and experiences of everyday life in the diaspora. In this circumstance, the ICT selection priority was to choose an easily accessible, familiar communications technology.

Given the potentially sensitive nature of her study, the text-based approach allowed participants a layer of privacy. Bishai used synchronous, near-synchronous, and asynchronous approaches so participants could, if desired, pause to reflect on the questions and their experiences before responding. While text-only communications might be considered "lean" according to Media Richness Theory, a recent study by Hertel and colleagues suggests that shy people (or those anxious about discussing sensitive issues) may be more forthcoming in text-based forms that allow time for thoughtful written responses (Hertel, Schroer, Batinic, & Naumann, 2008).

For participant recruitment, she used a snowball approach and relied upon word of mouth, and family and religious or cultural places where participants who met the study's criteria might be found. Participants were recruited through both online and face-to-face interactions and referrals.

Even with this network of referrals and contacts that would suggest certain known factors about the research participants, Bishai expressed some concern that some of the individuals she interviewed

Figure 2.1 Research map for "Blog Like an Egyptian."

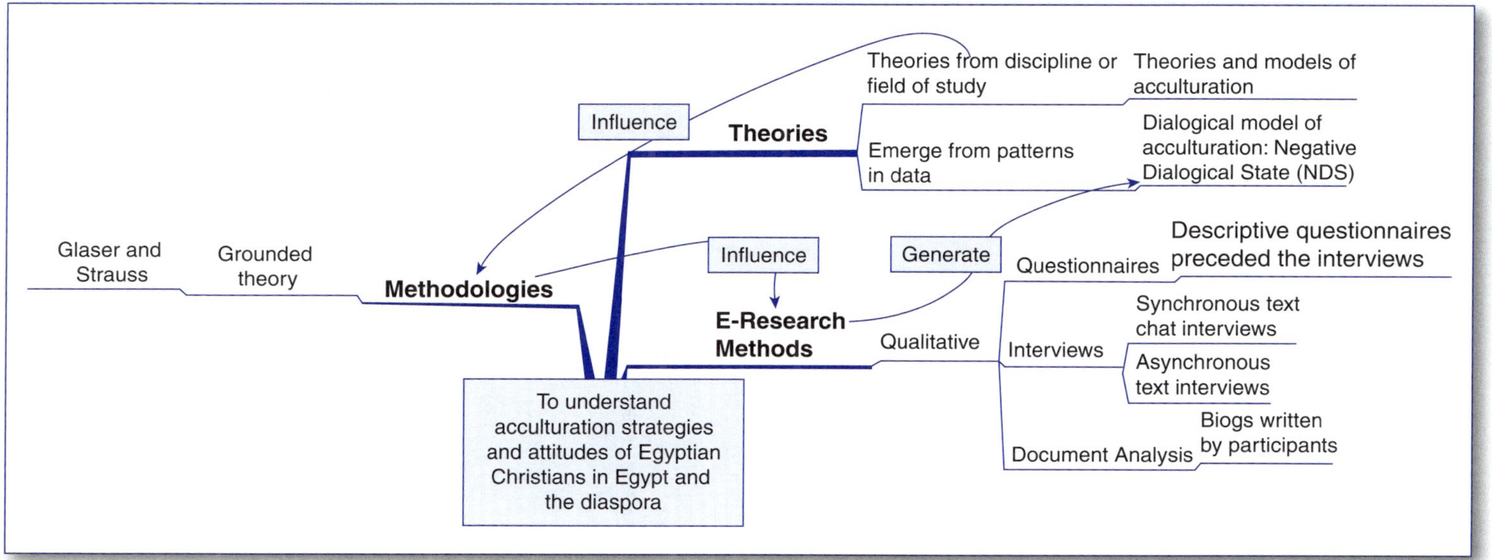

Theories from discipline or field of study

Theories and models of acculturation

Dialogical model of acculturation: Negative Dialogical State (NDS)

Emerge from patterns in data

Descriptive questionnaires preceded the interviews

Theories

Generate

Questionnaires

Synchronous text chat interviews

Asynchronous text interviews

Influence

Qualitative

Interviews

E-Research Methods

Blogs written by participants

Document Analysis

To understand acculturation strategies and attitudes of Egyptian Christians in Egypt and the diaspora

Methodologies

Influence

Grounded theory

Glaser and Strauss

65

may not have been fully honest in some respects. She decided that some possible misrepresentation was acceptable: "It did not matter to me if they had changed some details about themselves, because in this study, I sought the absence or presence of a particular something—a process, actually—and not the precise circumstances that brought it about." She felt that her larger, personal understanding of the research population—together with triangulation of the data from multiple sources and interactions—would make it possible to overcome minor discrepancies.

The researcher's ability to discern what was real or not, what mattered to the study or not, relates to the researcher's position vis-à-vis the study. She was an insider, someone who shares many characteristics and experiences with the research population. Using a metaphor for researchers' roles defined by Kvale, she "travelled with" the research participants to generate data (Kvale, 2007; Kvale & Brinkman, 2009). Stake describes emic issues in case studies as those research questions revealed by the actors of the case, who may include the researcher (Stake, 1995). While Bishai did not contribute data, her insight into the research population allowed for a level of understanding an outsider researcher may not have been able to achieve. This level of insight may have also allowed her to grasp the significance of research participants' responses, even through a lean, text-only medium of communication.

A key lesson learned from this study is the need for flexibility when conducting research online. If one technology did not work, Bishai shifted to another, selecting options that would allow for comparable data collection. She also noted the value of several shorter, more focused sessions, rather than try to cover all topics in one session. This point may be particularly true in text-based interviews, where keeping the participant's attention and interest in typing potentially long responses could be a challenge.

By using e-research methods, Dr. Bishai was able to collect data from far-flung research participants. Face-to-face interviews would have been logistically difficult and cost-prohibitive. It is hard to say whether she would have been as successful at collecting data on sensitive, personal issues with other interview approaches, such as telephone interviews. As a result of her study, a new theory is proposed and that may be of value to future researchers who are interested in the process and impact of acculturation.

Table 2.1 Summary: Key Factors in the "Blog Like an Egyptian" Study

Motivation for Choosing E-Research	Sampling and Recruiting	Interview Style and Structure	Technology: Issues, Features, Lessons	Ethical Issues
Bishai selected online research to enable interviews with geographically dispersed participants, and to foster dialogue on sensitive topics. Bishai selected online research methods to study phenomena that are not Internet related.	Criterion and snowball sampling were used with online and face-to-face recruitment.	Semi-structured and unstructured conversational interviews Synchronous, near-synchronous, and asynchronous text-based interviews	When synchronous interviews were not possible, Bishai offered an asynchronous option. She used text-based interviews; did not collect visual data.	Possible identity issues with participants were addressed by triangulating the data.

References

Glaser, B., & Strauss, A. (1967). *The discovery of grounded theory: Strategies for qualitative research.* Chicago: Aldine.

Hertel, G., Schroer, J., Batinic, B., & Naumann, S. (2008). Do shy people prefer to send e-mail? Personality effects on communication media preferences in threatening and nonthreatening situations. *Social Psychology, 39*(4), 231–243. (DOI: 10.1027/1864-9335.39.4.231)

Kvale, S. (2007). *Doing interviews.* Thousand Oaks, CA: Sage.

Kvale, S., & Brinkman, S. (2009). *InterViews: Learning the craft of qualitative research interviewing* (2nd ed.). Thousand Oaks, CA: Sage.

Stake, R. E. (1995). *The art of case study research.* Thousand Oaks, CA: Sage.

Stranger in a Strange Land

The Challenges and Benefits of Online Interviews in the Social Networking Space

Allison Deegan

California State University, Long Beach, USA

This chapter describes a study conducted online, using specific electronic methods (including real-time and e-mail interviews), as well as electronic adaptations of traditional methods. The purpose of the study was to examine the development of confidence in creative writing abilities by adolescents who were participants in an out-of-school-time (OST) creative writing and mentoring program. While the content and findings of the study are significant and, I hope, interesting to anyone striving to engage teens and guide them to form and achieve educational goals (including attaining entrance to college), it is the study's design, logistics, the evolution of the methodology, and the challenges I faced while conducting the research that I have highlighted here. I hope that this description of my adventures in the wild world of social networks and real-time online communication will provide guidance and support to others interested in using online methods for educational research.

My Social Network

I developed a social network overnight, and by accident. Due to my unfamiliarity with the conventions and processes for navigating the Facebook social network site, I invited everyone who has ever sent me an e-mail over the course of the past 10 years to be my Facebook friend. Shortly thereafter, I began receiving hundreds of messages confirming acceptance of invitations I was not aware I had sent. I recognized a lot of the names but many were not familiar at all. There were a few queries by people asking me who I was and how I knew them. In a matter of days, we were all bound together in a manner I had not yet had time to understand.

FACEBOOK

I had heard much about Facebook, of course. It is everywhere. I never participated because it did not appeal to me. I am not a Luddite; in fact, I am a former technology consultant. It was not my inability to operate the hardware and software that kept me from Facebook, Twitter, chatting, and texting. It is just not the way I prefer to communicate, especially with people I know. Like many of my friends and colleagues, I have gravitated toward e-mail for a significant portion of my communication, but when it is truly personal, I pick up the phone (to speak, not to text!).

The only downside of e-mail communication for me was that it was often far from synchronous (when I wanted that kind of communication, which I must confess I do not always want—sometimes the delay via e-mail is quite beneficial and preferable, even when communicating with those I know intimately). Facebook never called to me as an efficient way to stay in contact and, while that attitude made me seem out of the loop, I did not mind. Once my Facebook network was formed, however, I decided to delve in to see who was hanging out in my new online neighborhood.

Many of my new Facebook friends were people I knew well. Scrolling through the pages was fun at first, if a bit distracting, and I had no reason to think anything nefarious was going on. I enjoyed one Facebook group conversation with a bunch of college buddies over the course of several days that felt like I had attended a warm, endearing reunion. If that was Facebook, I was a fan. That is when I noticed the teens among the ranks of my hundreds of new Facebook friends.

WORKING WITH YOUTH

I am associate director and one of the founding members of a creative writing and mentoring organization called WriteGirl. Over the course of my 9-year tenure in that role, I have interacted with several mentees online in social networking sites (Myspace and Facebook) because it was the only way I could reach them and keep them in our program. In these communications, I sent and received messages through the sites' e-mail functions—I was not an active member or friend on their individual pages. As soon as I established regular communication with them in the real world, I stopped messaging them through the social networking sites and used e-mail or the phone.

During my invitation snafu, when I had invited everyone in my e-mail address book to be my Facebook friend, I had inadvertently solicited many of the alumni and teen participants from the WriteGirl program, since I had e-mailed them at one point or another. Nearly all of them accepted and were now part of my online social network.

PERCEPTIONS ABOUT FACEBOOK

As I explored the pages of these teen Facebook friends, I came to several anecdotal conclusions. First, they spent a lot of time on Facebook. Virtually every time I logged in during the course of my research, no matter what time of day, most of the teenagers in my network were active on their pages and in Facebook chat.

The second observation was that social networking communication can be isolating. Part of my reluctance to interact with program youth on social networking sites was born of concerns I have about truly connecting. I believed that the sites tended to foster the semblance of contact and connection when, in fact, they could create greater distances among young people (and people like me who were trying to reach them). If the only way I can reach a teenager is through Facebook, it seems like a problem to me, an indication that they may be unwilling or unable to participate in face-to-face communication.

Third, I observed how different the Facebook personas of the youth who had accepted my friend requests seemed to be from the real-world personalities and behaviors I had observed during their time in the WriteGirl program. They were self-creating new, hybrid identities for themselves. They had very active Facebook "walls," posted dozens of status updates daily on their pages (almost exclusively about mundane activities and observations), and some conducted what was tantamount to a datebook/texting roundup on a moment-by-moment basis right there in public, for *all* of their Facebook friends to observe, comment on, and presumably participate in.

I did not join in the discussions on any of these teens' pages because it did not seem appropriate to me. I did not want to be this kind of friend to them, no more than I would want to attend their slumber parties or listen in on their telephone calls. It felt like I was not supposed to see much of it, and yet there it was, in full view of the world, with their consent.

However reluctant a participant I was, I also came to see that the social network space could be a very rich environment for research. I turned my attention to the Facebook pages of WriteGirl alumni, all of whom are over 18 and in college or are college graduates. They were also very active and nearly all had hundreds of Facebook friends. However, perhaps because they were older and less amorphous as personalities, I did get the sense that the alumni pages represented who these young women had become. I was excited to have a window into their current lives, and wanted to learn how they had turned out.

The final conclusion I came to was that the ease and comfort with which some navigated the world of Facebook was a legitimate representation of their lives and social networks, and that I should not dismiss its value as an arena for social construction and communication just because it was not my preferred method. Thus, I designed my study to be conducted entirely online, in real time, within the world of Facebook, centered on interviews with alumni participants of the WriteGirl creative writing and mentoring program.

ABOUT THE WRITEGIRL PROGRAM

WriteGirl (www.WriteGirl.org) is a creative writing and mentoring organization based in greater Los Angeles. Founded in 2001, WriteGirl provides individual creative writing mentors to mentees in out-of-school-time settings. Mentees, aged 13 to 15, are drawn from more than 60 public and private high schools and self-select to participate, with many discovering the program through WriteGirl's public events, books, website, and outreach campaigns conducted at inner-city schools in Los Angeles.

WriteGirl does not screen girls for achievement, grades, or writing ability and accepts all girls who apply based on space availability.

Mentees work weekly with their creative writing mentor, and meet monthly for full-day creative writing workshops that present proprietary curricula that meet (but are not constrained by) California state educational standards (California Department of Education, 1998). Participants remain in the program by choice, most for more than 3 years. WriteGirl serves approximately 75 girls per year in matched mentoring pairs, 50 additional girls as occasional or drop-in participants at workshops, and 120 girls who participate in a related program serving pregnant and parenting teens. All participants for this study were drawn from alumni who were part of the core WriteGirl program, and were part of a mentoring pair for a year or more.

WriteGirl participants learn and refine creative writing skills, demonstrate significant gains in self-confidence, and produce work that is included in the program's award-winning books. They also work closely with a support team on college essays and applications. In May 2010, California Governor Arnold Schwarzenegger and First Lady Maria Shriver named WriteGirl California Non-Profit of the Year. By and in October 2010, the group launched its 10th year of programs for teen girls. The author serves as WriteGirl's associate director and is one of the founding members.

Study Design

This study used a single-case approach employing triangulation in data gathering (Yin, 2009), and was intended to test a theory about the connection between participants' experiences in WriteGirl and any resulting creative writing confidence. Interviews with alumni of the WriteGirl program were the primary source of data. Additional sources of data included document review of the program's records, review of physical artifacts, and program observations. This triangulation of data provided a rich library of information for analysis (Yin, 2009). Interview data were analyzed using an adaptation of the Listening Guide methodology (Gilligan, Spencer, Weinberg, & Bertsch, 2003).

This study included real-time interviews within Facebook and asynchronous interviews conducted via e-mail. These techniques were selected specifically to provide maximum comfort to study participants. I am a significant insider in the study's program site, and I am well-known to all of the study participants. I assumed that

I would be perceived as an authority figure. However, I wanted to both acknowledge and utilize my insider status to my advantage by putting myself (as the data gatherer) in a position to observe and analyze any layers of nuance in the communications with the participants. I did not believe that an objective third party could capture this critical data. However, I also wanted to provide what I came to think of as a "safe distance," letting me spend some time in the participants' comfort zone (their Facebook or online world) without being an actual presence who might have an undue influence on how they might respond (which was what I feared might happen with in-person interviews). In addition, I wanted them to interact with me using the same channels they used to communicate with their other online friends. I wanted to increase their freedom to be themselves and to respond without any filter. Having seen the ease with which they presented themselves on Facebook, I wanted to engage them on their home turf.

As planned, some of the interview questions would likely require some pondering to respond, and were well suited to a setting where participants could write their responses in their own time. I developed a semi-structured interview protocol that had the flexibility to expand or contract question areas, depending on the flow of the interview.

As a bonus, the speed and veracity of online communication with someone one knows well would make the whole process efficient and ultimately very accurate. I intended to interview each participant in Facebook chat and to conduct every other part of the data-gathering process online, including soliciting participants, securing consent, and distributing incentives. At the time the study plan was formed, literature on real-time online interviewing (James & Busher, 2009; Salmons, 2009) was just beginning to emerge and provided significant support for the process I envisioned. Because I knew the participants well, I felt that I could avoid some of the potential pitfalls of working online, such as not being able to verify the identity of the person you are communicating with. It was a solid plan, and then the fun began.

INSTITUTIONAL REVIEW BOARD

The initial Institutional Review Board (IRB) application for this was extensive because I was using emerging methods. I took the time to

Chapter 3: Stranger in a Strange Land   75

lay out exactly what I wanted to do, why the online space was a critical component of the study (and not just a convenience), and how
the tension between my insider status and my researcher's remove
would be fully addressed in the study and even catalogued and
offered as data, rather than a hindrance to objectivity. I explained the
recruitment process by which I would secure 20 participants from a
pool of approximately 180 program alumni, hoping to spread them
across an evenly distributed range of what are called dosage levels
(how many years they spent as members of the WriteGirl program).
This goal was important to represent the breadth of the WriteGirl
program and to identify any differences born of experiencing it from
1 to 5 years.

The initial response from the IRB was confusing. Apparently, I had
not accurately conveyed the context of the study and the board misunderstood some of the fundamentals, such as my being well-known
to all of the potential participants. Thus, they provided significant
guidance and requirements on how to keep participants anonymous.
They did not understand the focus of the WriteGirl program and
were concerned that participation might render the young women in
urgent need of psychological counseling, and thus required that I
provide access to these resources.

They also rejected the adequacy of electronic consent, concerned about my ability to verify the identity of participants
online. I had prepared for this concern by comparing it to that
which survey researchers face, where it is impossible to verify who
filled out the survey, or who mailed it or e-mailed it back. The
board was not convinced. Further, they requested that any communication sent electronically include a warning that it was not
secure.

The confusion, and the requirements for going forward, grew
from there. I am not entirely sure how the extensive document I
submitted came to be viewed as a plan for an entirely different sort
of study, as I had labored over being as explicit as possible because I
knew my data-gathering methods were unusual. I can only say that it
presented unfamiliar methods at a time when concern over privacy
and protection of research participants' identities was very high, as it
should be.

To resolve these issues, I met with IRB representatives and, with
the ability to respond to any questions and concerns, was able to
make the case for the study as I designed it. I had successfully
conveyed the critical relationship of the online space to the data

I hoped to gather. However, the rounds of back and forth consumed significant weeks under a very tight research schedule and ended up delaying the study by several months.

Purpose of the Study and Research Questions

The purpose of this study was to investigate and describe a connection between creative writing confidence and confidence/self-efficacy in other kinds of writing, and in educational goals and outcomes, among adolescent girls who have participated in the WriteGirl program.

The research questions asked whether participation in the creative writing program impacted participants' creative writing self-efficacy, overall self-confidence, and formation of educational goals (while enrolled) and outcomes (after their participation concluded).

Research Design Overview

CONCEPTUAL FRAMEWORK

In investigating how adolescents develop self-efficacy in creative writing, the study was framed around two major components: freedom and self-efficacy. These two conceptual pillars of freedom and self-efficacy describe the goal of WriteGirl's curriculum and the community that is created for teen participants.

Peter Elbow's (1973/1998) landmark treatise, *Writing Without Teachers*, was a foundational source for the freedom pillar of the conceptual framework. Elbow's ideas about freedom were examined in context with Dewey (1934), Freire (1970), Gilligan (1982), and Myhill (2001; Myhill, Fisher, Jones, Lines, & Hicks, 2008), to help describe the components of freedom and how it impacts the development of confidence for writers and spurs creativity.

The framework's second pillar, self-efficacy, was examined using the work of Pajares (Pajares, 2003; Pajares & Johnson, 1993, 1995; Pajares & Urdan, 2006; Pajares & Valiante, 1997), who studied writing self-efficacy among youth. Pajares's work is informed by the classic self-efficacy foundations of Bandura (1977) and creative writing confidence studies by Chandler (1999, 2002).

OPERATIONAL DEFINITIONS

Creative writing: Writing that is primarily for expressive purposes, grounded in genres such as fiction, poetry, creative nonfiction, memoir, and personal essay. Whether or not developed as part of an educational program, creative writing is distinct from academic, research, expository, diary, or reportorial writing, primarily in the sense that the author determines what to write without prescriptive guidance.

Educational goals and outcomes: In the context of this study, educational goals and outcomes include high school graduation and admission to college.

Out-of-school time (OST): Activities including educational and enrichment programming that take place outside of classroom instructional time. OST activities can take place in school buildings and may be conducted or led by teachers or certificated personnel, but students do not receive grades. Typically, attendance and participation are optional.

Self-efficacy: An individual's belief in their ability to complete a task or achieve a milestone.

Teens/adolescents: Participants between the ages of 13 and 18.

DATA COLLECTION STRATEGY AND TOOLS, POPULATION AND SAMPLE

Interview data were collected using online synchronous interviews and e-mail interviews with alumni participants of WriteGirl, conducted in Facebook chat and through participants' e-mail accounts. All alumni for whom WriteGirl had operational contact information were solicited to participate in the study via e-mail addresses provided by the program, and they were invited to join a WriteGirl alumni page in Facebook. Of the total pool of alumni of approximately 120, 70 young women joined the WriteGirl alumni Facebook page. In addition, I sent invitations to participate in the study via e-mail to several dozen more alumni who were my Facebook friends (using Facebook e-mail) or for whom I had non-Facebook e-mail addresses. My goal was to secure 20 participants for the study.

Dosage

Respondents were to be assigned to groups based on their WriteGirl program dosage (from 1 to 5 years of participation in the program). I planned to select randomly from each dosage group to achieve a study pool balanced across the full range from 1 to 5 years. In selecting across dosage ranges, I also hoped to include participants from each of the previous 8 years of WriteGirl programming. I took this approach because, in the OST world, the metric of dosage is a commonly used determinant of program quality. Higher dosage tends to indicate higher-quality programs or programs with significant outcomes (Piha, 2008), as participants, especially teens, are viewed as "voting with their feet"—if they do not want to be there, they will have low dosage.

Facebook Protocols

My initial plan was to send potential participants a solicitation through Facebook e-mail, and ask those who accepted the invitation to complete a preliminary demographic questionnaire (to provide basic contact information and program participation data, as a check against WriteGirl records), sent back and forth pasted into a Facebook e-mail window. In addition, informed consent forms and interview releases would also be sent via Facebook e-mail.

I sent all members of the WriteGirl Facebook alumni group a standard solicitation. Approximately 50 responded that they would participate. I followed up with these individuals and e-mailed them the informed consent documents approved by the IRB. The document exceeded the size limit of the Facebook e-mail window, so I had to break them up into multiple Facebook e-mails to each potential participant.

In addition to these efforts, I e-mailed (via Facebook e-mail) approximately 30 additional alumni who were not yet members of the WriteGirl alumni page on Facebook but who were either my Facebook friends or just individuals I had located on Facebook by searching for their names. Approximately 15 of these alumni contacted me back through Facebook e-mail, agreeing to participate in the study. I sent them the multipart consent form through Facebook e-mail. Further, I e-mailed another 15 alumni for whom I had e-mail addresses but who were not on Facebook (or were not using the names I knew them by on Facebook). Of this group, 6 agreed to participate. I was very pleased to have assembled a potential participant pool of approximately 70 participants from which to select 20 ultimate study participants across dosage groups.

First hurdle. In anticipation of conducting the interviews in the Facebook chat function, I conducted several pilot interviews. I chatted with personals friends, one of whom is a professional social networking consultant, asking her to provide technical assistance and Facebook cultural guidance. The tests went off without a hitch and I was pleased with the speed of the interaction (it felt very conversational) and the efficiency of having a transcript already constructed.

For the study's interviews, questions from the interview protocol were to be entered into the chat window by me, and the participants would add their responses thereafter. At intervals during the interview, I planned to cut the interview text and paste it into a Word document on my personal computer, thus never archiving or saving the chat transcript anywhere online. I wanted to do this periodically in case the chat window closed unexpectedly, so I would not lose any interview data. When the interviews were completed, no text would remain in the chat window and it would be closed. I developed 30 interview questions, following a semi-structured approach to allow for exploration, and several with multiple parts for potential follow-up, as necessary. I anticipated that most interviews would last between 30 and 60 minutes.

The first problem I encountered was that an interview participant had to be my Facebook friend (not just a member of the WriteGirl alumni Facebook page) to chat with me. Thus, I had to make a friend request to each potential participant that I wasn't already friends with. I encouraged those I had solicited outside of Facebook to join as my friend and to join the WriteGirl alumni Facebook group. These complications added time to the study and threatened to diminish the size of the potential participant pool.

Second hurdle. As I continued sending out multiple Facebook e-mails containing the parts of the informed consent documents, tried to round up new Facebook friends, and sent out e-mails, I was unsure if I had the time to reach all 120 alumni. The "automated" process I hoped to achieve using Facebook had turned into a very labor-intensive, somewhat manual process, as I had to cut and paste, and send and resend e-mails and messages that did not get through. Many of the potential participants who had first expressed interest in the study were visibly active on Facebook and yet had not responded to subsequent outreach. I did not want to badger any of them or communicate so much that I was talking them into joining the study, so I was left in limbo waiting for responses.

Banned From Facebook

While working late one evening, as I was going in and out of Facebook, sending various messages, I was logged off the service with no explanation. I tried to log back in and received a screen message that said I had been banned from Facebook. I tried multiple times to log in and was prevented. The next day, I reviewed Facebook's online documentation to try to find a reason for my banning. When I found nothing that explained what had happened, I used Google to research being banned from Facebook. I found references by many people who were banned from Facebook without knowing what they did wrong. Several alerted me to the site's warning not to try to create a new account under a different name (something I was considering, given the very short time window I had within which to collect data). Creating a new account under a different name, the site warned, would result in a lifetime ban!

Facebook's initial denial of access message provided a link to an appeal process. I filed an appeal by e-mail explaining that I did not know which rule I had violated and that I was a doctoral student in the middle of a dissertation study with intense time constraints. The banning notice had cautioned me that there was no timeframe within which they would review the appeal, and that making multiple entreaties asking for a quicker review would only delay the process. One had to just sit and wait for their verdict. I included a sense of urgency and pleading in my appeal, since I did not have time to wait. I resisted the urge to create a new identity and try to get an account, fearing both a lifetime ban and the need to recontact all of my potential participants, asking them to befriend my new account.

Regrouping

With only a few weeks to conduct the interviews to meet dissertation completion deadlines, I decided to revamp my participant recruitment procedure. I asked one of the other administrators of the WriteGirl alumni Facebook page to send out a message to page members asking them to contact me via my home e-mail address. Several of them contacted me right away but many did not. I e-mailed all of the potential participants for whom I had non-Facebook e-mail addresses and several of them responded. Again I feared I would not have a large enough pool from which to select 20 participants who covered the program dosage range I was seeking, something that seemed unlikely if I was relegated to a very small pool.

Population and Sample

Many of the 120 alumni I had originally contacted through Facebook and e-mail did not seem to be able to sort out the multiple messages they had received from me, especially since my communication about being banned from Facebook had been sent to them by someone else (and they could no longer reach me through Facebook). Even I was getting confused. After several weeks of trying to line up participants, I only had 20 confirmed, from whom I had collected electronically signed informed consent forms. I did not want to sit and wait for participants to respond and decided to go forward with the 20 participants I had. If the pool of participants turned out to be too narrow (especially in terms of dosage), I figured I could address that limitation in the analysis. I confirmed the participation of the 20 who had agreed by e-mail. While finalizing this process with the 20 participants, I reached out through a friend of a friend who worked at Facebook, asking that an additional appeal be communicated on my behalf. Shortly thereafter, Facebook restored my access. I never received an explanation about why I had been banned and will never know what led to my reinstatement.

I began to steer my 20 interview participants back to Facebook (much to *everyone's* confusion!), to set up the interviews in the chat function. I had to make sure everyone in the pool was my Facebook friend, which they all were. Each participant received a preliminary demographic questionnaire (sent via regular e-mail to avoid any issues with Facebook e-mail size limitations). The questionnaire sought information about their participation in the WriteGirl program (grades in school, years of participation, age, marital status, educational status, and other programs they participated in while in high school).

Ultimately, 18 alumni participated in the interviews and they did represent a range of participants across dosage levels and participation years. One potential participant completed the demographic questionnaire but did not complete the interview, and one did not complete either the questionnaire or the interview. No reasons were provided from the two who did not complete the process but they received the iTunes compensation ($10 gift cards) that all participants received. No information about them was included in the study.

Interviews

The study had been founded on the primacy of real-time online interviews within the social networking space, for the reasons outlined above. While I was required to transition some of my communication with participants to other methods (e-mail), due to being banned by the Facebook site, I still wanted to conduct the interviews in Facebook chat once I was provided access to the network again.

The interview protocol offered questions about participants' experiences in WriteGirl and in college. They were asked about the transition from high school to college, and whether the confidence they gained in WriteGirl (if they did indeed gain any) in both creative writing and their lives in general was maintained when they got to college. The interview instrument was developed based on my knowledge of the participants and the WriteGirl program. I also queried participants about their perceptions of self-efficacy, creativity, the contrast between creative and academic or school writing, and whether they were cognizant of any of these areas while a participant in WriteGirl (during high school) or now, as young adults in college or as college graduates. It was designed to get them to think deeply and to respond in depth if necessary.

Maintaining Focus Online

I developed a schedule for the interviews and made chat appointments with high expectations, but I had trouble in the very first interview. The Facebook chat function worked well enough and the participant arrived in the chat room on time, but there seemed to be a lag between questions and responses that undermined the conversational atmosphere I had hoped to create. The comfort and familiarity were there, the interview was warm and amusing at times, and I was convinced that the participant was expressing herself with no concern about saying what I wanted to hear. I had no indication or fear that I was chatting with someone other than the participant. Nevertheless, I was frustrated that the interview went so slowly.

The time lag kept taking *me* out of the conversation. I was waiting for responses for as long as 10 minutes. In my impatience, I began to ask the questions again, as if they were not seen or understood, and I typed "Are you there?" multiple times into the chat window. Eventually a response would come back and the conversation would start again. This was not a good start to what I hoped would be an organic, online version of a real, connected conversational interview.

The next several interviews played out in the same way. The jerky, start and stop exchange back and forth between me and the participant, conversational in content and tone but not in progress, provided me with the kind of data I was seeking but with little opportunity to conduct an actual conversation (a true, unscripted back and forth). I ended up covering the content of the interview protocol but did not have much opportunity to expand on it—just getting the questions covered became like pulling teeth.

Why not e-mail? At that point, I came to a participant who could not be interviewed over chat because of time zone differences. I sent the interview protocol to her via her personal e-mail and asked her to e-mail back her responses to any of the interview questions she chose to answer. She completed the interview and returned it to me the next day. She stated that she delayed a bit because she wanted to be thoughtful in her responses. Her interview responses were very conversational in tone, not stilted or formal in any way. A little pondering, I noticed, appeared to be a good thing. She provided more insight than some of the prior interviews conducted in Facebook chat. It was fast, efficient, personal, and insightful, and it was written, just what I had been seeking. There did not seem to be any deficit in the depth of the content just because it had been completed via e-mail rather than in chat.

I wondered why I had rejected the use of e-mail as an interview method. In retrospect, it may have seemed like a lesser degree of online contact when compared to real-time chatting. In addition, I feared that the process would be too formal, like completing a test or a questionnaire, rather than talking in an interview setting. I wondered if participants would spend a lot of time composing what they believed to be the "right" responses, rather than spontaneously offering up whatever occurred to them in the moment.

As I reviewed the completed e-mail interview, I began to see that this format might be the answer to many of my challenges. If I used e-mail interviews, I could control the process while keeping it open ended, with the interview protocol being a starting point but allowing the participant to say whatever they wanted. I could follow up if necessary, and participants could have contact at their own convenience. They would not have to contend with other distractions during the actual interview, as some had while chatting online. I would not have to tolerate the delay I had experienced in Facebook chat. Thus, I made plans to conduct the remaining two thirds of the interviews using e-mail.

I asked several participants whose interviews took place in Facebook chat why they had taken so long to respond to questions. They revealed, as was their usual practice, they were participating in multiple online activities during our interviews. Although we were directly connected, the line of communication was quite crowded with other requests for input and output on various other chats, websites, and even text-message sites. Thus, I decided to minimize the distractions and e-mailed the interview protocol to the remaining participants, via their personal e-mail addresses.

DATA ANALYSIS

Interview data were analyzed using an adaptation of the Listening Guide methodology. It was well suited for a group of writers who were part of a creative writing program designed to empower their voices since the Listening Guide is a voice-capturing method.

UNDERSTANDING THE LISTENING GUIDE

The Listening Guide methodology (Gilligan et al., 2003) was designed to elicit hidden or reluctant voices to emerge from interview transcripts. To use the Listening Guide, a researcher conducts participant interviews (using a protocol guided by a theoretical framework of the researcher's choosing) that are transcribed at completion. The researcher then conducts a series of four separate "sequential listenings" (Gilligan et al., 2003, p. 159), while reviewing hard copies of the interview transcripts. Throughout the process, the researcher marks comments, finds common themes and other indicators on the transcript, and records them using different colored markers. The result is a transcript rich in information for analysis.

Through the four steps, researchers "listen" to the transcripts for (1) the plot that seems to emerge from the interview; (2) "listening" for what are called I Poems (first person statements extracted in order from the transcript and composed into poems); (3) "listening" for contrapuntal voices (to hear and understand the different layers of a singular voice, based on the theory of music counterpoint, which is listening for single instruments in isolation while they play with others simultaneously); and (4) "listening" to compose an analysis of the whole interview, where the researcher synthesizes what has been heard, observed, and how he/she has responded to it (Gilligan et al., 2003).

Because the study participants are accomplished writers, I was interested in seeing how their interview data comported with the goals of the Listening Guide and whether an additional layer of data would be revealed for analysis. I also selected this methodology because of the primacy of the researcher in the process. As stated earlier, I am a key individual in the WriteGirl program and cannot be scrubbed (to any good effect) from the process of analyzing how the participants chart their experiences within it. Thus, the Listening Guide allows for personal interaction and reflection with and about the data collected and does not require that I remove my own impressions from the study, however subjective they may be.

I adapted the Listening Guide through the incorporation of electronic tools, including online interviews, e-mail interviews, NVivo qualitative data analysis software, and Microsoft Excel software (to extract themes from the transcripts, and to confirm themes identified during the interview and review processes).

Research Findings

The study found that most participants did indeed develop confidence in their creative writing abilities through their membership in the WriteGirl program (Deegan, 2010). They translated their creative confidence into other realms of their life and were guided to participate more in class, speak their minds, and try new things. They provided some interesting feedback into the nature of creativity and freedom (with some benefiting from the free environment of the program, but others commenting that creative people like to challenge restrictions as a way to spark their imaginations, so sometimes less freedom is good!). They made a strong connection between the development of their confidence and self-efficacy, in general and with regard to creative writing, in large part due to the supportive nature of the WriteGirl program and the mentors they worked with.

However, upon entering college, many had a vastly different experience with writing self-efficacy. College professors were not nurturing. Some participants who considered themselves strong writers encountered harsh criticism, especially in creative writing classes. In my estimation, this seemed to be more of a stylistic difference—their classes were not WriteGirl workshops, where a premium was placed on empowering them to achieve. Rather, the college classes outlined a static standard (however subjective that may be when "grading" creative writing), and professors determined that they either met it or they did not. Their journey as creative writers was of little concern to these professors. Many of the classroom practices described were antithetical to the WriteGirl environment, and to the notions espoused by Elbow (1973), that freedom is essential for achievement, and by Pajares and his colleagues, that self-efficacy is achieved in a supportive environment.

As someone who has devoted a great amount of time and effort into guiding these young women to develop confidence, this was very difficult data to review. I was a bit heartbroken that the bright, high-achieving young writers I had helped to nurture were being denigrated by some of their professors, at least in terms of creative writing. It was certainly not the experience of all of the participants, but it was for some and that was one too many in my mind.

Luckily, other participants were more resilient and used their WriteGirl-gained confidence to steel themselves against criticism from professors, over creative writing, writing in general, and broader college and life challenges. These participants reported that, when challenged, they would remember the confidence they had in high school, and the role models who had instilled it in them. This helped them to feel better and be better armed to work through self-doubts. Nearly all recalled using the confidence in their creative writing abilities as currency to develop confidence (or at least be brave enough to participate) in other areas of their lives.

The findings of this study indicate that, while there is a link between the WriteGirl curriculum and program and the development of creative writing confidence, the alumni need a cohesive, mutually supportive network to extend the reach of their confidence currency after they leave the program. I have already taken steps to deepen the alumni network (online through Facebook, of course, but also in real life) and have increased the number of alumni who intern in the organization's office and participate in leadership development activities.

Lessons Learned and Recommendations

Separate from the content of the study, many lessons were learned about working in the online world, especially in real time. As research conducted in social networking space becomes more common, both among anonymous participants and known group members, it presents a powerful and convenient resource, once the conventions are known to the researcher. Learning the specific conventions of each social network, and the culture of usage, would also be helpful. While my invitation to Facebook and a large network of friends, by accident, was the spark for this study design, I would have benefited from a longer timeline during which I could have tested and learned more about the operational aspects of the site. The fine print is quite difficult to grasp (especially on Facebook, where significant account options changed in the middle of my study), but knowing how to take full advantage and avoid pitfalls could have added to the richness of the study and an expansion of the pool of potential participants.

I would encourage researchers to be active members in the networks they seek to utilize for research purposes. As long as insider status is framed as such, openly and up front, being part of the network itself can minimize some of the concerns that arise when working with anonymous participants.

REFLECTIONS ON THIS APPROACH TO RESEARCH

Despite the challenges I faced conducting a research study entirely online, I have not been deterred from this approach, because (1) it is so efficient and (2) new tools that assist in the process are coming out every day. Thus, I recently completed a follow-up online study with participants drawn from the WriteGirl community, using a multipronged approach to data gathering. The topic was creative space, how it is defined, and how the perception of space impacts the WriteGirl program and members in their physical space.

For this study, I developed a 5-question online survey using the GoogleDocuments Forms function (www.google.com/google-d-s/forms/), which is free, simple to use, and has a quick-to-learn option for surveys. It offers a wide variety of survey design choices and also provides data analysis functionality. Participants are sent a link to an online form and, when they enter their responses, the GoogleDocuments Form function converts their answers into a downloadable spreadsheet.

I solicited for different participant classes using four different online settings and strategies.

First, WriteGirl teen alumni who are members of our Facebook WriteGirl Alumni page (www.Facebook.org) were contacted via a Facebook e-mail that provided the survey link.

(Continued)

(Continued)

Next, I solicited WriteGirl adult members using the BigTent community software (www.BigTent.org), which WriteGirl uses to manage member communications. This community software hosted the survey solicitation (with the GoogleDocuments link) on a "News" page visible to all members, and automatically e-mailed it to each of them using an option it calls "Blast."

I also sent the survey solicitation to current program participants who were high school seniors, via their individual e-mails. These were the only current WriteGirl mentees selected for participation (in part as practice for them in being responsive to important e-mails).

Finally, I e-mailed a 9-question interview protocol to 6 WriteGirl leaders who deal specifically with the issue of physical and creative space, offering them the chance to provide more in-depth replies to a longer series of questions.

After the solicitation text, survey questions, and e-mail protocol were developed, it took approximately one hour to set up the GoogleDocuments Forms survey, test it, and then distribute messages to alumni via Facebook, members via BigTent, and current mentees and program leaders via e-mail. That level of efficiency and speed is incredibly valuable when compared to traditional data-gathering methods. After a preliminary review, it looks like I have gathered a great deal of very rich data.

Conclusions

I predict that we will see an explosion in the use of the online research space, mimicking the manner in which communications (social, private, and commercial) have migrated there. It can be a powerful place to work, one that can yield rich data and unique opportunities to connect, but it can also present significant challenges, especially to the uninitiated. Now that I feel like a veteran user of Facebook, I am already planning further online research projects. It is where everyone seems to be.

See the Appendix for suggested readings and resources on the software, methodologies, and methods discussed in this case.

 Find More Materials on the Study Site! See the book website for related resources, materials, discussion, and assignment ideas.

References

Bandura, A. (1977). Self-efficacy: Toward a unifying theory of behavioral change. *Psychological Review, 84,* 191–213.

California Department of Education. (1998). *English-language arts content standards for California public schools, kindergarten through grade twelve.* Sacramento: California Department of Education.

Chandler, G. E. (1999). A creative writing program to enhance self-esteem and self-efficacy in adolescents. *Journal of Child and Adolescent Psychiatric Nursing, 12*(3), 70–78.

Chandler, G. E. (2002). An evaluation of college and low-income youth writing together: Self-discovery and cultural connection. *Issues in Comprehensive Pediatric Nursing, 25,* 255–269.

Deegan, A. (2010). *Creative confidence: Self-efficacy and creative writing in an out-of-school time program and beyond.* Unpublished doctoral dissertation, California State University, Long Beach. Retrieved from http://gradworks.umi.com/34/48/3448618.html

Dewey, J. (1934). *Art as experience.* New York: Capricorn.

Elbow, P. (1973). The pedagogy of the bamboozled. *Soundings, 56*(2), 247–258.

Elbow, P. (1998). *Writing without teachers* (2nd ed.). New York: Oxford University Press. (Original work published 1973)

Freire, P. (1970). *Pedagogy of the oppressed.* New York: Continuum.

Gilligan, C. (1982). *In a different voice: Psychological theory and women's development.* Cambridge, MA: Harvard University Press.

Gilligan, C. (2004). Strengthening healthy resistance and courage in children: A gender-based strategy for preventing youth violence. *Annals of the New York Academy of Science, 1036,* 128–140.

Gilligan, C., & Machoian, L. (2002). Learning to speak the language: A relational interpretation of an adolescent girl's suicidality. *Studies in Gender and Sexuality, 3*(3), 321–341.

Gilligan, C., Spencer, R., Weinberg, M. K., & Bertsch, T. (2003). On the listening guide: A voice-centered relational model. In P. M. Camic, J. E. Rhodes & L. Yardley (Eds.), *Qualitative research in psychology:*

Expanding perspectives in methodology and design (pp. 157–172). Washington, DC: American Psychological Association.

James, N., & Busher, H. (2009). *Online interviewing.* London: Sage.

Myhill, D. (2001). Writing: Crafting and creating. *English in Education, 35*(3), 13–21.

Myhill, D., Fisher, R., Jones, S., Lines, H., & Hicks, A. (2008). *Effective ways of teaching complex expression in writing: A literature review of evidence from secondary school phase* (Research Report No. DCSF-RR032). Exeter, UK: University of Exeter, Department of Children, Schools and Families.

Pajares, F. (2003). Self-efficacy beliefs, motivation and achievement in writing: A review of the literature. *Reading & Writing Quarterly, 19,* 139–158.

Pajares, F., & Johnson, M. J. (1993, April). *Confidence and competence in writing: The role of self-efficacy, outcome expectancy and apprehension.* Paper presented at the annual meeting of the American Educational Research Association, Atlanta, GA.

Pajares, F., & Johnson, M. J. (1995, April). *The role of self-efficacy beliefs in the writing performance of entering high school students.* Paper presented at the annual meeting of the American Educational Research Association, San Francisco, CA.

Pajares, F., & Urdan, T. (Eds.). (2006). *Self-efficacy beliefs of adolescents.* Greenwich, CT: Information Age.

Pajares, F., & Valiante, G. (1997). Influence of self-efficacy on elementary students' writing. *Journal of Educational Research, 90*(6), 353–360.

Piha, S. (2008, May). History of after school programs. In J. Jordan (Chair), *BOOST high school forum.* Symposium conducted at the meeting of the Best Out-of-School Time Conference, Palm Springs, CA.

Salmons, J. (2009). *Online interviews in real time.* Thousand Oaks, CA: Sage.

Yin, R. K. (2009). *Case study research: Design and methods.* Thousand Oaks, CA: Sage.

Sally Bishai

Making Friends With Facebook: A Brave New World (of Researchers)

I think it is safe to say that there were not any qualitative studies conducted on Facebook 10 years ago; there *could not* have been, because the site was launched just 8 years ago (in 2004). Since that time, feelings about the social networking site (and ramifications of its use) have been mixed. Some, for example, have embraced such features as connectivity, self-promotion, and time-killing/boredom-busting, while others have been concerned about privacy of information; negative or falsely positive effects on communication, identity, and/or self-image; and time-wasting, to name only a few.

Practical concerns like those aforementioned are not, however, the only considerations articulated by would-be users of Facebook: A simple Google search using such terms as "Orwellian Internet" or "Facebook conspiracy" will yield all sorts of interesting leads, but one theory seems to be everywhere. This theory—which may be an outrageous urban legend, or a mere understatement of a more disturbing truth—claims that Facebook is or was a source of information used to compile dossiers on individuals.

Many conspiracy theories about Facebook have surfaced since 2004, some plausible and likely, others almost psychotic in nature. For example, my informal poll of 21 graduate students at a large university in the southern United States revealed fears that Facebook was partially or completely owned and/or controlled by the CIA; that it kept a log of every message, wall posting, and preference ever set—even after the

(Continued)

(Continued)

setting or message was changed or deleted; and that some users were shills of the government, hoping to catch drug use or theft or other criminal activities. One of the zanier answers given was that Facebook had found a way to map body heat through a computer screen, so that "they" could gain biological information about the user, to break through any false identities that a user had created, to keep closer tabs on Facebook citizens. While unlikely, the notion did bring to mind a pre-web camera urban legend of the 1990s that had computer screens able to "see" what was in front of them.

As for actual facts regarding any skullduggery—governmental or otherwise—on Facebook's part, several viral videos and blogs have claimed that there are links between several venture capital groups and board members of the CIA, In-Q-Tel, the Defense Advanced Research Projects Agency (DARPA), the allegedly dissolved Information Awareness Office (IAO), and the CIA's injection of $12.7 million into Facebook. It should be noted that the stated mission of the IAO is

to gather as much information as possible about everyone, in a centralized location, for easy perusal by the United States government, including (though not limited to) Internet activity, credit card purchase histories, airline ticket purchases, car rentals, medical records, educational transcripts, driver's licenses, utility bills, tax returns, and any other available data.

It is unclear whether "everyone" refers to "everyone in the world," or "everyone in the United States."

Whether true or false, the theory—and Deegan's study—made a few things clear to me:

1. Where there are people, there are also stories.

2. Facebook claims to have over 500 million users on its site.

3. Most of these users are likely "strangers" to one another (and they certainly are to me, anyway, but maybe you are more popular than I am).

4. It is possible to sift through the 500 million and find people of a certain demographic or interest group using Facebook.

5. It is possible to contact and even "friend" (or "un-stranger," anyway) said people using Facebook.

6. Apart from its potential ability for communication (however choppy) and matchmaking (in any sense), Facebook could, theoretically, be a fair-to-middling source of information; on the other hand . . .

7. Facebook profiles sometimes make people I know into strangers who look nothing like the photos on "their" pages.

So basically, Facebook *could* be a researcher's best friend. Deegan's fascinating study demonstrated, in fact, Facebook's potential as a research tool; however, it also revealed opportunities for the growth of three distinct entities. Taking these opportunities would minimize or prevent (for all three entities) any future frustrations with Facebook-based research.

The first entity that needs an update is the Institutional Review Board (IRB). As Deegan articulated in her chapter, the IRB had quite a time accurately understanding her intentions and procedures, and—after my similar experience with an IRB half the world away from Deegan's—I am convinced that any miscommunication was the result of IRB members who were not up on the intricacies of emerging methods such as Facebook-based or online research.

After all, if the IRB is made up of scholars from different fields, and if qualitative online research lends itself more generously to the work of social scientists than to our brothers and sisters in geology and engineering and biochemistry, then it is safe to presume that we (researchers schooled in qualitative and/or online research methods) will necessarily be in the minority on most boards. This is not to say that our friends in geology and biochemistry are dolts because they couldn't immediately visualize proposals coming from researchers like Deegan (and me), only that they may not have had the reason and/or opportunity to explore it as a viable option for their own work and are, therefore, behind the times in some respects. As Deegan's chapter demonstrated, however, it is possible for dedicated, talented, and brave scholars to acclimate (however painfully! But that's where the braveness comes into play) to a new world that promises virtually endless possibilities for research.

The second entity is the researcher him/herself. While many today would describe themselves as "tech-savvy," the truth is that there aren't enough hours in the day for a person—any person—to keep up with every single online tool in the whole world. This is to say nothing of the fact that a great many of today's qualitative (or quantitative, for that matter) researchers are at least a tiny bit over 24ish years of age. What this means is that they have not grown up with text messages and YouTube and Facebook and have had to, therefore, adjust to these wonderful and terrible technologies during adulthood. For example, while my friend's 12-year-old daughter may have known the difference between "friends" and "likes" and "group members" when she was knee-high to a grasshopper, Deegan (by her own admission) did not at first, while I—and this is a huge understatement—am *still* not acquainted with this intricacy of Facebook.

Speaking of which, Facebook itself is the third entity that needs to adjust to emerging methods of online research—though I am not suggesting that they need to adjust to make themselves more *accessible* to researchers. Rather, I believe that Facebook's oft-changing privacy policy and terms of use should address the notion of using their website for a purpose that is neither social nor commercial.

I am, of course, referring to the sudden and unexplained blocking of Deegan's account.

After much thought over (and many rereadings of) Deegan's chapter, a certain suspicion suggested itself to me, and I wondered if Facebook had banned Deegan due to the fact that she attempted to paste in and send multiple similar messages within a brief period of time.

Recommendations for the Three Entities

All in all, I want to reiterate that researchers *necessarily* have wildly varying levels or types of education, technological skill, and online experience—not to mention our different thresholds of frustration with lethargic, tenacious, and/or temperamental Internet connections. This is a good thing, and helps us achieve triangulation in various fields—not to mention classic and emerging research methods.

We should not use these wondrous, strange differences as excuses for laziness and/or stagnation, however. Therefore, my recommendation for the first two entities can be summed up in one word—TRAINING. It would behoove researchers to learn more about online research in general, and Facebook (or other common sites) in particular.

To put it another way, IRB members should stop being strangers to Facebook and online research, while researchers can try to make friends with new tools or skills on a regular basis. I believe that if Facebook's "powers that be" examined ways researchers used Facebook, the company's policies and/or legal documents could be improved to either (1) make the site more research friendly and also reflect emerging methods of research, or (2) make it very clear that research is not allowed on Facebook. Thus, members with scholarly inclinations would know up front what behaviors are off-limits, so that they could avoid such actions—and the confusion of not knowing why a sudden and unexplained disciplinary action was taken.

A New Formulation of Some Old Formulas

Deegan's research spoke to me on quite a few levels on themes such as patience, identity, membership, increased confidence levels based upon the number of "public displays of Facebook affection" (or "Facebook PDAs"), and the culturally determined role of respect in communication (including qualitative research).

Ironically, however, thinking through such concepts as those found in and inspired by Deegan's study has actually inspired me with two interview-related things: the first, thoughtfulness-of-response, made me think of percolation, brewing, and steeping. I particularly liked her conclusion that "a little pondering . . . is a good thing"—especially after seeing a transcript of my online conversation with Deegan. Her remarks (each) consisted of several well-thought-out, cohesive, and elegant sentences, while mine were delivered in real-time, the exact way I would have said them out loud. On the other hand, though, while my comments were far from concise, they did get me thinking about the topic from a different angle, and helped me weed through the mental sheaves of thoughts that swirled in my brain as I later revisited the questions she had e-mailed me. So, which is more helpful, then—the brainstorming, half-baked and real-time responses, or cohesive, properly punctuated, and elegant ones?

Actually, it was the elegance of Deegan's communications that led me to the second thing: multitasking (aka inconsiderate) participants. I'm an Egyptian—a traditional one. Even though some Egyptians my age may be all Westernized and "modern," I am the original, old-school, high-context, indirect, resourceful, and polychronic beast. A chief characteristic of a polychronic culture is the ability to multitask; another way to describe a person subscribing to the polychronic way of life is that we are workaholics who cannot sit still.

Well, thinking about all that made me wonder if the participants who were multitasking actually did have ADHD (attention-deficit hyperactivity disorder) or ADD (attention-deficit disorder). If so, I can see how a lag between the arrival of Deegan's next set of elegant sentences could trigger a burst of "maybe I can e-mail my professor in the next 30 seconds!"

In any case, the idea is actually just a recycled, reworked method of data collection—a method more basic than brilliant, perhaps, and more foundational than fantastic—but as my preliminary attempts have already suggested, it can increase the effectiveness and output of qualitative interviews, yielding a bonanza of accurate, rich, real, *and* thoughtfully considered data. Very simply, the *repeated reframing method of data collection* involves an in-depth, asynchronous interview flanked by a large number of online, qualitative, synchronous interviews.

ORIGINS OF THE REPEATED REFRAMING METHOD

Drawn from the "sensitized groups" method and the "depth motivational study" favored by some marketing researchers (Thomas, 1998), the repeated reframing method is perfect for any qualitative researcher, though it's particularly suited to studies using grounded theory and/or immersion and crystallization.

Using participant data to create and/or validate a model or instrument is nothing new, of course. Haven't researchers been "testing, tweaking, retesting, retweaking" (ad infinitum) for hundreds or thousands of years? The difference here lies in (1) the strategic refocusing of topics (which facilitates an intra-participant triangulation of information about the topic of interest), (2) the arrival of an "all-talked-out-about-this-topic" point in the series of discussions, and (3) the cooling-off segment of the discussion (which isn't unlike the technique of crystallization—or the practice of stepping back from a relationship to gain some perspective about it).

More specifically, the repeatable 7-step process begins after a topic (or population) of interest has been identified. It is important to remember that the topic of interest is just a place to begin the journey.

The first step consists of a *brainstorm* by the researcher. This brainstorm may look like a preliminary laundry list of interesting themes, or may contain a dozen perfectly worded and ready-to-go interview questions. Is there a wrong way to put this brainstorm together? In a word: NO.

The second step involves several synchronous, semi-structured or unstructured, in-depth interviews, which take the form of online chats between researcher and participant (who have both pledged to

NOT multitask during the sessions). The actual number of chats is left up to the researcher (and participant), but something between 10 and 20 is ideal. Also ideal is the variation of the time of day—and length of time spent chatting. Such variations are designed to eliminate staleness in the conversation, but also to access different moods, circumstances, and energy levels.

These preliminary *sensitizing chats* accomplish several goals that make subsequent steps more productive. First, they establish rapport between researcher and participant; second, they sensitize the participant to the topic of interest; third, they inspire the researcher with questions, comments, themes, and/or related topics that may enhance or otherwise impact discussion on the main topic of interest—or that may lead in another direction altogether; fourth, these chats allow the participant to vent, to think out loud (sort of!), to organize her or his thoughts on the matter, and—in a way—to get "all talked out."

The third step can be very welcome or very tough, depending on the level of rapport between researcher and participant, and the proximity of either or both to the topic of interest. Beginning once the fountain of thoughts and feelings has dried up, it has researcher and participant taking a break from the topic—and from one another. (Though the participant should be instructed to make a notation of any research-related thoughts, feelings, and/or ideas had during the time apart.)

Following this *cooling-off period* (which may last one day or 100), the researcher gets back to work and undertakes the fourth step, which involves the reading, organization, consolidation, and *streamlining* of thoughts, questions, and themes inspired by the participant's sensitizing chats. This may take quite a bit of time, since the number of chat-transcript pages might be hovering around the 300s at this point.

Upon completing the task of streamlining data, the researcher gets to begin the fifth step of *synthesis.* True to its name, this step involves the synthesis of information appearing in the first four steps. The result should be an asynchronous questionnaire with open-ended questions.

Sending the *synthesized document* to the participant through e-mail (or other asynchronous means) is the sixth step.

Once the document is completed and returned to the researcher (together with the record/log kept in Step 3), the seventh step of *dissection* can begin. In it, the questionnaire is read and dissected for exemplars, heretofore-undiscussed themes and/or examples, and key elements.

At this point, the researcher begins at Step 1 all over again, only from a slightly different (i.e., reframed) angle. The difference might be content-based (i.e., if conversations have been centered upon nonverbal communication, one could shift to verbal communication), perception-based (i.e., if conversations have focused upon all of the positive, affirming experiences a WriteGirl had on Facebook, one could shift to the positive experiences she had in the WriteGirl program, or as an Arab American), or based upon any number of other differences.

At the end of the second go-round, the researcher should have two sets of very valuable documents ready to go: the synthesized documents from Step 5, and the completed/dissected questionnaires from Step 7. These documents may be used as is with other participants, or might be compared with the documents of past and/or future participants from the same group.

Final Thoughts

At the end of the day, how is the method of repeated reframing more effective than its predecessors? Very briefly, let me say that "it's not, necessarily."

This method is, after all, rather time-consuming, emotionally draining, and difficult to find people for. On the other hand, the preliminary chats get participants thinking, researcher time isn't wasted while participants multitask, and participants have the time and preparation needed to craft thoughtful responses to questions. The time apart sometimes results in numbness to the topics of interest, or depression (since extended chats about significant issues often result in catharses, and can, moreover, foster deep feelings of friendship and/or dependence, among other things), but it frequently results in mental conversations with the "other-in-the-self," or a fantasy version of a real person (Caughey, 1984; Hermans, 2008). These conversations sometimes provide us comfort or advice, but can also trigger critical thinking, logical analysis, and/or varied perspectives. In the case of one of my study's main bloggers, our intense chats and time apart (though unintended) contributed to his emotional breakthrough (according to him).

For studies like Deegan's, one reframed repeat might be enough, since she had a particular agenda (confidence levels and WriteGirls), whereas my study could (and did) benefit from dozens of markedly different conversations (i.e., the baby version of a reframed repeat) with certain participants (most of them afflicted with the negative dialogical state, come to think of it).

All in all, I was sad that some WriteGirls were dismissed by their professors. I was mad that some of these very same girls had dared to multitask while discussing important things with Deegan. I was cross over the fact that people posted uncharacteristic photos (resembling strangers) on their profiles, and that they allowed their mood and/or self-esteem to rise or sink based upon the overall level of activity on their Facebook pages (i.e., the number of communications received from strangers—over a given period of time).

But I must confess that I was energized by the thought that—despite the difficulties with the IRB and with Facebook—big advances could be made in online research. I am glad to think that perhaps Deegan's untimely banning was the result of an anti-spam policy, and was NOT caused by an anti-research clause in the social networking site's ever-changing fine print. Most of all, however, I am grateful for the many points of inspiration, wisdom, and advice offered by Deegan in her chapter—and in the conversation that made the very strange land called Facebook a little less strange.

References

Caughey, J. L. (1984). *Imaginary social worlds: A cultural approach.* Lincoln: University of Nebraska Press.

Hermans, H. M. (2008). How to perform research on the basis of Dialogical Self Theory? *Journal of Constructivist Psychology, 21*(3), 185–199. (doi: 10 .1080/10720530802070684)

Thomas, J. W. (1998). *Motivational research.* Retrieved from http://www .decisionanalyst.com/publ_art/motive.dai

CHAPTER 3
FRAMEWORK COMMENTARY: "STRANGER IN A STRANGE LAND: THE CHALLENGES AND BENEFITS OF ONLINE INTERVIEWS IN THE SOCIAL NETWORKING SPACE"

Janet Salmons

In this single-case study, Dr. Allison Deegan looked for connections between self-confidence and creative writing and developed recommendations for the WriteGirl program based on her findings. She chose to interview WriteGirl alumnae in Facebook. While recruitment occurred online, Deegan worked within an existing sample frame: former program participants.

Deegan decided to conduct interviews online because it reflected the study purpose as a site of significant identity creation and offered a practical way to communicate with participants. Her study explored alumnae reflections on a face-to-face program, so she did not enter into the research with the intention of studying Facebook per se. However, the choice of Facebook chat evolved into more than a simple selection of interview setting. In Facebook, she discovered an entirely new culture of communication and exchange, and at the same time, a proprietary commercial environment with its own ever-changing rules and access issues.

In Facebook, Deegan gained additional perspectives about the participants, soon realizing that they were offering a great deal of personal information about themselves that extended beyond the scope of her study. This kind of consent scope creep can present an ethical dilemma to a researcher. A researcher must decide whether publicly available information is subject to consent, whether to stretch the boundaries and use data not explicitly covered in the agreement or whether to go back to the participant (and the IRB) and renegotiate the agreement. Dr. Deegan, after a struggle to gain IRB approval, and with a focus on other topics, chose to largely ignore the pictures and comments posted in plain sight. She commented: "I did not want to be this kind of friend to them, no more than I would want to attend their slumber parties or listen in on their telephone calls. It felt like I was not supposed to see much of it, and yet there it was, in full view of the world, with their consent."

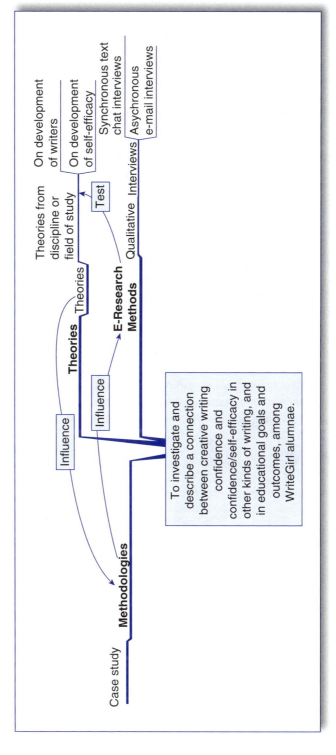

Figure 3.1 Research map for "Stranger in a Strange Land: The Challenges and Benefits of Online Interviews in the Social Networking Space."

Deegan's interviews covered the full spectrum of the time-response continuum. Some were real-time synchronous, some truly asynchronous, some in between (see Figure 3.2). The spectrum of interview synchronicity emerged from a dilemma Dr. Deegan encountered due to a lag time in the Facebook chat. It was unclear whether response delay was a technical problem, or whether participants were simply doing other things instead of promptly responding. Dr. Deegan hoped for focused synchronicity in "an organic, online version of a real, connected conversational interview," yet in an apparent mismatch participants' expectations were that other chatting or activities could occur at the same time. The near-synchronous exchange was not satisfactory to the researcher, who ultimately opted for asynchronous e-mail for some of the interviews.

Deegan's position as an associate director of WriteGirl placed her in an insider position in terms of knowledge of the program under investigation; however, in the role of researcher her position could be better described as etic. Stake (1995) defines etic issues as those initiated or brought in from outside the case. As someone from another generation and experience, she did not share essential characteristics with the research population and came with a different set of priorities about the need to understand program outcomes. From this vantage point, Deegan took the research role defined as the gardener. In this role, the researcher seeds the interaction with questions, and cultivates a response with follow-ups, prompts, and encouragement.

Figure 3.2 Deegan's interviews on the Time-Response Continuum.

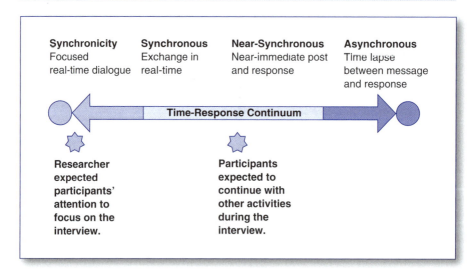

Synchronicity	Synchronous	Near-Synchronous	Asynchronous
Focused real-time dialogue	Exchange in real-time	Near-immediate post and response	Time lapse between message and response

Time-Response Continuum

Researcher expected participants' attention to focus on the interview.

Participants expected to continue with other activities during the interview.

Table 3.1	Summary: Key Factors in the "Stranger in a Strange Land: Online Interviews Within the Social Networking Space" Study			

Motivation for Choosing E-Research	Sampling and Recruiting	Interview Style and Structure	Technology: Issues, Features, Lessons	Ethical Issues
Deegan selected online research to interview participants who favor text chat. Deegan selected online research methods to study phenomena that occur on- and offline.	Purposeful, criterion-based sampling was used. Participants who were alumni of a face-to-face program were recruited online.	Semi-structured and unstructured conversational interviews Synchronous, near-synchronous text-based, and asynchronous e-mail interviews	Deegan chose to conduct research in an arena her participants were familiar with: Facebook chat. Deegan confronted erratic access issues and loss of contacts in proprietary community. After unsatisfactory lag time in chat, Deegan used e-mail.	Difficulty with IRB regarding use of anonymous participants who consent via electronic forms. Deegan set parameters and did not collect data (including pictures) from other parts of participants' Facebook lives, even though it was publicly available.

Dr. Deegan described a follow-up study in the concluding section of the chapter, conducted using some different tools and approaches. It is clear that the study described in this chapter stimulated new areas of inquiry for her, and the trials and errors she encountered will undoubtedly be instructive to other researchers who might view Facebook as a potential research setting.

Reference

Stake, R. E. (1995). *The art of case study research.* Thousand Oaks, CA: Sage.

PART II

INTERVIEW RESEARCH IN VIRTUAL WORLDS

A *virtual world* is "a synchronous, persistent network of people, represented by avatars, facilitated by computers" (Bell, 2008, p. 2). Second Life and Wonderland are popular immersive virtual worlds, but there are other environments including private worlds created for specialized instruction or work, or games that involve individuals or groups of players.

People joining a virtual world create their own cartoonlike "avatar," which may look very realistic or completely fanciful. The avatar represents the user in the 3-D world. Participants travel around the various online environments and interact with one other. Avatars can explore, meet other residents, socialize, participate in individual and group activities, participate in experiential and educational activities, and create and trade virtual items and services with one another.

Second Life users can create buildings and campuses that may be realistic or based on fanciful imagination. Participation in Second Life is free and open to anyone who registers. Participants can choose to purchase virtual items or property. Games and other virtual worlds may require special equipment or fees.

From early on, researchers were drawn to virtual worlds like Second Life to conduct observational research to learn about the actions and behaviors of avatars. More recently, researchers have started to conduct interviews in virtual worlds. The virtual environment offers the chance to seemingly sit down with someone for a text or audio conversation in a way that can approximate "being there."

Virtual worlds allow the researcher to consider options not usually possible in the face-to-face world through other kinds of online interaction. Unique options include the ability to visit, explore, demonstrate, or simulate some aspect of the research phenomenon in the context of the research interview. Techniques drawn from sociology, anthropology, or ethnography (and visual ethnography) can be adapted to a study of individuals' perceptions and experiences of virtual culture. Using the language of the Typology of Online Visual Interview Methods (Salmons, 2010), it is possible to transmit images, and view or navigate the environment for the purpose of visual elicitation, communication, and/or collaboration (see Table 1).

| **Table II.1** | Typology of Online Visual Interview Methods (Salmons, 2010) |

Researchers can do the following:	In order to achieve the following interactions with research participants:
Transmit visual images. Image or media files, links to images posted on a server or website, or images captured in the moment are sent to the other party during the interview. ***View*** visual representation of phenomena together: Researchers can view photos, graphics, artifacts, or media during the interview. ***Navigate*** in a visual virtual environment. Observe and experience websites, software applications, or 3-D virtual environments. ***Generate*** visual images. Access shared tools that allow researchers and/or participants to create drawings, diagrams or visual maps, snapshots or videos.	***Visual communication*** describes the use of images to communicate abstract concepts, relationships between concepts or data, or examples of research phenomena. ***Visual elicitation*** refers specifically to the process of using visual stimulus to draw out a verbal or a visual response. The scenery or events in an immersive virtual environment navigated by researcher and participant, the images or media viewed together, or the graphic generated during the interview may stimulate response. ***Visual collaboration*** refers to a collaborative approach to either stimulate new thinking or create responses in relation to visual representations of the research phenomena. Researchers and participants can create, edit, or embellish images together during the interview.

As the four chapters in this section of the book show, virtual worlds offer new potential for interview research. At the same time, the use of virtual worlds raises new dilemmas about the identity of both researcher and participant when they are represented by avatars, and the protection of the avatar and what Cabiria (Chapter 4) calls its "human operator." The researchers who contributed to this section are developing solutions to these dilemmas—and they raise new questions that researchers and those who assess their work will need to consider as these approaches become more commonly used.

SUGGESTIONS FOR PLANNING A VIRTUAL WORLD INTERVIEW

Since Second Life communication can occur through text, considerations about text interviews mentioned in the introduction to Part 1 would apply here a ding teleporting and sharing items with other avatars.

- Decide where and how to conduct the interview. If you create a space, consider making it private and requiring permission to enter (make sure the space is large enough so that voice chat is out of range of others who could eavesdrop).
- If it is not your own property, make arrangements to use it for interview purposes. Make sure to schedule and plan to minimize the likelihood that others could be present and eavesdrop.
- If you select a place like a library or academic meeting area, determine what ethical expectations are established by the setting.
- Make sure the participant has all information needed, including meeting place.
- Offer to meet ahead of the interview, so both researcher and participant are familiar with the location and features. If you decide to meet on the participant's property, ask to visit in advance of the interview.
- Decide whether to use text chat or audio features for dialogue in the interview.
- If using VOIP or telephone, check audio operations. Arrange for audio recording.

References

Bell, M. (2008). Toward a definition of "virtual worlds." *Journal of Virtual Worlds Research, 1*(1). Retrieved from http://journals.tdl.org/jvwr/article/viewFile/283/237

Salmons, J. (2010). *Online interviews in real time.* Thousand Oaks, CA: Sage.

Interviewing in Virtual Worlds

An Application of Best Practices

4

Jonathan Cabiria, PhD
Walden University, USA

I t is clear that technological advances in recent decades have changed our approaches to even the most basic of activities. From document preparation, sharing, and storage to daily communications, things have changed dramatically. So, too, have things changed in how psychological research can be conducted, especially given the expanded access that researchers now have to potential study participants, venues, and topics. In the following study, I explored a virtual community called Second Life, seeking to understand how this new environment could be used for the benefit of marginalized people.

Second Life is a virtual online community that is built by its members. Avatars, which are graphical representations of the people engaging in virtual-world activities, may participate in a variety of activities that include creating the virtual environment, exploring social interactions with other avatars, using various entertainment options, and/or seeking some level of personal fulfillment. This study specifically looked at this virtual world as a possible venue for marginalized people to engage in developmental redirection, that is, exploring developmental experiences and milestones that may have been unavailable to them in real life.

The activities that occur in Second Life are as varied as those in real life, and the purposes for which people use Second Life are also diverse. Of these many activities and purposes, I analyzed how my study participants used virtual resources to help them deal with real-life issues, including identity development. It was anticipated that people who experienced multiple negative effects in real life, as a result of their marginalized status, would find therapeutic benefit that transferred back to the real world by engaging in online virtual social communities.

Fredrickson's (1998) broaden-and-build theory of positive emotions and Festinger's (1957) theory of cognitive dissonance provide the framework for this study. Qualitative grounded theory and some descriptive statistics were used to explore the narratives of the participants in an attempt to theorize what happens when marginalized people engage in positive virtual-world activities. Of special interest were the challenges in conducting the research interviews in a virtual-world environment in which adjustments had to be made to account for privacy, participant identity verification, and even discussions on the human nature of avatars.

Research Purpose and Questions

Over the past 3 years, there has been a dramatic rise in participation in virtual communities such as Second Life, and a similar increase in special interest groups and social communities in these venues (Flowtown, 2010). What has not been adequately studied is the effect of participating in virtual community groups that support marginalized classes of people, or whether participation in virtual-world communities can be a recommended activity to ease the harmful effects of real-life marginalization.

Some marginalized people, as a result of their social status, can suffer from psychological problems. For example, gay and lesbian people who keep their sexual orientations hidden can experience heightened effects of isolation, loneliness, depression, low self-esteem, and pessimism (e.g., D'Augelli & Patterson, 1995; Garnets & Kimmel, 2003; Perez, DeBord, & Bieschke, 2000). These same researchers also indicated that finding similar others with whom to gain support and companionship (whether in person or through mediated technologies) provides positive benefit.

Finding social support is an important source of positive well-being and is needed to cope effectively with stressors. Jones et al. (1984) noted that aligning one's self with similar others provides two important coping functions: (1) it allows one to exist within a non-stigmatizing environment, and (2) it provides support against the negative effects of the stigmatizing external society.

Social evaluation theory (Pettigrew, 1967) proposes another way of looking at the coping skills of stigmatized people. Stigmatized people who seek out and actively participate in welcoming and supportive groups, and who develop a strong sense of community as a result of this participation, evaluate themselves in comparison with those in their group who are like them rather than with those of the dominant and stigmatizing culture. The group validates and normalizes what the general society would consider to be deviant experiences (Thoits, 1985), providing the stigmatized person with a new perspective on his or her place in the world and, thereby, allowing the possibility of increased self-esteem (Garnets & Kimmel, 1991; Meyer, 2003). It would appear that what is most important is that one surround her- or himself with supportive others, regardless of the formal nature of the group.

There is little formal research to date that has explored the benefits of virtual-world societies for marginalized people. Furthermore, there is also little formal research that looks at the use of virtual-world societies as a developmental enabler for marginalized people, as well as a safe harbor from which to explore identity deconstruction and reconstruction, or transportation of positive experiences gained in a virtual world back into real life. The goal of this study was to see if there were any changes in self-perception of real-world senses of loneliness, isolation, depression, self-esteem, and pessimism when compared to virtual-world perceptions.

This research also sought to propose theories and applications regarding the experiences of marginalized people in virtual worlds and the effect of those experiences, if any, on their real-world lives. Potential emergent theories were expected to arise from the following research questions:

1. What are the experiences of selected participants from marginalized groups in their Second Life activities?

2. What are the benefits, if any, that the participants gain in Second Life?

3. Are these benefits transferable to real life?

4. Can Second Life be recommended as a therapeutic tool for certain marginalized people?

Research Design Overview

This study sought to uncover the meaning that could be derived from the virtual-world experiences of the participants. A grounded theory approach guided the analysis, using software analysis tools and manual coding for category creation that help to develop theories about virtual-world utility for marginalized people. Quantitative analysis was used for some minor descriptive statistics.

When thinking about which methodological approach should be considered for this unique study, existing literature was explored, and the types of study participants, the context within which the participants interacted, and the goals of the study were taken into consideration. To help guide the methodological decision making, a checklist by Marshall and Rossman (2006) was used, which indicated that qualitative research was an appropriate choice because the following research conditions existed:

- elicited multiple constructed realities, studied holistically
- explored tacit knowledge and subjective understandings and interpretations
- delved in-depth into complexities and process
- explored little-known phenomena or innovative systems (p. 53)

The data were collected from questionnaires and semi-structured interviews. The analysis of individual questionnaire responses helped to shed more light on the meaning that participants gave to the intersection of their real and virtual lives, and content analysis of the open-ended responses helped to discover emerging themes during the process of comparing and contrasting participant responses.

METHODOLOGY

Qualitative methods can be used to explore substantive areas about which little is known or about which much is known to gain novel understandings (Stern, 1980). In addition, qualitative methods can be used to obtain the intricate details about phenomena such as thought processes and emotions that are difficult to extract or learn about through more conventional research methods (Strauss & Corbin, 1998). Given the complexities of the lives of marginalized people in Western society, and given the relatively unexplored phenomenon of virtual social communities and their psychological effects on marginalized people, qualitative, grounded theory approach was an appropriate methodology for this study.

The grounded theory method consists of systematic, yet flexible guidelines for collecting and analyzing qualitative data to construct theories grounded in the data themselves (Charmaz, 2006, p. 2). The goal of the research was to discover themes that could contribute to the development of a new theory or the modification of an existing theory, making the choice of a qualitative grounded theory method the most obvious option. Using several preexisting questionnaires related to the research as foundations from which to build semistructured interviews, a number of themes were uncovered that appeared to describe real-life and virtual-life contrasts and comparisons.

An important technique in grounded theory research activities is to think comparatively. By comparing incident to incident in the data—in this case, similar real-world and virtual-world experiences—the researcher is better able to stay grounded in them. Additionally, to reduce researcher bias and misinterpretation of the data, existing literature is used to find examples of similar phenomena (Strauss & Corbin, 1998). In looking for phenomena, the researcher remains alert to repeated patterns of happenings, events, or actions/interactions that represent what people do or say, alone or together, in response to the problems and situations in which they find themselves (Strauss & Corbin, 1998). In this study, emergent patterns from the narratives indicated changes in effect between real-life experiences and similar virtual-world experiences, as well as changes over time in real-life experiences that could have been influenced by virtual-world experiences.

SAMPLING APPROACH

There are many approaches to grounded theory and ways of deriving samples from emergent data to further explore. Basically, there are three processes from which sampling arises: open coding, axial coding, and selective coding. Theoretical sampling is based on theoretically relevant constructs (Charmaz, 2006). Initially, limits on what is being studied are not overly restrictive in order to discover what "bubbles up" from the data (open coding). Once it has been determined that coding derived from the text (questionnaires and interviews) reveals promising categories, then sampling of the preliminary data commences to create categories from the codes. As coding continues, the research is able to connect relationships between the categories (axial coding). Finally, core categories are revealed after an iterative process of data gathering, coding, more data gathering, and more coding. Once a point of saturation is achieved, in which the data reveals no further useful information, the researcher will choose which categories to analyze to arrive at possible theories (selective coding).

At this point, the researcher incorporates information from the literature, experiences, research journals, and other relevant sources to either confirm or disavow the relationship between categories that were evinced during the earlier coding process. Participants are then selected from the population that supplied the data, and their narratives inform the core categories.

Participants for this study were solicited primarily through several targeted venues:

1. Second Life Educators Group (SLED)

2. Various special interest groups in Second Life

Note that the choice of these specific venues is important and will be further discussed under the section exploring special challenges in online interviewing.

Potential participants for the study were selected based upon several criteria that were obtained from the demographic survey they filled out. The study participants were restricted to people over the age of 18, and only to those who indicated on the demographic survey that they belonged to a marginalized class. Furthermore, only English-speaking participants from the United States, Canada, or Great Britain were asked to participate.

It was necessary for potential participants to be active users of Second Life—active being defined as using Second Life for 15 or more hours in the previous month, and that they had been members for at least 6 months prior to engaging in the study. All of these requirements were addressed in the demographic survey.

Potential participants from the above-listed groups received electronic notecards summarizing the study and asking for their participation ("notecard" is the term used for public communication in Second Life, similar to an e-mail distribution list). It was estimated that between 4,500 and 5,000 people received a notecard. Group lists are public within Second Life and accessible to any Second Life member who is also a member of the specific group. These lists are not available or accessible to nonmembers of Second Life or nonmembers of the group.

Interested persons responded via in-world (within Second Life) instant messaging. Interested potential participants were sent a request-to-participate letter and a website link to the research study information packet, which described the study and participant rights, following institutional review board (IRB) guidelines. Potential participants were required to electronically sign these documents with their avatar name, acknowledging that they read and agreed to the terms of the study before proceeding as a participant. Note here that avatars were being treated as proxies for their human controllers, which will be further addressed later in this chapter. Those who expressed an interest to continue were sent a link to an online demographic questionnaire. For tracking purposes, participants placed their avatar name on this and each subsequent questionnaire they filled out.

DATA COLLECTION

The initial pool of participants were selected from those people who filled out the demographic questionnaire and who met the criteria of the study based upon their questionnaire responses, those criteria being age, country, self-identified marginalized class, Second Life membership of more than 6 months, and use of Second Life more than 15 hours in the past month.

Those who completed the demographic questionnaire were scheduled for the first interview, during which their lives in the real world were discussed, after which they were sent a link to the Real Life Questionnaire, which asked them about various experiences and psychological effects in their real-world lives. The purpose of the first meeting was twofold: (1) to review the study details and address questions and/or concerns, and (2) to engage in a conversation about their real-world lives as they pertained to being a marginalized person. Since this was a study that explored expressed negative effect in the real world, conversation transcripts and notes were reviewed to determine if the participant had indicated such negative effect. Those that did moved on to the next phase of the study. This remaining pool of participants was considered to be the population of research participants upon which this study was based, and on which coding of their responses would occur.

These participants then engaged in a second interview, after which they were provided with a link to a questionnaire that addressed their experiences as marginalized people in Second Life. When this second interview was finished, and all questionnaires had been completed, the participants were asked if they were willing to participate in further interviews should the analysis of the then-current data reveal the need for clarifications or further exploration.

These interviews were conducted in a secured Second Life environment created specifically for this study. The virtual interview space was created in a way to deal with concerns regarding privacy, realism, and usability. It was tested on volunteers until all concerns were addressed. In this virtual environment, avatars (graphical representations of the human beings who operate them from a computer keyboard) interact through voice and through text chat (similar to instant messaging). This will also be discussed in detail in upcoming sections.

DATA ANALYSIS AND TECHNOLOGY CHOICES

Once the participants had filled out the questionnaires, the data were downloaded from the survey website into a spreadsheet. The open-ended questionnaire responses were exported to a text analysis software program called SPSS Text Analysis for Surveys for content categorization, and the demographic questionnaire responses were analyzed by using SPSS for Windows v15 to show descriptive statistics. The text chat from the interviews was exported to SPSS Text Analysis for Surveys for extraction of meaningful terms and categorization. The text was also hand coded for meaningful terms and categorization. The results of hand coding and software coding were compared and contrasted as the analysis progressed.

In qualitative research activities, it is important that steps be tracked through every phase of the study. This provides the transparency that allows other researchers to understand how conclusions are made (Strauss & Corbin, 1998). This process is called an *audit trail*, which is the recording of the researcher's actions and decisions to help develop a decision-making history of the research. This aids the researcher in tracking the evolution of the study and providing a history of when decisions were made, why they were made, and how they were implemented.

Ethical Issues and Institutional Review Boards

When conducting research, it is important to ensure that all participants understand that they are able to freely participate or not participate in the study. The guidelines followed were those of the Fielding Graduate University Institutional Review Board, which monitors research projects that involve human subjects. Although interactions were with avatars, which are graphical representations, it was an important consideration that they were being operated by human beings. While an avatar cannot be "harmed," there were concerns about protection of the human being behind it. To that end, privacy issues had been identified and addressed along every step of the research project, including the use of research data in the future. It is worthwhile to note that all communications between the researcher and the participants were anonymous.

Members of Second Life have identities that exist only in Second Life. Participants could only be known by their fictitious avatar names. Linden Labs, the owner of Second Life, does not reveal real-life names or information about its members. Participants were also told that real-life identifying information would not be solicited or recorded, and this statement was included in the information packet given to all participants.

Linden Labs does not have an official document regarding doing research in Second Life. Linden Labs clarified its position regarding research surveys in Second Life (see Second Life's *Knowledgebase*, 2007). This is important information for those planning on doing research in Second Life and whose IRB or other research governance body wants official documentation. In this research study, there was great reluctance on the part of the IRB to accept this study venue without a formal declaration from Linden Labs that a study could be conducted in Second Life. The above information, and this study, helped set a precedent for further formal research in virtual-world spaces.

One special consideration by the IRB, however, was the issue of the need for avatar privacy protections. Since this was relatively uncharted territory at the time of the study, it was unclear if an avatar was a person or a non-person. Certainly, the avatar object was a non-person and, as such, required no protections. The debate, therefore, centered on if the human controller of the avatar could be harmed by the research process if she or he were not protected.

Originally, the IRB was inclined to think that protections were not warranted. The researcher made a point that the human controller can have an emotional connection to the avatar, as an extension of self, and that damage to the reputation of the avatar in the Second Life environment could result in potential psychological issues for the human controller. In addition, the Second Life avatar was often part of a virtual society and had a "virtual reputation" that, if damaged, could affect its ability to socially interact as it had prior to the research. Again, this could have repercussions on the human controller. In the end, it was determined that the avatar, in the case of this study, required human protections from psychological harm. The study, therefore, proceeded as it would have if the participants were flesh-and-blood humans.

Interview Experience and Challenges: Lessons Learned and Recommendations

With virtual-world interactions come special considerations when attempting to build and maintain relationships with study participants. Due to the lack of various sensory and social communication cues, people engage in behaviors that can be perceived as dysfunctional in the real world but that have utility in the virtual world. Increased self-disclosure can serve to quickly establish one's identity and reduce social discomfort, while disinhibition, paired with anonymity, can provide a means of avoiding real-world labeling and establishing a new identity framework. In attempting to relate to others, one might engage in solipsistic introjections, creating a mental image and identity of the virtual other as a way of establishing a contextual space for interactions to occur. With anonymity comes extreme behavior, in which people might espouse radical ideas, resist rules and authority, and engage in atypical activities that could be considered psychologically and socially unhealthy. It has been proposed that these more radical activities are a response to the loss of sensory and social cues, and a reaction to the loss of real-world identity and sense of self (Suler, 2004). For the researcher, these social and sensory cue replacements can bring challenges to the process since participants may not be who they say they are, or may not respond in a way that is typical of them in real life.

To help deal with the possibility that participants would not be who they said they were, the researcher sought out groups within Second Life that were known to have an established reputation. These groups consisted of other researchers and academicians, as well as those from marginalized classes who formed in-world groups for mutual support. It was assumed that the chances of misrepresentation would be lower than soliciting from the general Second Life population. In addition, the questionnaires were designed to capture irregularities in responses, and the interview transcripts were compared to the questionnaire responses as well. Any participant information that raised red flags was not used in the study.

An additional concern was that, in Second Life, there was the potential that text chats and voice communications could be read or overheard by other avatars who were in the immediate vicinity. In addition, many spaces were open to the public unless settings to ban entry were created. To protect the privacy of study participants and the integrity of the study, a special interview space was created in the upper reaches of Second Life, the ceiling as it were, which did not have a published Second Life address and could only be reached by a special flight accelerator, which most Second Life members did not have. As a result, not one interview was disturbed by accidental or purposeful intruders.

Since text chat was the communication tool of choice, it was important to allow for enough time to explore concepts with participants, recognizing that the flow of information would be slower than voice communications. Keeping this in mind, sessions were limited to one hour to avoid fatigue, and several sessions were scheduled with each participant to provide the opportunity to dig deeper into their responses. To keep participants motivated to stay in the study, sessions were scheduled as soon as the participants were available for interviews.

There were several potential technology issues that needed to be considered prior to conducting the study. The two primary ones were that Second Life servers were unpredictable, and that the interviews could be interrupted at any point due to sudden lag (slow or unresponsive avatar movements), malfunctioning chat, and/or being suddenly logged out of the system. On the participant and researcher end, there could be disruptions with personal Internet service providers and overheated computer graphics cards. Several times during various interviews, either the researcher or the participant froze or was logged out. As a backup, participants and the researcher used external (to Second Life) instant messaging to reconnect and determine next steps (to log back in or to reschedule). In using new technologies, it is important to identify a backup plan should technological issues arise.

Research Findings

This study looked at two areas of the participants' lives: their real-world experiences as marginalized people and their virtual-world experiences as marginalized people. The purpose of the real-world phase of study was twofold: (1) to see if the participants' experiences as marginalized people were similar to those reported in various studies conducted over the past few decades (e.g., D'Augelli & Patterson, 1995; Garnets & Kimmel, 2003; Perez et al., 2000), and (2) to establish a point of reference in comparing real- and virtual-world experiences. The results of the real-life portion of this study indicated that the participants' experiences were in line with the results of previous studies, and that these experiences led to the expected emergent themes of loneliness, isolation, depression, low self-esteem, withdrawal, and lack of personal authenticity. Specifically, these expected results dealt with developmental obstruction, negative psychological effect, the power of social-normative forces, and compartmentalization, to name a few. While not every participant indicated all emergent themes, each participant experienced multiple effects in meaningful ways, as demonstrated by the representative excerpts from the interview transcripts and the questionnaire responses.

The purpose of the Second Life phase of the study was also two-fold: (1) to see if there were any differences between stated real and virtual experiences with regard to being marginalized, and (2) to see if the broaden-and-build theory of positive emotions had applicability. It appeared from the analysis that there were several differences between real and virtual experiences and that several themes emerged from the data, namely belongingness, connectedness, improved well-being, higher self-esteem, optimism, sense of personal authenticity, and evidence of transferable positive benefits. It was conjectured that cognitive dissonance, the gap between how one perceived one's self and how one behaved, became uncomfortably evident as participants explored virtual lives that contrasted dramatically with their real-world lives. The research indicated a clear juxtaposition in constructs of real and virtual, in that several participants stated feeling more "real" in their "artificial" lives and more "fake" in their "real" lives. Evidence was also found to support the broaden-and-build theory of positive emotions when participants indicated how discrete positive events in Second Life empowered them to seek positive change in their real lives. Theories that emerged from the study were that there are positive benefits to virtual-world engagement, and that positive virtual-world engagement has transferable positive effects into the real world.

RECOMMENDATIONS FOR FUTURE RESEARCH

Research into the effects of virtual-world experiences on marginalized groups, such as those with physical or mental challenges, lesbian and gay populations, or racial and ethnic groups, to name a few, is in its infancy. For example, at the time of this research, there had been no published, formal research exploring the positive benefit of the redirection of developmental paths of marginalized people in virtual-world environments, or of the transferability of their positive effects from their virtual-world to their real-world lives. However, this is just the beginning step. A purpose of a grounded theory qualitative study is to explore uncharted territories and to propose hypotheses. As future researchers build upon this information, the collective body of research will, at some point, be able to claim findings that are generalizable to larger populations, as well as provide insights into the uniqueness of each individual experience.

Conclusions

Research methods and procedures in virtual-world environments overlap many of the real-world approaches. However, there are some special considerations that need to be explored prior to conducting the research. Of special note is the willingness of the institutional body governing research ethics to keep an open mind to the unclear or unstated policies for conducting research in a virtual-world venue. Additionally, when dealing with participants who are virtual representations, it has to be determined if the representations require certain ethical considerations, and at what level. In this study, given the nature of the research, it was important to afford the avatars full ethical protections guided by institutional IRB policies. This included creating a safe and private space to conduct interviews.

In choosing participants who are virtual representations and whose human controllers are anonymous, it is important to develop approaches that can help reduce the potential for false representation of self and of one's experiences. To this end, potential participants should be solicited, when appropriate, from known and legitimate groups where there would be an interest in the outcomes of the research.

By carefully designing the study, the researcher was able to feel secure in the knowledge that the data was largely uncorrupted by misleading data. Consequently, the study was able to show, with a fair level of confidence, that engagement in virtual-world environments by some marginalized people produced positive effects. Furthermore, these positive effects were transferable and could aid in reducing negative real-world effects caused by marginalized social status.

See the Appendix for suggested readings and resources on the software, methodologies, and methods discussed in this case.

Find More Materials on the Study Site! See the book website for related resources, materials, discussion, and assignment ideas.

References

Charmaz, K. (2006). *Constructing grounded theory: A practical guide through qualitative analysis.* Thousand Oaks, CA: Sage.

D'Augelli, A. D., & Patterson, C. J. (Eds.). (1995). *Lesbian, gay, and bisexual identities over the lifespan.* New York: Oxford University Press.

Festinger, L. (1957). *A theory of cognitive dissonance.* Stanford, CA: Stanford University Press.

Flowtown. (2010). *The 2010 social networking map.* Retrieved from http://www.flowtown.com/blog/the-2010-social-networking-map

Fredrickson, B. L. (1998). What good are positive emotions? *Review of General Psychology, 2,* 300–319.

Fredrickson, B. L. (2001). The role of positive emotions in positive psychology: The broaden-and-build theory of positive emotions. *American Psychologist, 56*(3), 218–226.

Garnets, L. D., & Kimmel, D. C. (1991). *Lesbian and gay male dimensions in the psychological study of human diversity.* Washington, DC: American Psychological Association.

Garnets, L. D., & Kimmel, D. C. (Eds.). (2003). *Psychological perspectives on lesbian, gay, and bisexual experiences* (2nd ed.). New York: Columbia University Press.

Jones, E. E., Farina, A., Hastorf, A. H., Markus, H., Miller, D. T., & Scott, A. S. (1984). *Social stigma: The psychology of marked relationships.* New York: Freeman.

Marshall, C., & Rossman, G. B. (2006). *Designing qualitative research* (4th ed.). Thousand Oaks, CA: Sage.

Meyer, I. H. (2003). Prejudice, social stress, and mental health in lesbian, gay, and bisexual populations: Conceptual issues and research evidence. *Psychological Bulletin, 129,* 674–697.

Perez, R. M., DeBord, K. A., & Bieschke, K. J. (Eds.). (2000). *Handbook of counseling and psychotherapy with lesbian, gay, and bisexual clients.* Washington, DC: American Psychological Association.

Pettigrew, T. F. (1967). Social evaluation theory: Convergences and applications. *Nebraska Symposium on Motivation, 15,* 241–311.

Second Life. (2007). Knowledgebase. Retrieved on August 23, 2007, from
    https://secure-web16.secondlife.com/community/support.php

Stern, P. H. (1980). Grounded theory methodology: Its uses and processes.
    Image, 12, 20–23.

Strauss, A., & Corbin, J. (1998). *Basics of qualitative research: Techniques and
    procedures for developing grounded theory* (2nd ed.). Thousand Oaks,
    CA: Sage.

Suler, J. (2004, June). The online disinhibition effect. *CyberPsychology &
    Behavior, 7*(3), 321–326.

Thoits, P. A. (1985). Self-labeling processes in mental illness: The role of
    emotional deviance. *The American Journal of Sociology, 91,* 221–249.

CRITIQUE AND ANALYSIS OF CABIRIA'S "INTERVIEWING IN VIRTUAL WORLDS: AN APPLICATION OF BEST PRACTICES"

Ann Randall

This study distinguishes itself by contributing to a major issue in virtual-world interviewing—the issue of human subject protection. Cabiria recognizes throughout the account of his research that avatars are graphical representations of human beings, who are vulnerable to harm during the research process. He adds a further dimension to the concept of avatar vulnerability by pointing out that anything that can harm an avatar's virtual-world reputation can have negative repercussions on its human operator.

Widespread use of Second Life (SL) at the time of this study was relatively new, and the Institutional Review Board (IRB) apparently did not fully understand this human–avatar connection. Avoiding the IRB approval process would have been easy. I found it commendable that Cabiria pressed the issue, resulting in the IRB's recognition that the nature of the research brought this study under their purview. The documented outcome of the IRB's decision now adds to literature supporting what seems to me to be the critical first step in assuring ethical research in virtual worlds—to recognize that research involving avatars is always research involving human beings and always requires taking the second step of reviewing the nature of the research.

Virtual-World Research Challenges

Other aspects of this study I found instructive were some of the techniques used to address issues that are of particular concern in virtual worlds. Two of these issues are anonymity and privacy.

Anonymity. In the study I conducted in SL, anonymity was not essential to the phenomenon of interest, since the phenomenon has been documented in normal qualitative interviews. My reasons for preserving anonymity were to honor the culture and to reach a more diverse group of participants. In contrast, the phenomena Cabiria studied were dependent on the anonymity of the SL environment—particularly for participants who in real life had not identified with a stigmatized group that they openly associated with in SL. Preserving anonymity, therefore, required no justification.

The threats to credibility inherent in anonymity, however, were challenges that had to be addressed in both studies. In common, we addressed this challenge by recruiting potential participants from established SL groups. Both of us used one or more educator-oriented listservs to recruit participants, and Cabiria added to his recruitment pool existing in-world SL support groups for marginalized real-life populations.

Cabiria took an additional step beyond limiting his participant pool, however; he triangulated his data by conducting a separate survey of all participants that linked data to their avatar names. By comparing survey data with interview data linked to the same names, he was able to eliminate data with apparent discrepancies, further decreasing the risk of false data and increasing the validity of the research findings. This type of precaution is particularly important when participants are compensated for their time, since the promise of payment can attract individuals who do not meet the research criteria.

Privacy. The range for hearing normal text chat in SL is 20 virtual meters . To reduce the likelihood that conversations would be interrupted or overheard, Cabiria conducted interviews out of range of normal avatar travel in SL. This provided a no-cost alternative to leasing virtual land where access could be restricted. For researchers who choose to interview within restricted-access virtual land, this technique is worth considering to provide an additional layer of privacy protection.

Conducting interviews at the virtual ceiling of SL is not foolproof, however. Cabiria acknowledges that avatars can wear aids to enable sound to travel beyond the normal 300-virtual-meter limit (http://wiki.secondlife.com/wiki/Flight), and I suspect that the use of such devices is more common now than it was at the time of his study. Since all avatars are shown on the SL map by green indicators regardless of how high they are positioned (http://wiki.secondlife .com/wiki/KB2/The_world_map_and_mini-map), it might be worthwhile to add an additional privacy protection by monitoring the vicinity for approaching avatars, either by using an avatar radar device (http://wiki.secondlife.com/wiki/Display_Names_Radar) or by accessing SL with one of the virtual-world viewers that can be configured to detect avatars entering chat range.

Another tool that either of us could have used to keep SL interviews private is the instant messaging (IM) tool. However, since IM conversations must be conducted in a separate communication window instead of the more convenient chat field at the bottom of the screen, they have the potential to decrease participants' sense of comfort and informality and could adversely affect their candor. Though it might be worthwhile to offer IM as an alternative to public chat for participants who prefer it, I would be hesitant to make IM the primary method of interviewing.

Congruence of Subject and Environment

The characteristic of this study that most impressed me was how well the research topic matched the research method. Not only does it make sense to study virtual-world phenomena in the environment where they occur, sometimes data for such phenomena cannot be collected accurately any other way. Cabiria chose to study what I consider one of the most interesting aspects of virtual worlds—the refuge they provide to human beings with real-life challenges. In my personal experience in virtual worlds, the proportion of inhabitants who deal with disabilities, illnesses, trauma, or prejudice in real life is unusually large. Where better to find out what these individuals gain from virtual worlds than to go into one of these worlds to study them? In this study, the decision to conduct the research within the chosen virtual world, Second Life, was essential. The anonymity and persona identity so integral to the phenomena being studied could not have been preserved or observed as well in any setting outside SL.

CHAPTER 4
FRAMEWORK COMMENTARY:
INTERVIEWING IN VIRTUAL WORLDS:
AN APPLICATION OF BEST PRACTICES

Janet Salmons

In this grounded theory study, Dr. Jonathan Cabiria explored Second Life experiences of a group of people marginalized in real life, to learn whether the experiences transfer from the virtual to the real and to determine possible therapeutic options. He chose to carry out the interviews in Second Life, in essence conducting the study about Second Life within a virtual field setting.

As a researcher, Cabiria experienced the virtual world with the research participant as a fellow traveler. According to Kvale (2007; Kvale & Brinkman, 2009), the researcher as a traveler journeys with the participant to discover insights. Research in virtual worlds is uniquely well matched with the traveler metaphor since like the participant, the researcher operates in the form and persona of an avatar, within the virtual world and environments under investigation. While he shared some characteristics with the educators being studied, he took a largely etic stance since he introduced real-world concerns and questions from outside the case (Stake, 1995).

Cabiria used text chat to communicate during the interviews. While he observed the visual nature of the environment, he did not use data collected from the visual representation of the avatars.

Cabiria contributed to the knowledge base about the experiences of marginalized people in an environment that operates by different cultural and social norms, and the implications of these findings for real-world individuals and organizations. Additionally, the obstacles Cabiria encountered in his efforts to win IRB approval for this study spurred new thinking about human subjects and avatars, and that new thinking may be one of the study's valuable outcomes. Drawing on his background in new media psychology, he described key positions in the debates about whether an avatar is a person or a nonperson, and the relationship to the "human controller" of the avatar. Perhaps most interesting, he was able to elucidate some of the kinds of harm that could result to the human controller as a result of harm

Figure 4.1 Research map for "Interviewing in Virtual Worlds: An Application of Best Practices."

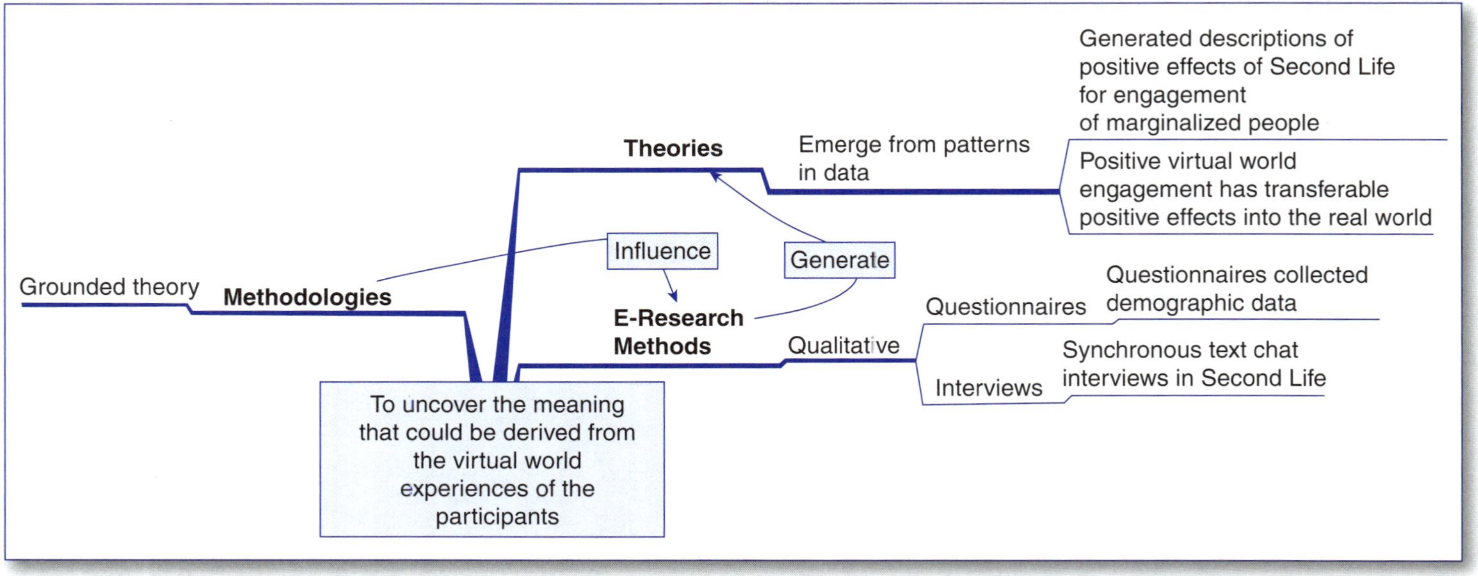

Methodologies

Grounded theory

To uncover the meaning that could be derived from the virtual world experiences of the participants

Influence

Theories

E-Research Methods

Generate

Emerge from patterns in data

Generated descriptions of positive effects of Second Life for engagement of marginalized people

Positive virtual world engagement has transferable positive effects into the real world

Qualitative

Questionnaires

Interviews

Questionnaires collected demographic data

Synchronous text chat interviews in Second Life

to the avatar—or harm to the avatar's distinct identity, friendship, or professional networks in-world. Any researcher with an intention to interview avatars would benefit from reading his explanation of the relationship of human and avatar, and implications for real and virtual research participant(s).

| Table 4.1 | Summary: Key Factors in the "Interviewing in Virtual Worlds: An Application of Best Practices" Study |

Motivation for Choosing E-Research	Sampling and Recruiting	Interview Style and Structure	Technology: Issues, Features, Lessons	Ethical Issues
Cabiria selected online research methods to study online experiences and their influence on life off-line.	Purposeful, criterion-based sampling was used. Participants were recruited online in Second Life, through membership lists of established groups.	Semi-structured interviews were used. Cabiria also collected data using questionnaires. Synchronous interviews conducted using text chat in Second Life	Cabiria conducted interviews in a private, secure Second Life environment created specifically for this study.	Difficulty with IRB about the use of anonymous participants who consent via electronic forms With IRB agreement: research participants could remain anonymous. Consent provided by virtual notecard.

References

Kvale, S. (2007). *Doing interviews.* Thousand Oaks, CA: Sage.

Kvale, S., & Brinkman, S. (2009). *InterViews: Learning the craft of qualitative research interviewing* (2nd ed.). Thousand Oaks, CA: Sage.

Stake, R. E. (1995). *The art of case study research.* Thousand Oaks, CA: Sage.

Beneficial Interview Effects in Virtual Worlds

A Case Study

Ann Randall
University of Idaho, Boise, USA

Participation in multi-user virtual environments (MUVEs) is becoming part of the American culture, particularly since virtual worlds were made popular by the advent of Second Life (SL), a three-dimensional world introduced in 2002 in which participants can socialize, create artifacts, and buy and sell. As the use of virtual worlds increases, their importance to educational researchers also increases. The educational community's participation is significant in SL, which lists more than 130 educational organizations with an active presence on its grid (http://edudirectory.secondlife.com/). The immersive nature of virtual worlds, along with their cultures and social interactions, also make them fertile ground for research. The procedures to conduct such research are, therefore, an important area of investigation.

This chapter is a case study of a qualitative research project conducted in SL in 2008. The case illustrates some of the procedures, benefits, and challenges to consider when conducting qualitative studies in virtual worlds.

The Case: Studying Interview Effects in Second Life

This study began as an assignment for a doctoral course: conduct a pilot research study related to your dissertation topic. Since my dissertation research plan was too complex to carry out within a semester even as a pilot, I proposed an alternative that could investigate the same basic research question using a quicker, more manageable method, which was to conduct the study in the virtual world Second Life. SL provided a ready-made pool from which to solicit participants, and made the logistics of interview appointments much easier. In addition, by using text-based interviews, I was able to eliminate the time-consuming process of transcribing voice recordings.

Study Purpose and Questions

The primary purpose of the study was to investigate positive effects of qualitative interviews on interviewees—an effect referred to throughout this chapter as *beneficial interview effects*. The limited research available on beneficial effects of qualitative interviews (Berger & Malkinson, 2000; Hiller & DiLuzio, 2004; Mills, 2001; Ortiz, 2001) is based on face-to-face interviews, leaving a gap in the literature about the effects of such interviews conducted at a distance through electronic technology. This created a clear justification for conducting the study in a virtual environment. The focus of the study was further narrowed to text-based interviews in immersive three-dimensional virtual environments.

The primary research question of the study was, do beneficial interview effects occur in text-based qualitative interviews in virtual worlds? A secondary question was, if such effects do occur, what are the characteristics of the interviews in which they occur?

Design Overview

THEORETICAL AND PHILOSOPHICAL FRAMEWORKS

The words used to describe beneficial effects of qualitative-style interviews—words such as profound (Patton, 1997), serendipitous (Ortiz, 2001), empowering (Mills, 2001; Shamai, 2003), and therapeutic (Hiller & DeLuzio, 2004; Ortiz, 2001)—immediately evoke the powerful effects in Mezirow's (1991) transformative learning and seem to illustrate his observation that "we give meaning to experience in large part by participating in dialogue with others" (p. 58). A phenomenon so deeply rooted in dialogue owes its philosophical roots to Buber's (1970) I–Thou perspective.

METHODOLOGY

The qualitative methodology chosen for the study was basic interpretive, employing some techniques and approaches from both phenomenological and case study traditions (Creswell, 2007), and following some of the principles of the ethnography tradition.

SAMPLING

Participant selection for the study was purposive, limited to adults with a professional interest in virtual worlds. Qualification as an adult was assumed based on the SL membership restriction to individuals 18 and older. The professional interest limitation was addressed by recruiting participants through two SL-sponsored e-mail lists—one for educators, and one for educational researchers.

DATA COLLECTION

Data was primarily collected through two semi-structured interviews with each participant. Since research on beneficial interview effects (Hiller & DiLuzio, 2004) identifies one factor in beneficial interview effects as "subject matter deemed important by the participants," the interview protocol for the first interview included the one topic all participants had in common—an interest in virtual worlds. I asked them to identify what drew them into SL, and what they were looking forward to when they logged on. The focus of the second interview was to find out how the first interview had affected the participants.

A second source of data was the SL profile of each participant. As illustrated in Figure 5.1, information in the avatar's profile includes such SL data as the date the individual began using SL, group memberships, interests, locations of interest, and sometimes information about the avatar's real life. A third source of data was comments the participant may have contributed to the listservs from which they were recruited.

Figure 5.1   Avatar profile.

DATA-GATHERING TECHNOLOGY AND ANALYSIS

To gather interview data for the study, I chose text-based interviews, which provided two advantages. First, they gave me an opportunity to study whether the phenomenon of beneficial interview effects that had been observed in face-to-face voice interviews was present in text-based interviews; second, they allowed me to conduct and analyze more interviews within the limited time frame for my study.

The preference settings of the SL viewer I used allowed me to opt to save to my computer the two types of text conversations available in SL: chat, which can be read by avatars within 30 virtual meters of the conversation; and private instant messaging (IM), which can only be read by avatars invited to the conversation. Since I gave participants the option of participating in the interviews at a place of their choosing or at a private location leased for the study, I opted to log both chat and IM messages.

To analyze the textual interviews, I used TAMS Analyzer software (http://tamsys.sourceforge.net/), with which I coded and created a database of themes. As themes began to emerge, I recoded the data until I felt satisfied I had identified the major themes emerging from the interviews.

Ethical and Credibility Issues

IDENTITY

In virtual-world research, ethics and credibility are intertwined. Although the identity of research participants is generally associated with credibility, anonymity is part of virtual-world culture. Therefore, limiting research participants to those willing to forgo anonymity eliminates a significant sector of the population along with the perspective that population might provide. I therefore proposed to allow participants to remain anonymous. This meant that participants would not be required to affix live signatures to the consent form, as I explained to the Institutional Review Board (IRB), so that research participants could remain anonymous. Therefore, as an alternative to returning consent forms by e-mail, consent forms could also be returned to me by way of a notecard transfer within Second Life, with the date and the avatar's name added.

PRIVACY

Closely related to the issue of participant identity in virtual worlds is that of privacy. In SL, this can be particularly sensitive for SL residents who participate in SL activities that carry social stigma, such as virtual sex or Gorean role-play. I handled this potential hurdle in two ways: first, by stating in both the letter soliciting participants and the consent form that we would be discussing activities that participants found "appealing or important in Second Life"; and second, by ensuring privacy during the interviews either by location or texting method.

DISCLOSURE

A second ethical issue often faced in studies is that the researcher is unlikely to get an accurate picture of the phenomenon in question if participants are aware it is being observed. Cohen, Manion, and Morrison (2007) state that deception in research may be justified if it "serves the public good" and "prevents bias" (p. 66); and Creswell (2007) suggests that in cases where full disclosure of the research purposes would be counterproductive, the researcher may provide "general, not specific information about the study" (p. 142). Therefore, in my IRB application, I explained that although I would inform participants, "the study is about interviews in Second Life, I will not tell them until after the interviews that the aspect of interviews I am studying is the positive effects" such interviews can have on participants. Accordingly, the consent form gave only general information about the purpose of the interviews by stating simply, "The purpose of this research is to study the effects of research interviews in a virtual environment."

The Research Experience

SELECTING PARTICIPANTS

Once my project had met with IRB approval, my next step was to recruit participants. I recruited from two e-mail lists, the Second Life Educators (SLED) list (https://lists.secondlife.com/cgi-bin/mailman/listinfo/educators) and the SL Researcher list (SLrl, at http://list.academ-x.com/listinfo.cgi/slrl-academ-x.com). In my e-mail to members of these two lists, I introduced myself and stated that as part of my PhD program I was planning a qualitative research study in SL. The e-mail netted responses from 11 individuals. Of these, only one was straightforward from the first about his real identity. Seven of the remaining participants used their real names on the consent form. Although three chose to conceal their real names, I was able to reasonably verify their backgrounds and ages during the interviews based on their mature communication styles and their broad understanding of such subjects as educational theory and philosophy, technology and virtual-world history, and the liberal arts.

During the recruitment and interview process, two participants identified themselves as relatively new to SL. As the interviews progressed, I realized that only seasoned SL residents would have the expertise to discuss the questions in my study and eventually excluded the newcomers.

CONDUCTING THE INTERVIEWS

Preparation

About a month prior to beginning the research, I created an alternative avatar (alt) to prevent interruption during interviews by friends of my primary avatar or announcements from the many groups my primary avatar had joined.

To create a private setting for the interviews, I leased a piece of virtual land that was adjacent to an inaccessible sea. Locating the interview spaces next to the sea on the beach distanced them at least 30 virtual meters from the inland property borders to prevent chat from being overheard.

Another action I took in preparation for the interviews was to send each participant a "friend" invitation in Second Life. This enabled us to know when the other was online, and allowed us to easily communicate in-world through IM. It also made it simpler for me to give them access to the private location I had created for the interviews.

To make it convenient to communicate with participants who did not wish to use e-mail, I set my SL viewer preferences to forward IMs to my e-mail address. Since IMs received by e-mail can be answered by e-mail, I was able to respond to IMs without logging into SL.

Scheduling

All interviews were scheduled in Second Life Time (SLT), which is equivalent to Pacific Time, enabling both the participants and me to use the same time zone, regardless of our physical locations. Most appointments were made by e-mail, but the individuals who chose not to use e-mail communicated from SL by IM. I kept a table of my appointments in a spreadsheet, stated in both SLT and my own time zone.

Setting

Since my intent was to ensure participants felt comfortable in the interview setting, I allowed them to choose where the interviews would be conducted. Three chose their own locations—virtual structures they had built or occupied as virtual homes. The other six met at the virtual property I had leased. I informed participants that I had set privacy settings to exclude visitors and had added the interviewee as the sole resident allowed in the area.

The interview spaces I created were made to appear informal and comfortable—one space allowing the avatars to sit on rocks or stumps around a beach fire pit and the other providing reclining chairs by a fireplace in a beach house (see Figures 5.2 and 5.3). The one difficulty I found in conducting interviews at locations other than those I had created was that two of those interviews were interrupted by visitors—in one case effectively ending the interview.

Interview Meeting

At the time of the meeting appointment, I offered the participant transportation to my location or asked them to transport me to

Figure 5.2 The interview setting.

Figure 5.3 A private virtual interview space.

their location, depending upon where the interview was being held. This type of transportation in SL is called teleporting, and is quick and easy to use.

Once we were in the same place, I invited the participant to sit down and attempted to help her or him feel at ease.

> This introductory exchange is typical of the initial conversation:
>
> Me: Hi!!
> Participant: hello
> Me: nice to meet you
> Participant: likewise
> Me: feel free to have a seat
> Participant: thanks
> Me: you can sit on the stump if you want
> i've restricted access temporarily so we can speak privately
> oh and have some coffee if you'd like
> right click on the coffee pot

The original capitalization and punctuation above illustrate another frequent practice in virtual worlds—simply omitting unnecessary keystrokes such as the shift key and periods.

FIRST INTERVIEW

After introductions, I began the interview by confirming that the date indicated in the participants' SL profiles accurately represented when they had begun participating in SL. The format for the interviews was semi-structured, with the interview protocol being used as a guide rather than a script. Knowing that interviewees could not gauge my continued attention by facial expressions or body language, I frequently interjected text expressions to show I was still there, listening, and interested.

Research on beneficial interview effects (Hiller & DeLuzio, 2004) indicates that one factor in such effects is subject matter importance to participants. For this reason, I followed subjects of interest to interviewees more carefully than the interview questions themselves, attempting to engage in what Holstein and Gubrium (1995) call "active interviewing," in which "interviewer and respondent collaboratively construct the meaning of interview narratives" (p. 59).

So while there was a set of basic questions, the interview did not proceed through them in a linear fashion. I allowed myself to enter into the stories, listening to the direction participants were going and pulling them further down those paths. At least some degree of success was confirmed by one participant's comment—"You're very skilled at following up with additional questions"—and another participant's reflection that the first interview "did not seem to be an interview. It seemed more like a meeting—Q and A for discovery."

In addition, I allowed myself to empathize with interviewee viewpoints in order to yield data of more depth. Although this could be considered a threat to neutrality, I adhered to Lincoln and Guba's (1985) argument that objectivity is untenable in qualitative research, except in the sense that the research audit trail makes data *comfirmable*. I therefore kept detailed records and solicited participant feedback to confirm the data.

Field Notes

These records included a description of the setting where the interview took place and notes about the visible characteristics of the avatar who represented the research participant. I noted, for instance, whether the avatar had attached hair and attached shoes, wore a commercially created skin, and its general appearance, as well as some details of the body shape. Since the participant had chosen all of these characteristics, they all had the potential to inform me about the person behind the avatar. I kept these notes in the spreadsheet with the interview schedule, along with any real-life information the respondent had shared during the interview and information retrieved from each SL profile. The result was a table of details about all the interviews and interviewees (see Table 5.1).

SECOND INTERVIEW

The second interview took place between 6 weeks and 2 months following the initial interview. Since I had not disclosed in the first interview the specific interview phenomenon I was studying, I followed the advice of Cohen et al. (2007) by providing a thorough debriefing in the second interview. I thoroughly explained the beneficial interview effects phenomenon and asked participants to think back to the first interview to anything that stood out in their minds. In some cases, I read or summarized statements from the previous interview that seemed to indicate metacognition.

The concept of beneficial interview effects explored during the second interview intrigued several of the participants so much that

Table 5.1 Table for Organizing Interview and Participant Information

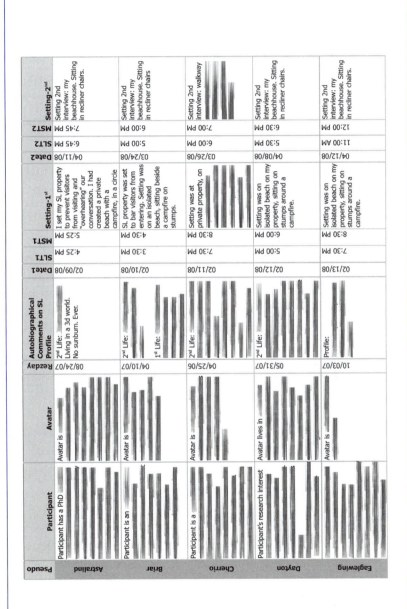

Pseudo	Participant	Avatar	Autobiographical Comments on SL Profile	Rezday	Date1	SLT1	MST1	Setting-1st	Date2	SLT2	MST2	Setting-2nd
Astralind	Participant has a PhD	Avatar is	2nd Life: Living in a 3d world. No sunburn. Ever.	08/24/07	02/09/08	4:25 PM	5:25 PM	I set my SL property to prevent visitors from visiting and "overhearing" our conversation. I had created a private beach with a campfire, in a circle	04/11/08	6:45 PM	7:45 PM	Setting 2nd interview: my beachhouse. Sitting in recliner chairs.
Briar	Participant is an	Avatar is	2nd Life:	04/10/07	02/10/08	3:30 PM	4:30 PM	SL property was set to bar visitors from entering. Setting was on an isolated beach, sitting beside a campfire on stumps.	03/24/08	5:00 PM	7:00 PM	Setting 2nd interview: my beachhouse. Sitting in recliner chairs
Cherrio	Participant is a	Avatar is	1st Life: / 2nd Life:	04/25/06	02/11/08	7:30 PM	8:30 PM	Setting was at private property, on	03/26/08	6:00 PM	7:00 PM	Setting 2nd interview: walkway
Dayton	Participant's research interest	Avatar lives in	2nd Life:	05/31/07	02/12/08	5:00 PM	6:00 PM	Setting was on isolated beach on my property, sitting on stumps around a campfire.	04/08/08	5:30 PM	6:30 PM	Setting 2nd interview: my beachhouse. Sitting in recliner chairs.
Eaglewing		Avatar is	Profile:	10/03/07	02/13/08	7:30 PM	8:30 PM	Setting was on isolated beach on my property, sitting on stumps around a campfire.	04/12/08	11:00 AM	12:00 PM	Setting 2nd interview: my beachhouse. Sitting in recliner chairs.

the interview ran past the time originally allotted, and even seemed to elicit more pronounced beneficial effects than the first interview.

After the interview, I sent participants a thank you note by e-mail or IM and offered to share the results of the study with them. All participants asked to see the results.

Interview Results

My analysis of the interviews suggested that the beneficial interview effects phenomenon did indeed occur in virtual-world text-based interviews. Based on the participants' assessments, supplemented by my analysis of the two interviews, I concluded that at least two thirds of the participants had experienced some measure of the phenomenon I was studying.

The coding of the interviews identified three main themes: (1) an interview subject that was important to the participant, (2) an interview dynamic in which interviewer and interviewee co-constructed meanings, and (3) an interview setting that felt comfortable and nonthreatening. However, I found very little to differentiate between the interviews that yielded beneficial effects and those that did not.

After writing up the results of my analysis, I sent copies by e-mail to all the participants. Although only one participant provided feedback, the feedback was positive and affirmed both the data and my tentative conclusions.

Lessons Learned From the SL Research Experience

PARALLELS WITH TRADITIONAL RESEARCH INTERVIEWS

While the issues I encountered in the SL interviews often had unusual twists, they were usually fundamentally similar to issues in traditional qualitative research. As with traditional research, the research in virtual worlds required establishing criteria for participation, proposing a study design, securing IRB approval, obtaining consent from participants, scheduling interviews, dressing appropriately, locating interviews in private settings, putting participants at ease, establishing an atmosphere of trust, using good interview techniques, analyzing data, checking the accuracy of data with participants, and sending them thank you notes.

SPECIAL CHALLENGES OF VIRTUAL-WORLD INTERVIEWING

Virtual worlds do, however, have some unique challenges. The primary one brought to my attention during the research project was cultural credibility.

Cultural Credibility

In qualitative research, the issue of researcher as instrument ties in with credibility, which is the qualitative research counterpart to internal validity (Lincoln & Guba, 1985). One of the requirements in credibility is to conduct the research in a way that "the probability that the findings will be found credible is enhanced" (Lincoln & Guba, p. 296). This includes investing sufficient time to understand the culture where the interviews will take place. Lincoln and Guba point out that "the mere fact of being a 'stranger in a strange land' draws undue attention to the inquirer," and assert that "unless the inquirer began as an accepted member of the group or agency being studied, distortions can never be overcome" (p. 302).

The practical application of this in SL research is for the researcher to gain sufficient experience in the virtual environment being studied to fit in. As the researcher in this study, I had been active in SL for more than a year and wore the trappings of an experienced SL resident—commercially purchased virtual clothing, skin, shoes, hair, and an animation overrider (AO) attachment to make my movements appear more natural. I also had become familiar with text chat—learning shorthand expressions such as *afk* for "away from keyboard" and *brb* for "be right back," as well as conventions such as starting a chat line with */me* to indicate thinking as opposed to talking, and using ellipses at the end of chat lines to indicate an unfinished thought.

The importance of these preparations in establishing credibility was confirmed by one respondent who, while inspecting my avatar, noted, "It's not a bad skin. I was looking at it closely— :) It's got a nice make up, good definition on the hands, and the collar bone shows up nicely." Then she went on to say,

> Here where ppl [people] can look just how they want . . . is where a lot of educators lose credibility. Most . . . never worry about shape, skin, hair. About one-third of them don't even consider an AO. So—you walk like a duck, stand like a stick, look like a dork, and wonder why people think you're an idiot?

Because virtual worlds have their own cultures and norms, the credibility of research in such environments can be severely hampered by ignoring the importance of what Creswell (2007) refers to as the "key concern" of qualitative research—understanding the phenomenon being studied from the "insider's perspective" (p. 6).

Voice or Keyboard

Another decision that must be made when conducting interviews in virtual worlds such as SL involves the option of communicating by voice. Since voice more closely resembles in-person interviews, it is intuitive to assume voice would be the communication mode of preference; but this is not necessarily so. Those who follow the Second Life Educators (SLED) listserv are aware that educators have sharp disagreements about whether to use voice or text in SL. Some SL residents refuse to use voice, and their views would be excluded from interviews that required the use of voice. On the other hand, some residents have a strong preference for voice or are unable to communicate effectively using text.

In my study, all participants were willing to use text, although a couple of them preferred voice. Ideally, however, participants should be able to choose their preferred mode, unless the mode of communication is a factor being studied.

Preparation Costs and Skills

The two primary sources requiring expenditure and knowledge or skill are avatar appearance and the interview setting.

Avatar appearance. While I highly recommend spending a few dollars to buy professional-looking virtual clothing, skin, and AO, it is possible to find some free items that look quite good. Few researchers would have the time or artistic skill to create high-quality clothing or skins, and importing the images for these items also costs a few cents per item.

Interview site. Although the cost of leasing virtual land for interviews is not a necessity, since using IM instead of chat solves privacy problems, being a landowner does offer certain advantages. As the owner of the land where the interview occurs, the researcher can block visitors, preventing interruptions and distractions. In addition, researchers who have acquired the necessary skills can construct and furnish an interview space to give an appearance of warmth and comfort.

The "land" I used for my study cost approximately $23 to purchase and $11 in monthly fees, and I had the skills to terraform the edge of it to create a beach, furnish it with casual seating, and build a beach house with ocean views. Researchers lacking the funds or the skills to create an inviting interview setting may be able to find appropriate research locations through the SLED or SL Researcher list (SLrl) listservs.

THINGS I WOULD DO DIFFERENTLY

Participant Selection

I quickly realized that I had not narrowed my selection criteria sufficiently. The success of my study depended upon interviewees having a strong interest in virtual worlds, so it did not occur to me that interest itself was insufficient, without the experience to understand and discuss virtual worlds. If I repeated the study, I would limit participation to people who had been active in SL for at least 6 months.

Interview Interruptions

I am still not certain I would insist on conducting interviews at my own site, but I would at least make sure that the location chosen could exclude visitors during the interview. I would also suggest that participants change their SL status to *busy* during the interview to avoid receiving distracting messages.

Interval Between Interviews

The interval of 6 or more weeks was too long for participants to remember their experience during the first interview accurately. If I were to repeat the study, I would conduct the follow-up interview much sooner. An interval of 1 or 2 weeks would probably yield better data.

Data Bias

Although disclosing the underlying purpose of my research near the beginning of the second interview resulted in some very interesting discussions, it also likely distorted the recollections of the participants. Were I to redesign the second interview, I would not discuss the phenomenon of beneficial interview effects until at least midway through the interview.

Mutual Trust

Trust grows over time and is an essential element of the phenomenon I was studying. This may at least partially account for the more pronounced beneficial effects in the second interview. Were I to repeat this study, I would strongly consider conducting three interviews. In an environment where it is so easy to present a false persona, the advantages of conducting repeated interviews might be more important than in a physical setting. That in itself may be a question for further research.

RECOMMENDATIONS FOR RESEARCHING IN VIRTUAL WORLDS

Based on my experience conducting qualitative interviews in a virtual world, I recommend that researchers spend a period of time learning the culture, becoming proficient with text conversations, and learning enough about the skills used by residents to discuss them intelligently. Unless the research is to be confined to the educational community, acculturation also requires exposure to life outside the educational circle.

TIPS FOR LEARNING THE CULTURE

1. *Do some homework.* Before you join SL, watch the videos embedded at http://secondlife.com/whatis/; and then check out the Showcase at http://secondlife.com/destinations/ for places to visit when you get there.

2. *Go through SL orientation.* Start your SL experience on Orientation Island and complete all the tutorials before moving on.

3. *Get outfitted.* Acquire commercial quality shoes and hair, an animation overrider (AO) or walk animation, and clothing.

4. *Go exploring.* Visit some of the destinations you found when you did your homework.

5. *Join groups.* Look for groups that focus on subjects of interest to you at http://secondlife.com/community/groups/. Search terms to consider are music, jazz, poetry, politics, role-play, sci-fi, coffee, or "causes" (using quote marks). Be sure to pick groups that have at least 100 members.

6. *Strike up a conversation.* Start with a simple "hello" to someone at a concert, coffee shop, dance club, museum, or shopping mall.

7. *Learn the language.* Get familiar with abbreviations used in SL text communication. Take a look at a glossary of SL terminology (http://wiki.secondlife.com/wiki/Viewerhelp:Glossary) and refer back to it when needed.

One of my alt avatars is an elf, belongs to an elf group, and dances with elves. My primary avatar turned a hobby into an SL profession, joining artist groups and displaying vector art in a gallery. SL has groups for many interests. Sometimes, learning about the non-education virtual world is as simple as striking up conversations with avatars who are shopping for similar merchandise or attending the same event.

A second recommendation is to pay attention to appearances. In an environment whose main attraction is visual, appearances are important. Many people identify closely with their avatars, and it is important to respect the appearance they have chosen. It is also important to keep in mind that virtual objects and scenery can have real effects. So the appearance of the interview location is important.

Another recommendation is to keep in mind that in text-based communication, the cues that exist in real life, such as body language, eye contact, and voice inflection, are missing. These missing cues are the reason behind text cues, such as smiley faces, and abbreviations such as *lol* for "laugh out loud." If such symbols and slang seem trite or silly, it helps to remember that they serve a purpose. Even researchers who choose not to use them need to show respect for those who do, while taking care not to say things in jest that could be misinterpreted.

A final recommendation for researchers who plan to conduct virtual-world interviews is to keep in mind that behind each avatar is a person. The same rules of respectful research still apply, even if the avatar is shaped like a rabbit. As the interview begins to evolve, the unusual appearance an avatar may have chosen takes second place to the human interaction expressed in words.

Conclusions About Interview Effects in Virtual Worlds

The pilot study described here—researching beneficial effects during qualitative interviews in a virtual world—did appear to yield results similar to those that have been observed during in-person interviews. The themes that characterized the beneficial virtual-world interviews included (1) a topic of intense interest to the interviewees, (2) a dynamic of trust between researcher and participant, (3) an informal setting imitating a comfortable setting in the physical world, and (4) an interview style designed to encourage reflective thinking.

These conditions of meaningfulness, trust, comfort, and reflective dialogue appeared to enhance the potential for human connection and meaningful interchange and generate rethinking of ideas and problems interviewees might not otherwise have considered. This reevaluation of meanings can lead to the transformative learning that Mezirow (1991) argues should be "a cardinal objective of adult education" (p. 111).

For distance educators, the evidence that the beneficial interview effects observed during in-person interviews can also occur in virtual worlds holds a secondary promise of another way to increase engagement of online learners by borrowing strategies from virtual-world qualitative interviews.

 See the Appendix for suggested readings and resources on the software, methodologies, and methods discussed in this case.

 Find More Materials on the Study Site! See the book website for related resources, materials, discussion, and assignment ideas.

References

Berger, R., & Malkinson, R. (2000). "Therapeutizing" research: The positive impact of family-focused research on participants. *Smith College Studies in Social Work, 70*(2), 307–314.

Buber, M. (1970). *I and thou* (W. Kaufmann, Trans.). New York: Scribner.

Cohen, L., Manion, L., & Morrison, K. (2007). *Research methods in education* (6th ed.). New York: Routledge.

Creswell, J. W. (2007). *Qualitative inquiry and research design: Choosing among five approaches* (2nd ed.). Thousand Oaks, CA: Sage.

Hiller, H. H., & DiLuzio, L. (2004). The interviewee and the research interview: Analysing a neglected dimension in research. *Canadian Review of Sociology and Anthropology, 41*(1), 1–26.

Holstein, J. A., & Gubrium, J. F. (1995). *The active interview.* Thousand Oaks, CA: Sage.

Lincoln, Y. S., & Guba, E. G. (1985). *Naturalistic inquiry.* Beverly Hills, CA: Sage.

Mezirow, J. (1991). *Transformative dimensions of adult learning.* San Francisco: Jossey-Bass.

Mills, J. (2001). Self-construction through conversation and narrative in interviews. *Educational Review, 53*(3), 285–301.

Ortiz, S. M. (2001). How interviewing became therapy for wives of professional athletes: Learning from a serendipitous experience. *Qualitative Inquiry, 7*(2), 192–220.

Patton, M. Q. (1997). *Utilization-focused evaluation* (3rd ed.). Thousand Oaks, CA: Sage.

Shamai, M. (2003). Therapeutic effects of qualitative research: Reconstructing the experience of treatment as a by-product of qualitative evaluation. *Social Service Review, 77*(3), 455–474.

Effects in Virtual Worlds

Chapter 5 describes an interesting study focused on interviews of educators in a virtual-world environment in order to investigate the *beneficial effects* of qualitative interviews on interviewees. Building on existing research, where face-to-face interviews were the basis of data collection, this study explores the use of interviews conducted via Second Life. The study illustrates several methodological topics of interest to others considering online research in virtual-world environments.

Study participants, nine adult members of the educational community, were recruited from e-mail lists of Second Life educators and researchers. All were experienced Second Life users. Two interviews of each participant took place over a 6- to 8-week period. The first interview was aimed at identifying what drew the interviewees into Second Life. The second interview focused on how the first interview affected the participants. The research addressed two questions: Do beneficial interview effects occur in text-based qualitative interviews in virtual worlds? If such effects do occur, what are the characteristics of the interviews in which they occur? All interviews were conducted using text-based chat between the interviewer and interviewee avatars in Second Life.

For those readers not familiar with beneficial effects research, it would be helpful if the author provided some background and examples on the topic. It would also be interesting for the author to share some details on the questions or topics that were used in the interviews to encourage and elicit the discussion with participants in Second Life.

Based on the analysis of interview data, the author concludes that the beneficial interview effects phenomenon did occur in this study, yielding similar results to those observed during in-person interviews. Three main themes emerged that characterize beneficial virtual-world interviews: (1) an interview subject that was important to the participant, (2) an interview dynamic in which interviewer and interviewee co-constructed meanings, and (3) an interview setting that felt comfortable and nonthreatening. Again, some examples or highlights of the researcher's analysis and findings leading to these conclusions would clarify the topic of the beneficial effects of qualitative interviews.

Chapter 7 in this volume, titled "Guides and Visitors: Capturing Stories in Virtual-World and Interactive Web Experiences," describes our project, which also used interviews in a virtual-world environment. Group interviews, rather than individual interviews, were conducted to solicit feedback from users of a prototype story-sharing application in OpenSim that was under development in collaboration with an American history museum. Although the objectives were quite different, both chapters highlight some of the same methodological issues of using virtual worlds, often with different perspectives and outcomes. Following are some of the themes that emerged in both chapters.

PARTICIPANT EXPERIENCE WITH VIRTUAL WORLDS

Chapter 5 provides a summary of lessons learned from the author's experience, including things that parallel traditional in-person interviews as well as a discussion of some of the special challenges of conducting interviews in virtual-world environments. The author points out that it was necessary that she establish credibility as a member of Second Life. Credibility in this case includes being able to navigate in-world, having a suitable avatar appearance, and demonstrating proficiency using the lingo and conventions for chat-based communications. At the time of the study, the author was already an experienced Second Life resident with an "insider's perspective" of the community. All of the interviewees were selected, in part, because they were seasoned members of the Second Life community of users.

In contrast, Chapter 7 focused on participants with relatively little experience in virtual worlds. In fact, two group training sessions were conducted prior to the story-sharing/interview session to introduce the participants to basic navigation skills, including flying and teleporting, and encouraged modifying the appearance of participants' avatars (after selecting one from a small library of predefined avatars). It was felt that these skills were necessary for participants to partake in the storytelling activities, interactions, and ultimately, the interview at the end of the session.

Questions for future research revolve around the need for expertise in virtual worlds. How much is familiarity with Second Life, or
other virtual-world environments, necessary to conduct interview
research in the environment? Could an "outsider" interview members of the community to achieve similar beneficial effects? Does this
change if the interviews migrate to more observational activities or
multiple interviewees?

PARTICIPANT IDENTITY AND PLATFORM SELECTION

The Chapter 5 author used Second Life for her interview research.
Second Life is an open environment with members from many different places and interests. This provided a pool of potential participants for the research project. The author recruited participants
from public e-mail lists focused on education. Some of the participants were concerned with revealing their identities. As an open
environment, interviews could be interrupted by other visitors. The
author leased virtual land where the interview could take place as an
approach to address privacy issues.

The study outlined in Chapter 7 used OpenSim on a private network. This was necessary to ensure an environment where the project
could experiment with technology prototypes (and potential intellectual property) in a nonpublic online environment. The study participants were all members of museum staff and even though they did not
necessarily work with one another, their identities were known to one
another. In addition, some of the participants were members of the
project team, and so had ongoing interactions with the researchers.

These two studies utilized different virtual-world environments
based on very different research goals and objectives. Questions for
research may focus on if, and how, research results based on one
virtual-world environment can be applied in other environments.

INDIVIDUAL AND GROUP INTERVIEWS

The Chapter 5 author conducted one-on-one interviews with the
participants over the course of two interview sessions. The interviewer and interviewees did not know each other prior to the study.
The interviewer had to establish rapport and build trust in a relatively
short amount of time. The author used a semi-structured, "active
interviewing" approach to collaboratively construct the interview
with the interviewee.

In contrast, the Chapter 7 study utilized a group interview approach following participation in a curator-led story-sharing session. The authors here also took a semi-structured approach, choosing to let participant responses guide some of the discussion. Participants were enthusiastic volunteers in the study, interested in exploring the use of virtual worlds in general, as well as the prototype concepts under development for applications in their respective areas of expertise. The interactions during the session and subsequent interview were very dynamic and often humorous, with participants making references and connections to their own perspectives and experiences.

SHARING INTERVIEW RESULTS WITH PARTICIPANTS

Upon completion of the Chapter 5 study, the author shared the results of the data analysis with the participants, taking this as an opportunity to solicit their feedback. Although only one participant provided feedback, this can be an important approach to gain additional insights into participants' perspectives.

In the Chapter 7 study with museum staff, and studies we've conducted in various other contexts, sharing findings and encouraging a discussion about results with participants is a valuable way to build trust with participants as well as to clarify and inform our understandings. In the collaborative study with the museum, we shared study findings via a web conference with the team. This proved to be an opportunity to refine our findings and discuss next steps for the project.

Virtual worlds offer an environment that can be leveraged by researchers to encourage interactive sharing and in-world discussion of research findings. What kinds of tools and applications are needed to enable these kinds of interactions?

TEXT-BASED CHAT

The Chapter 5 author raises the topic of choosing text-based chat instead of voice chat. In her study, the participants were willing to use text. The author chose text, although voice was available. As noted, one of the benefits of using text-based chat is that a record of the interaction (the chat file) can be used for data analysis, effectively streamlining analysis by eliminating the need for time-consuming translation of video and/or voice recordings.

Text-based chat was also used in the Chapter 7 study with the museum, finding similar benefits. The version of OpenSim that was used did not have voice capability (initially viewed by some of the researchers as a limitation). However, it became evident that having a record of the chat, which included up to 12 avatars (8 participants and 4 researchers), was immensely valuable. Creating a transcript of this interaction could have been quite complex with 12 potential voices to distinguish. The transcript of the session captured the rich interactions among participants during the event, with an increasing number of comments among all participants as the session progressed.

During a group interview (via chat) at the close of the story-sharing session, participants indicated that their favorite part of the session was the interaction among participants and the topics raised for discussion during the storytelling. An interesting observation made by the participants was that text chat enabled them to scroll back up and reread content they might have missed. Although they suggested voice-based chat as a desired future system enhancement, all did quite well using text-based chat, even though all participants were relatively new to the 3-D environment.

Another observation regarding text chat is that it can require considerable parsing and interpretation as the conversations unfold among multiple participants. All the comments from multiple threads of conversations appear in one chat window. These may be intertwined based on the order they were submitted to the window, requiring the participants to parse (or unpack) the comments that are relevant to the conversation(s) of interest to them. In addition to chat, the participants found the actions of their colleagues' avatars, for example, gestures (typing) and proximity and movement in relation to one another, provided important visual cues to the interaction.

This raises several questions about communication in virtual worlds and how researchers can most effectively conduct interview-based research in the environment. Which modalities are most effective (voice, text, sketching, gesture, or a mix of these) and for what kinds of interviews? What about interviews that cross into observation or visual description of an activity?

This brief commentary on Chapter 5 attempts to highlight some considerations in conducting interview research in virtual-world environments. It is an exciting time for virtual-world communities and the people who study them. We have highlighted a few methodological themes that intersect two chapters in the book. We hope our effort to provide insights based on the different approaches and rationales used in each will encourage further research and discussion.

CHAPTER 5
FRAMEWORK COMMENTARY:
"BENEFICIAL INTERVIEW EFFECTS
IN VIRTUAL WORLDS: A CASE STUDY"

Janet Salmons

In this exploratory pilot study, Ann Randall explored beneficial interview effects of interviews conducted in virtual worlds. As could be expected, the interviews were conducted in Second Life, a virtual world. The purposive sampling focused on participants who were educators, recruited online from existing sample frames, in this case, membership in related professional groups.

She conducted the interviews using text chat. She observed the visual representations and profiles of the avatars. She discussed visual perceptions of the avatar characteristics, styles, and manners in the context of interviewer credibility. In other kinds of online interviews, the interviewer may have to decide whether to be visible to the interviewee via webcam or photographs. In such cases, the interviewer may be attentive to appearance and attire. But when the interviewer is represented by a self-designed avatar, other considerations come into play. While Randall shared some characteristics with the educators being studied, she took a largely etic stance since she introduced real-world concerns and questions from outside the case (Stake, 1995).

Randall's observations about the interviewer as avatar point to the role Kvale describes as a traveler. According to Kvale (2007; Kvale & Brinkman, 2009), the researcher as a traveler journeys with the participant to discover insights. In interview research conducted in Second Life, the interviewer needs to be able to appear and function convincingly as a fellow traveler. It is clear that a learning curve exists and the interviewer without Second Life experience would probably need a bit of time to develop a credible avatar and to gain the confidence needed to conduct research in this environment.

This small study, conducted as an assignment for a class, yielded valuable insights for prospective researchers. The findings suggest a positive potential in regard to beneficial interview effects. Randall makes useful recommendations for researchers, in particular some specific steps that can help in preparation for the role and practice of

Figure 5.4 Research map for "Beneficial Interview Effects in Virtual Worlds."

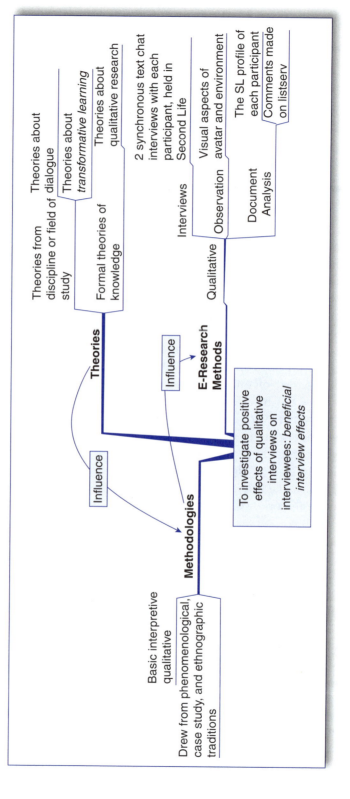

Second Life interviewer. Her work surfaces numerous other aspects of the interview process in virtual environments that other researchers, I hope, will explore. These include the use of text versus voice for interviews, the employment of a research-specific setting or a setting determined by the participant, and the collection and interpretation of visual information.

Table 5.2	Summary: Key Factors in the "Beneficial Interview Effects in Virtual Worlds: A Case Study" Study			
Motivation for Choosing E-Research	**Sampling and Recruiting**	**Interview Style and Structure**	**Technology: Issues, Features, Lessons**	**Ethical Issues**
Randall selected online research methods to study the effects of online interviews.	Purposeful, criterion-based sampling was used. Participants were recruited online in Second Life, through membership lists of established groups.	Semi-structured interviews Synchronous interviews conducted using text chat in Second Life	Randall conducted interviews in settings chosen by participants or a private Second Life environment created specifically for this study. Randall used observations and information gleaned from the avatar's profile as part of the data.	With IRB agreement, research participants could remain anonymous. Consent provided by virtual notecard. Used consent agreement to spell out privacy boundaries.

References

Kvale, S. (2007). *Doing interviews.* Thousand Oaks, CA: Sage.

Kvale, S., & Brinkman, S. (2009). *InterViews: Learning the craft of qualitative research interviewing* (2nd ed.). Thousand Oaks, CA: Sage.

Stake, R. E. (1995). *The art of case study research.* Thousand Oaks, CA: Sage.

Learning to Work In-World

Conducting Qualitative Research in Virtual Worlds Using In-Depth Interviews

Taryn Stanko
Lunquist School of Business,
University of Oregon, Eugene, USA

Jonathon Richter
Center for Learning in Virtual Environments,
University of Oregon, Eugene, USA

This chapter aims to provide insight into the benefits and challenges associated with conducting interviews in online three-dimensional environments (e.g., Second Life) using as its foundation a case study conducted in a virtual-world setting. We examine how such an online interview approach supports research efforts that allow us to authentically capture and depict the behavior of participants and other constructs of interest, as well as allow others to interact with and actively build upon our findings and disseminate such findings to a broad audience. Our goal is to use our own experiences as a lens for describing the process of gathering data in virtual settings. In particular, we hope to convey some of the powerful and

Author's Note: This research is supported by the National Science Foundation, Grant Award #0838550.

far-reaching potential that using media-enriched digital environments have, while at the same time acknowledging and discussing ways to mitigate key challenges of conducting in-world interviews. By working *in*—not simply *on*—these virtual settings we seek to better understand the work routines used by the participants interviewed in our study. Through such direct participation in virtual collaborative work, we hope to gain a better appreciation for the phenomena under study and the nuances of conducting work in a virtual setting.

In this case, we first describe the qualitative study that serves as a foundation for sharing insights into the process of conducting interviews in-world. After describing the core research questions explored, the methods, and the findings, we discuss the key advantages and disadvantages inherent in this approach. Finally, we conclude with ideas and thoughts on potential next steps in using virtual environments for disseminating research.

Study Description

Technology is often ignored in organizational research (Orlikowski & Scott, 2008), despite the fact that its use is becoming more prevalent, indeed almost ubiquitous in organizations. This raises a number of questions for organizational researchers, in particular around identity and the evolution of work routines within organizational contexts. Identity offers "a general, if individualized, framework for understanding oneself that is formed and sustained via social interaction" (Gioia, 1998, p. 19). Given that technology is often used on a daily basis to communicate and interact with others, this research examines routines around daily use of technology for work (Pentland & Feldman, 2005) and how they relate to individual identity. This research further seeks to understand how these patterns of use change over time and explore the implications of these changes.

The sociomateriality perspective (Orlikowski, 2007; Orlikowski & Scott, 2008) forms the theoretical foundation of this study. *Sociomateriality* is a theoretical framework that suggests that the social and material worlds are inextricably intertwined and cannot be understood in isolation from each other (Orlikowski, 2007; Orlikowski & Scott, 2008). This approach differs from previous views that focused primarily on how technology affects humans, to instead focus on how such technologies and the material are "intrinsic to everyday activities and relations" (Orlikowski & Scott, 2008, p. 455). An important pillar of the sociomateriality perspective is the belief that the technical and the social are so thoroughly intertwined that together they shape each other in a temporally emergent way, an idea captured by the term "mangle of practice" (Orlikowski & Scott, 2008; Pickering, 1993). In practical terms, a sociomaterial research approach looks for patterns in everyday work processes and does not try to artificially separate the technical from the social. We believe the sociomateriality approach is particularly appropriate to study identity in the context of the technology that individuals use.

Consistent with this approach, Turkle (1995) argued that identity and technology use are wrapped up in one another and that we are "increasingly intertwined with the technology and with each other via technology" in "technologically enmeshed relationships" (p. 21). This study focuses on individual identity and routines as well as the relationship between the two when individuals become immersed in using technology for work. While there are many types of individual identity that can be examined, the main focus here is on an individual's work identity, or how an individual defines himself or herself at work (Wrzesniewski & Dutton, 2001).

Our study examines the relationship between identity and routines among individuals who use virtual worlds in the process of conducting work. Virtual worlds (e.g., Second Life, Open Wonderland, and World of Warcraft) are three-dimensional computer environments that allow individuals to graphically represent a customizable version of themselves in a computer-mediated environment and to interact with others in real time. Virtual worlds allow individuals to create an avatar, or digital self-representation, that is displayed to the self and others in the virtual environment and there are frequent opportunities for interaction with others. While virtual worlds are often used for nonwork purposes, organizations increasingly see business value in conducting work in virtual worlds, including activities such as meetings, brainstorming sessions, and conferences (Driver & Driver, 2009), and use of virtual worlds is poised for dramatic growth (Strategy Analytics, 2009).

In addition to offering a place to explore identity issues, virtual worlds may also act as a window into how work is accomplished. One lens through which to view how work is accomplished is through organizational routines, or the "repetitive, recognizable patterns of interdependent actions, carried out by multiple actors" (Feldman & Pentland, 2003 p. 95) that function as core vehicles for getting work done in organizations. Pentland and Feldman (2005) describe organizational routines as consisting of both conceptual understandings as well as specific behaviors, which they respectively call the ostensive and performative dimensions of routines. The *ostensive* component represents "the abstract, generalized understandings of the participants" in a routine (Pentland & Feldman, 2007 p. 787) and plays an important role in allowing the various actors performing the work to reproduce a routine anew in varied circumstances. Thus, of interest is investigating what "different someones" are thinking while they perform their part in a routine. The *performative* dimension, on the other hand, refers to the concrete, specific performances that work entails—including the adjustments and variations required to fit the routine to the particular situation (Pentland & Feldman, 2007). Therefore, it is important in our study to understand not only how individuals think about the work they are doing in these three-dimensional immersive spaces, but also what specific behaviors they are enacting to get work done.

Importantly, an examination of the routines developed in working in-world may offer insight into work identity, and vice versa. We argue that the routines individuals use in virtual worlds and their work identities are not separate phenomena, but instead that routines and work identity may shape each other. The idea that the work we do is closely intertwined with our sense of self is consistent with early theory developed by Bandura (1978), which suggests that the environment, psychological processes, and behavioral processes each shape one another. Specifically, work activities provide opportunity for identity building (Van Maanen, 2009) and organizational routines in particular entail self-reflective behavior (Feldman & Pentland, 2003). Thus, the routines developed while working in a virtual world will likely have implications for one's sense of work identity (see Schultze & Leahy, 2009). Conversely, identity may also play a role in what routines are adopted (e.g., Kane, Argote, & Levine, 2005). For example, in a study of 144 students, Kane and her colleagues found that when groups shared a superordinate identity with a new member they were more likely to adopt routines superior to routines currently used by the team. When a shared identity with the new member did not exist, however, even superior routines were not likely to be adopted. Thus, by studying both routines and identity as they evolve and are enacted in virtual worlds, each may provide critical insight into the other.

Therefore we focus on three overarching questions. First, what is the nature of routines in virtual work environments? In particular, what patterns of activities do individuals develop to accomplish work, provided the set of affordances and constraints found in a particular virtual environment? The second question focuses on the emergence of work identity. While identity is often thought of and examined as a relatively static construct, it may be more accurately conceptualized as a "temporary, context sensitive, and evolving set of constructions" (Alvesson, Ashcraft, & Thomas, 2008, p. 6). Given the particularly flexible and customizable nature of the online work environment, how does an individual's work identity emerge and evolve through collaborative work processes within a virtual world and how does it differ from offline work identity? Finally, it is important to know not only how work routines and identity emerge in online work environments, but also how they are mutually constitutive of one another, or how they shape and are shaped by one another.

Methods

We take a qualitative approach to examine these questions using interview data from members of teams using virtual worlds to work and interact with distant colleagues as our main form of data. The participants in our study come from organizations involved in software development, the sciences, and the educational sector. A total of 25 in-depth interviews (McCracken, 1988; Seidman, 2006; Spradley, 1979; Weiss, 1995) were conducted with 14 participants, for an average of two interviews per person. The interviews focused on work routines and identity in virtual worlds. They lasted between 60 and 90 minutes each. For five participants, only one interview was conducted due to scheduling constraints; in two other cases, however, we were able to conduct a third interview to follow up on topics that were raised in earlier interviews.

While interview data forms the primary source of data for this study, to help us examine our questions of interest we relied on several additional types of data, including participant observation, photos, and *machinima,* or digital recordings created in-world. Participant observation data were gathered while attending developer meetings with a team creating a virtual-world platform called Open Wonderland. We collected participant observation data from 13 meetings with developers, for approximately 25 hours total. During these sessions, detailed notes were taken regarding the content and flow of the meeting, who attended, and what tools were used. We also collected all public text messages that occurred during the course of the session.

During both the interviews and participant observation, we took digital photos of individuals' avatars, the tools they used or created to accomplish work, and the environments in which they conducted their work. Interviewees also submitted pictures and written descriptions of virtual-world work routines when possible. Over the course of collecting data, we took 449 pictures (104 taken during participant observation and 345 taken during interviews in Second Life) of the interviewees, the tools they used, and the environments in which they worked. Finally, we took machinima of 4.5 hours' worth of interviews from a subset of three interviewees to capture use of the virtual environment for work in a richer way than photos alone provide.

DATA COLLECTION

We collected data via two interviews for each participant conducted at two different points in time. Two separate interview protocols were used—one that focused on the work routines that emerged in online work, and one that asked questions about identity formation in virtual environments and how this related to the everyday work. For convenience, we will refer to the first protocol as the routines protocol and the second as the identity protocol. During the first meeting, we asked background questions regarding age, experience with virtual worlds, and information on the organization for which the individual worked. The remaining questions during the first meeting focused on the routines protocol. In this first interview, we asked interviewees to walk us through several work routines they used in-world, and as they stepped us through the process we asked probing questions about what tools were used, why they were used, what problems or challenges the interviewee faced in that routine, how the routine evolved over time, among others. The second protocol focused on a set of questions around identity: How did they develop their avatar, how did they express themselves online, was their offline sense of self changed by their work in-world. Conducting two separate interviews allowed us to discuss emerging themes from the first interview before conducting the second, pick two or three routines to follow up on in the second interview, and identify any issues where we felt follow-up questions were needed. All interviews were conducted by both authors in-world in Second Life. In cases where it was only possible to schedule one interview with the participant, a condensed version of both interview protocols was used in one sitting.

DATA ANALYSIS

To analyze our data we used a grounded theory approach using multiple iterations of coding (Strauss & Corbin, 1998). Interviews were taped, then transcribed and imported into NVivo qualitative analysis software. Each interview was coded according to a number of categories (nodes) that emerged. Both authors read and coded the interviews. Three rounds of coding were conducted. The first round was focused on identifying the most fundamental level of nodes, which are categories under which text can be organized, called open coding (Strauss & Corbin, 1998).

FINDINGS

Our data suggest that individuals initially try to bring offline work routines into the virtual setting, but often the experience of work is truly transformed in virtual settings. This creates a tension between what routines are important to borrow from the offline world, and what work or routines should be done in new ways, making the most of the technology affordances found in the virtual setting. The benefits of borrowing old routines and ways of doing things from nonvirtual environments seems to be that people are more familiar and comfortable with them, but the downside is that using old routines may suppress individuals' ability to reap possible benefits from the affordances that virtual worlds offer. One of our interviewees stated, for example, that,

> Over time I totally, or as much as possible, abandoned a lot of the ways I used to work. And I actually prefer most of the methods I've developed or systems that I've found in SL [Second Life] and as much as possible I've brought them into my office and encouraged other people to try them out . . . because what I've found is that things in the virtual environment can move so much more quickly, so you need tools that facilitate that kind of really fast collaboration.

So, how do you balance the need for familiarity with the potential benefits of new ways of working? is a question frequently heard from virtual-world users.

Additional findings we discuss here revolve around key themes that emerged from this work, many unsurprisingly focused on what appear to be critical affordances of virtual worlds that alter ways that work is performed and experienced. Patterns of work routines naturally change and consequently have potential impacts on the identities and relationships of those performing such work. First, a key affordance of virtual worlds is the plasticity/immediacy with which the self and the virtual world are experienced. This is the idea that the environment and the appearance of one's avatar are very easy to change at a moment's notice. A second key affordance we see routines developed around is back-channel communication opportunities. One of the affordances that make virtual worlds unique is the ability to communicate via multiple channels simultaneously. Audio, 3-D objects, group chat, individual instant messaging (IM), embedded webpages, and stigmergic activity (where one person's avatar leaves objects or messages behind for others to interact with and further manipulate) can all be used simultaneously to communicate in a fluid and rich way. These 3-D environments thus constitute a very rich collaborative space. Finally, the third key affordance that we see routines developed around is what we call dynamic interaction feedback loops. Each of these three key themes as well as how each of these shape identity will be discussed in more detail below.

PLASTICITY AND IMMEDIACY

The first theme revolves around the affordance of plasticity and immediacy in virtual worlds. There are many opportunities to change one's appearance online. This could involve switching from one avatar to another (termed using one's "alt"), or changing an outfit, hair color, putting glasses on—for the purpose of meeting with another group or another person where you want to be viewed in a certain way, perhaps as more creative or more professional. In Figures 6.1, 6.2, and 6.3, the interviewee was a male offline, a senior scientist at a museum. He started out in Second Life and chose to be a woman, just to see what it was like, as he termed it—"a social experiment."

This led to changes in the patterns around how he interacted and spoke with others in the virtual world. He tried to communicate and behave in a way that was consistent with his avatar's gender so that people wouldn't know he was a male. To this end, he tried to be more sympathetic and more open and gentle, more consistent with his avatar's gender and found that people responded well to that, with very few realizing his offline gender. In the photos taken during one

Figure 6.1 Plasticity in appearance (male scientist in creative garb).

Figure 6.2 Plasticity in appearance (male scientist in professional garb).

of our interviews with him, there is an example of him in his creative garb (Figure 6.1), used to talk with students; his more professional garb in Figure 6.2 (an official Chanel outfit), used to meet with more professional audiences; and finally his alternate avatar (see Figure 6.3), who is male, who he used to meet with more conservative audiences who might not be comfortable with a male person using a female avatar.

| Figure 6.3 | Plasticity in appearance (male scientist using alternate avatar). |

Importantly, these routines around changing appearance can have implications for one's identity. One interviewee spoke of feeling more open and willing to experiment in general after regularly experimenting with her online appearance. In the case of our example here, the interviewee felt that he became more approachable and sympathetic and that his way of communicating with others changed and became more open. He also stated that his female coworkers changed their opinion about him after interacting with him over time in-world. After these online interactions with his female avatar, his coworkers then viewed the scientist as being more sympathetic and understanding, someone whom they would go to for advice in ways they never would have before.

BACK-CHANNEL COMMUNICATION

One of the patterns of action we see again and again in our interviews was around the use of informal communication channels (see Figure 6.4). Such back-channel communication has become a part of everyday communication patterns in that individuals use text chat to participate in group meetings, conferences, lectures, roundtable

Figure 6.4	Back-channel communication in an Open Wonderland setting.

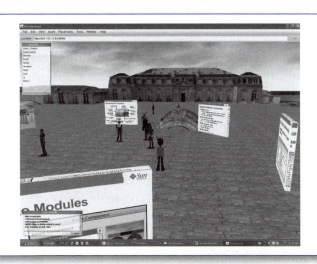

discussions, even one-on-one discussions to communicate thoughts, concerns, feedback, and questions in real time.

What we heard about the informal back-channel communication affordances that Second Life allows is how much easier it is to speak up at meetings in a less formal way (even if you're not an expert, for example, or if you don't want to interrupt a prestigious speaker). Back-channel communication can change the direction of a conversation when a participant raises a question or important issue that the group may not have yet considered. Our interviewees relayed stories of back-channel communication being used for everything from one-on-one communication and casual group meetings, to presentations and lectures.

One of our interviewees talked of giving lectures while using these back-channel affordances to better interact and engage with the audience. This way he could know if audience members did not understand or what key questions they had. One technique he successfully experimented with was using a second person to handle all of the back-channel communication when he was speaking to a large audience and couldn't manage both speaking and answering all of the questions that came in from texting.

Interviewees describe their belief that engaging in this type of behavior again and again eventually led them to feel more confident in groups, more willing to speak up, more comfortable interacting with others. Interviewees saw examples where this affected a person's overall sense of confidence. For example, one of our interviewees felt that features such as texting and other back-channel communication methods in the virtual world allowed her to move beyond her current skills and abilities, to grow and learn. She said the fact that "I have the screen to hide behind gives me the ability to go beyond my comfort zone and over time those comfort zones change for me in real life, just like they did virtually."

DYNAMIC INTERACTION

This final theme builds on elements of the two above affordances—the plasticity of the avatar, the plasticity of the environment, the immediacy, and the back-channel communication ability, which combine to afford what we call *dynamic interaction,* or continual feedback loops—iterative communication. Routines were developed around these affordances that allow for increased learning and on-the-fly changes to do real-time adjustment. For example, our interviewees talked about creating objects that multiple people can walk around, observe, comment on, simultaneously edit, give feedback on, and learn from in an extremely dynamic way.

In Figure 6.5, an interviewee is teaching us about the scales on a butterfly wing. From the starting point visible in this picture, the interviewee goes on to show the observers in steps what the scales

| Figure 6.5 | Dynamic interaction: Learning about the scales of a butterfly wing. |

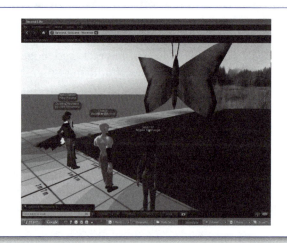

look like up to a magnification of 10,000 nanometers. At each level of magnification, observers can ask questions or view the scales from different angles using their zoom. The objects in the environment can also be used to display and demonstrate the points he is trying to get across. We heard many stories of the fast pace of interaction and real-time adjustment in planning, creating objects, and teaching that involved this highly dynamic, highly interactive pattern of work.

The importance of this real-time feedback, this continual adjustment and flexibility based on a group's learning or communication needs, was evident among our interviewees. Analysis of our data suggests that people feel more empowered in their work and have a greater sense of self-efficacy from engaging in these routines over time.

Challenges and Lessons Learned

In this section, we focus on some of the core challenges and lessons that we have learned along the way from a research methods perspective. A core challenge we faced in this project and that touched every aspect of our study involved the idea of working *in* virtual worlds and not just *on* virtual worlds. In other words, we believe that to adequately understand our interviewees' experiences and behavior it is critical to immerse ourselves in the virtual worlds under study. This meant conducting our research directly in-world.

One resulting challenge that we then faced as a research team was that one coauthor was an expert in the area of virtual worlds while the other was a relative neophyte. In this case, we found that this pairing was both a strength and a weakness. One strength of this pairing was that it was actually quite helpful to have one expert and one "newb" to get both perspectives—to have the expert to help navigate and the "newb" to make sure that questions are asked that might be obvious to and taken for granted by the expert, but still need exploring. However, the neophyte faced a learning curve in navigating Second Life, from mastering such simple tasks as walking and viewing objects from different angles, to understanding Second Life lingo (e.g., *newb* means neophyte; *rez* refers to the quality and speed with which graphics are displayed in a virtual world). For one author, it felt as if she was slowing down the process and perhaps took the focus off of what was really interesting by not always being able to navigate and view objects gracefully and subtly. By contrast, the other researcher was challenged to simultaneously embrace both the breadth of the phenomena under study and the time and effort required for his research colleague to gain sufficient experience and context to work well in virtual settings.

Given that we had not collected data in-world prior to this study, one concern was the lack of ability to see facial expressions and other types of body language that would be evident in face-to-face interaction. Interestingly, while there were minor difficulties encountered in using the technology, during the process of conducting the interviews in virtual environments we felt that rich data were still communicated. This might be worth taking note of, especially for those researchers who are used to interviewing face-to-face: Despite the fact that in-world interviews are not conducted in a traditional face-to-face setting, these interviews can be rich and data intensive and still include some body language and facial expressions (mediated through the avatar).

For both expert and neophyte, however, learning to conduct research in an online environment involved a steep learning curve, and both of us (even the expert!) faced several important challenges as we learned critical lessons in the process of conducting this research. For example, in a manner reflective of the lived perspective of participants in the research, the research team encountered a learning curve in bridging the virtual world and adapting offline research methods to the virtual world. We regularly assessed what new techniques might help us collect data in this new context (e.g., pictures, machinima, wikis) and which techniques to use from offline research. Importantly, early in this project the author team became a virtual team ourselves when one author moved to another state. This was another impetus for us to learn to work *in* virtual worlds and provided us with further perspective on the nature of geo-distributed teams collaborating in virtual worlds to get substantive work done.

Working *in* virtual worlds allowed us to harness the unique tools that virtual worlds offer to collect data, therefore collecting multiple types of data using multiple tools in this environment was critical. This necessitated finding appropriate and sufficient tools adequate for collecting the data corresponding to the rich, media-enhanced interactions to be found in these virtual worlds. It also entailed exercising an open mind so that we could view the possibility of using new ways of collecting data to help us approach our research questions from multiple angles and in richer, more authentic ways. For example, the pictures taken of people doing work in-world allowed us to capture the context and then replicate these situations in virtual research presentations. These photos then, annotated with notes and key features highlighted, provide the in-world viewer with an authentic sense of what work is done within these contexts. The machinima were also extremely helpful in allowing us to capture action and have a record of how online tools were used by interviewees instead of relying solely on interviewee descriptions. Given the focus here on gathering multiple types of in-world data, it may be especially important for researchers to work in pairs so that one person can focus on leading the interview, while the other can focus on taking notes, taking pictures and machinima, and being the point person to solve technical problems as they arise.

A third and related challenge that arose conducting research in-world involved overcoming technical issues, such as sound problems, delays in graphics "rezzing," or showing on the screen, and in some ways starting over at the bottom of the learning curve when a new version of Second Life was introduced midstream. Generally speaking, it became the norm to experience technology-related problems and the key became to take them in stride and find work-around solutions whenever possible. For example, when sound problems cropped up this caused time delays that we were very sensitive to as, at the very least, these problems took away from the time we had to talk with interviewees. We quickly came to rely on Skype as a backup technology to use when Second Life sound functionality did not work properly. We did not find an easy solution to the problem of delayed rezzing and when this problem occurred, in some cases we were not able to take pictures of the interviewee's avatar and lost time opportunities to gather data.

In addition to learning important lessons in the process of conducting research in a virtual environment, we also faced some interesting ethical questions. While acquiring Institutional Review Board (IRB) approval went smoothly for this project, what we experienced during the course of this study suggests that given the newness of this research context a greater onus falls on the researcher to be sensitive to ethical issues than one might often expect from an IRB for research conducted in a more traditional setting. As part of our protocol, we assured participants that their responses would be completely confidential and their names and identities would be disguised in papers resulting from the study, except where permission was explicitly obtained. In the process of collecting data during the interviews, however, several privacy issues came up. One involved taking pictures and machinima. We found that although we asked permission to take photos before the interviews began, it was important to emphasize to the interviewee that if an object or situation emerged that they did not indeed want us to take pictures of, they should let us know and we would stop taking pictures and destroy any pictures that the interviewee did not want used. This happened with one interviewee when she took us into a protected space in Second Life that blocked all outsiders and showed us a scheduling tool that had sensitive information displayed. We encourage researchers to be sensitive to the need to get permission for taking pictures, and to double-check that the study participant is comfortable with sharing on an ongoing basis.

Another, perhaps much broader issue was raised by one of our participants about ownership of the "self" in virtual worlds. When using an avatar for work purposes, there is human and social capital and reputation linked to the avatar. One senior scientist said, "When people think interactive science exhibit they think [his avatar's name]." The avatar, and the particular user account that the avatar is associated with owns buildings, tools, clothing, and many other resources that may belong to or be closely intertwined with an organization. What implications does this have for us as researchers? It may be especially important in this context to be proactive in obtaining permission from the organization as well for use of pictures of avatars or machinima or work being conducted. This context can obscure the need for permission because the virtual world does not always look or feel like a traditional work setting. One way of thinking about it is that being in a virtual world is like being in a glass house, where we are allowed to view more than we would be able to offline. Therefore, it is important to take into consideration whether the organization is aware of your research and be sensitive to the need to get permission from the organization to collect and use data in the virtual setting.

Like Boellstorff (2008), we continue to underscore the importance of performing research directly in virtual worlds to better understand the perspectives of those doing work in these contexts. Again, investigation of virtual worlds necessitates doing such work to some large degree within the virtual worlds, themselves. Not only do we seek participants, gather data, and examine phenomena in virtual worlds—but we live, play, experiment, and work in-world, too. Further, we believe that it is in many ways of equal importance to use the virtual world to collect data and as an authentic and complementary place to convey our research findings. Journal articles, conference presentations, and book chapters (like this one), while tried-and-true methods for doing scholarly work, convey, like any medium, certain forms of information well but render other forms of understanding clumsily or even obscurely. Virtual worlds are not only constructed 3-D spaces that allow others to experience a digital "built environment," but they may further be co-constructed environments that integrate the multiple sensory and communication modalities used and experienced by these very individuals. Use of a virtual-world space as a means for disseminating research findings for those doing virtual-world research is a possible advantage, as they reflexively provide perhaps the most distinguishing means to convey our interviewees' lived experiences and perceptions.

To this end, we have created a virtual collaboration laboratory, or "Collaboratory," for use in integrating our work. We foresaw the Collaboratory as a virtual environment to collect and organize tools and other work-related objects sampled from the collaborative workplace of volunteering participants for the public to see, interact with, and make suggestions and contributions to. With guidance from architectural and technology experts, our research team participated in a design charrette to converge on a set of specifications for a virtual layout for the Collaboratory that would best represent our purposes. Our design specifications—(1) to open a portal connecting Open Wonderland and Second Life for users, (2) to construct a virtual exhibition hall for displaying and showcasing exemplary instances of virtual collaboration as well as the results of our own social science research, and (3) to build a virtual social science laboratory where geo-distributed collaborations can be conducted and studied in real time—were then put into form by an architect and computer scientist. From that functioning model, we then created a Google Sketchup file for use in creating our Open Wonderland Collaboratory, a mirror image set in a different world with a different set of affordances and constraints.

Such virtual collaboration spaces allow us to invite virtual workers to demonstrate their work from within their respective environments, providing a venue and opportunity for others to compare and contrast, and potentially add their own way of using a tool or practice. Notecards, questionnaires, live filmed events, a "digital dropbox," and other ways of direct participation can be used to elicit contributions from visitors to either the Open Wonderland or Second Life Collaboratory location. This, in effect, offers an open prototyping method for contributing and describing virtual-world work routines and articulating patterns of action that may contribute to the knowledge base on virtual work. Permutations of virtual-world work routines may be visually arranged and displayed for visitors to view, and annotated machinima may be placed in each Collaboratory to highlight the dimensions and factors thought worthy of conveying.

This virtual environment situates the tools, avatars, work events, and perspectives drawn from our research as a sort of "pattern language," wherein narrative texts and synthesized themes can be contextualized alongside the tools and performances to represent the thinking and actions of participants about the work done while using these tools in collaboration routines. Thus, the ostensive aspects of routines, or the generalized understandings participants share, can be developed and placed in the Collaboratory in-world respective to the virtual routine in question. Annotated machinima, movies filmed within the virtual environment and affixed with notations made by the researchers at various points on the film's timeline, likewise represent the participants' use of these tools in the workplace contexts. This situates the performative aspects of the routines, or the ways routines are performed, too. Wiki pages, notecards, and other texts placed in-world represent the ostensive, while machinima, illustrations, photographs, and the objects themselves represent the performative. Together they constitute families of routines with permutations along functions.

The Collaboratory represents our intent to ecologically situate our knowledge in a way that is reflective of the rich digital environments from which we draw our experiences and stems from a methodological approach aligned with an emergent, critical understanding of the medium itself (Pink, 2001). We believe that if sufficient numbers of people become active there, our research may, through joint enterprise and mutual engagement, become a useful and shared repertoire of communal resources to form an evidence-based Community of Practice (Wenger, 1998). Through systematic representation of the people, practices, values, and technologies embedded in these virtual work environments, we hope this occurs through the development of a virtual "information ecology" that may shed light on the ways people and technology are interrelated (Nardi & O'Day, 2000).

Conclusion

Virtual worlds are potentially transformational in that they allow people a great deal of flexibility and power in developing an expression of the self online as well as the ability to adopt or create new work routines. As the use of virtual worlds grows dramatically

(Strategy Analytics, 2009), researchers may be increasingly drawn to use them as settings in which to gather data. Researchers are already conducting fascinating work in-world (e.g., Turkle, 1995; Yee & Bailenson, 2007, 2009). We believe work in this area will continue to provide insight into phenomena of interest, but it is critical to keep in mind both the strengths and limitations of these new environments.

From the perspective of evolving research methods, our goal with this project is to explore rigorous research methods commensurate with the goals of our study and outline key lessons learned. In-world research methods allow us to capture behaviors of interest in ways not only consistent with the phenomena of virtual work routines and virtual work identities, but also as an enriched set of inquiry processes to capture such lived experiences. Virtual environments as a form of online research media allow us to triangulate data and document these "third places" between work and play (Steinkuehler & Williams, 2006) and also to share knowledge in a richer way, reach a broader audience, and allow others to learn from and build on our findings. Alongside these potential advantages, it is important to keep in mind and plan for the sometimes steep learning curve involved with conducting research in these evolving environments, to tread carefully with ethical issues of heightened importance in virtual worlds, and to be open-minded with respect to gathering different types of data using multiple forms of technology. If researchers are able to balance these benefits and challenges, the potential to successfully harness virtual worlds as settings to conduct research will continue to grow.

 See the Appendix for suggested readings and resources on the software, methodologies, and methods discussed in this case.

 Find More Materials on the Study Site! See the book website for related resources, materials, discussion, and assignment ideas.

References

Alvesson, M., Ashcraft, K. L., & Thomas, R. (2008). Identity matters: Reflections on the construction of identity scholarship in organization studies. *Organization, 15,* 5–28.

Bandura, A. (1978). The self-system in reciprocal determinism. *American Psychologist, 33,* 344–358.

Boellstorff, T. (2008). *Coming of age in Second Life: An anthropologist explores the virtually human.* Princeton, NJ: Princeton University Press.

Driver, E., & Driver, S. (2009). *ThinkBalm immersive Internet business value study.* Retrieved from http://www.thinkbalm.com/2009/05/26/think balm-publishes-business-value-study/

Feldman, M. S., & Pentland, B. T. (2003). Reconceptualizing organizational routines as a source of flexibility and change. *Administrative Science Quarterly, 48,* 94–118.

Gioia, D. A. (1998). From individual to organizational identity. In D. Whetten & P. Godfrey (Eds.), *Identity in organizations: Developing theory through conversations* (pp. 17–32). Thousand Oaks, CA: Sage.

Kane, A. A., Argote, L., & Levine, J. M. (2005). Knowledge transfer between groups via personnel rotation: Effects of social identity and knowledge quality. *Organizational Behavior and Human Decision Processes, 96,* 56–71.

McCracken, G. (1988). *The long interview.* Newbury Park, CA: Sage.

Nardi, B., & O'Day, V. (2000). *Information ecologies: Using technologies with heart.* Boston: MIT Press.

Orlikowski, W. J. (2007). Sociomaterial practices: Exploring technology at work. *Organization Studies, 28,* 1435–1448.

Orlikowski, W. J., & Scott, S. V. (2008). Sociomateriality: Challenging the separation of technology, work, and the organization. *The Academy of Management Annals, 2,* 433–474.

Pentland, B. T., & Feldman, M. S. (2005). Organizational routines as a unit of analysis. *Industrial and Corporate Change, 14,* 793–815.

Pentland, B. T., & Feldman, M. S. (2007). Narrative networks: Patterns of technology and organization. *Organization Science, 18,* 781–795.

Pickering, A. (1993). The mangle of practice, agency and emergence in the sociology of science. *American Journal of Sociology, 99,* 559–589.

Pink, S. (2001). *Doing visual ethnography: Images, media, and representation in research.* Thousand Oaks, CA: Sage.

Schultze, U., & Leahy, M. M. (2009). The avatar-self relationship: Enacting presence in Second Life. *International Conference on Information Systems,* Phoenix, AZ.

Seidman, I. (2006). *Interviewing as qualitative research* (3rd ed.). New York: Teachers College Press.

Spradley, J. (1979). *The ethnographic interview.* New York: Holt, Rinehart & Winston.

Steinkuehler, C. A., & Williams, D. (2006). When everybody knows your (screen) name: Online games and "third" places. *Journal of Computer Mediated Communication, 11,* 885–909.

Strategy Analytics. (2009, June 15). *Report: Virtual worlds growth to skyrocket.* Retrieved from www.virtualworldsnews.com/2009/06/report-virtual-worlds-growth-to-skyrocket-.html

Strauss, A., & Corbin, J. (1998). *Basics of qualitative research: Techniques and procedures for developing grounded theory* (2nd ed.). Thousand Oaks, CA: Sage.

Turkle, S. (1995). *Life on the screen: Identity in the age of the Internet.* New York: Simon & Schuster.

Van Maanen, J. (2009). Identity work and control in occupational communities. In S. B. Sitkin, L. B. Cardinal, and K. M. Bijlsma-Frankema (Eds.), *Control in organizations: New directions in theory and research.* Cambridge, UK: Cambridge University Press.

Weiss, R. S. (1995). *Learning from strangers: The art and method of qualitative interview studies.* New York: Free Press.

Wenger, E. (1998, June). Communities of practice: Learning as a social system. *Systems Thinker.* Retrieved from http://www.co-i-l.com/coil/knowledge-garden/cop/lss.shtml

Wrzesniewski, A., & Dutton, J. (2001). Crafting a job: Revisioning employees as active crafters of their work. *Academy of Management Review, 26,* 179–201.

Yee, N., & Bailenson, J. (2007). The proteus effect: The effect of transformed self-representation on behavior. *Human Communication Research, 33,* 271–290.

Yee, N., & Bailenson, J. (2009). The proteus effect: Implications of transformed digital self-representation on online and offline behavior. *Communication Research, 36,* 285–312.

Jonathan Cabiria

In this study by Stanko and Richter, compared to the study by Cabiria (see Chapter 4), what is immediately striking is the transformative power of the virtual-world environment on individuals. Stanko and Richter noted not only how workers transformed their ways of thinking and performing when engaged in work-related activities, but also how they were transformed behaviorally and perceptually. In Cabiria's research, the virtual-world participants sought out the virtual environment for relief from real-world oppression and found a transformation as well. In attempting to expose this transformative process, all authors utilized qualitative approaches, specifically grounded theory, to discover emergent themes in the virtual experiences of their participants. A grounded theory approach is a perfect choice for virtual-world studies, given the relative newness of the technologies. It allows researchers to explore new territories with an open mind, letting the experiences of the participants reveal the how-and-why of these transformations; offering insights into not only the virtual experience, but into the contrasting real-world activities that precipitated the transformations.

The research results of both studies run roughly parallel to each other, even though the research questions and participants were completely different. Stanko and Richter looked at how workers adapted their work behaviors and processes in virtual worlds and Cabiria looked at how marginalized people adapted their social behaviors in virtual worlds. In each case, participants discovered virtual worlds to be safe havens for identity exploration, even when the goal of exploring the virtual environment had a different initial objective. Over time, both groups shed old ways of doing things to experience the affordances that virtual safe havens offered. As Stanko and Richter noted, plasticity—the ability to quickly change—was a key affordance that enabled participants in both studies to make immediate changes in their behaviors to suit the conditions of the virtual environments, and to suit individual needs.

Conducting virtual world research is both a familiar process and a unique one. Certainly, the traditional approaches to qualitative research hold true and grounded theory models are easily adapted to the virtual environment. Information is still gathered through interviews and observations, coding occurs in the same manner, and emergent theories are identified the same way. What is unique is the extra care needed to ensure that the virtual-world participants and data meet other real-world standards. One of these concerns the Institutional Review Board (IRB) application. The IRB exists to ensure the integrity of the research process and the protection of the research participants. Stanko and Richter appear to have had an easy time with their IRB application review. There is no indication of any committee conflict with regard to protection measures for avatars. Cabiria's IRB review, on the other hand, generated quite a bit of controversy. Questions arose as to what level of protection was required for avatars. Could the avatar suffer harm? How much recognition should be given to the avatar–human connection? Could it be known who or what was actually being protected given the anonymous nature of the avatars? For Cabiria's IRB, after several months of reflection and debate, there were several key decisions that were made:

1. The human controller of the avatar could suffer emotional harm as a result of harm to the avatar.

2. The human controller could be harmed in his or her real life if his or her connection to the virtual world avatar was publicly revealed.

3. An avatar has a social, professional, and family life within the virtual environment that can be harmed, inhibiting its ability to function as desired by its human controller.

4. Researchers must take steps to verify, in some way, the legitimacy of the avatar/human controller (is it who it says it is?).

5. Avatar participants should be afforded the same rights and protections in research studies as human participants would.

It appears that all researchers in these two studies arrived at the same conclusions, although the process was different. In the case of Stanko and Richter, the onus of protection was placed upon the researchers, and in the Cabiria case, it was directed through the IRB committee. Key to future researchers is that, apparently, it is better to treat the avatar as one would treat a human being when it comes to research protections.

Beyond the planning challenges associated with virtual-world studies, such as IRB approvals, there are the actual challenges of dealing with missing sensory cues and with technologies. Both studies noted the importance of conducting the research completely in-world, with researchers also engaged in the process through their avatars. It was quickly apparent that concerns over loss of communication subtleties, such as vocal intonation, body movement, eye gaze, and overall presentation of self were expected to possibly impede the depth of data that might otherwise be available in real-world studies. While some of this is true, to a certain extent, the data that came out of both studies indicated that it was possible to "fill in the gaps" of missing sensory input. For example, avatars do have the ability to amplify text-based communications with scripted body movements, limited only by the skill of the human controller to engage them in a meaningful manner. In addition, since how one dresses sends sensory signals, and since there is a preference for people to create avatars and dress them in an idealized manner, a researcher can draw observational inferences based on the body type and clothing choices made for the avatar. Finally, given some sensory and identity deprivation, human controllers often engage in psychological behavior called "excessive self-disclosure" in which the human controller, through the avatar, discloses more information, and in a shorter amount of time than would normally occur in a real-world face-to-face interview. Stanko and Richter and Cabiria all found that the sensory limitations were compensated for by other communication approaches (gesturing, appearance, disclosure) that aided in the creation of rich data from which to mine useful information. For future researchers, the takeaway is to realize that people, being social creatures, will develop ways of effective communication, when sensory deprivation occurs, by compensating through other channels of expression. Researchers just need to be aware and open to these channels.

The second challenge, aside from the sensory cues, is that of technological instability. Both studies indicated that problems could occur at any point along the communication chain, but most often related to performance issues of the virtual-world servers. It became clear early on that researchers need to have backup plans due to the certainty that the virtual world would "rez" slowly (long delays in graphics appearing and/or slow movements of avatars) or would freeze completely, necessitating closing down the program and reentering (rebooting). A best practice approach for any virtual-world research would require that several alternate plans be in place, and discussed with research participants beforehand, so that should an obstructive event occur, both parties (researcher and participant) would know what to do next. Options such as instant messaging, e-mail, Skype, rebooting, and moving to a low-rez load location are all possible options, depending upon the issue that arises.

Based on these two studies it appears that the qualitative approach is a good fit for virtual-world research. The relative ease and immediacy of the transformational process provides researchers with quick access to real-world versus virtual-world comparisons and contrasts. This allows for explorations into identity development and redevelopment across personal and organizational lines. The research process itself, while not without challenges, is eminently workable. Keeping some key best practice approaches in mind, such as applying human protections to avatars, keeping open to communication compensations, and planning for technological mishaps, can assist the virtual researcher in developing a good qualitative research model.

CHAPTER 6
FRAMEWORK COMMENTARY: "LEARNING TO WORK IN-WORLD: CONDUCTING QUALITATIVE RESEARCH IN VIRTUAL WORLDS USING IN-DEPTH INTERVIEWS"

Janet Salmons

Taryn Stanko and Jonathon Richter's grounded theory study of virtual work routines offers new ways to think about the "work" of the researcher who intends to collect data in virtual worlds. They observe that "individuals initially try to bring offline work routines into the virtual setting, but often the experience of work is truly transformed in virtual settings." This point may apply to researchers, as well. The "routines" of interview researchers must adjust, when, for example, they must first develop a credible identity as an avatar, and select voice or text, as well as environments conducive to private conversation.

Stanko and Richter point to two interrelated challenges: on one hand, the researcher needs to find "appropriate and sufficient tools adequate for collecting the data corresponding to the rich, media-enhanced interactions to be found in these virtual worlds." On the other hand, they note that "it became the norm to experience technology-related problems and the key became to take them in stride and find work-around solutions whenever possible." Again, the researcher needs flexibility and the ability for agile in-the-moment changes of modality.

While some interviewers conduct the interview in the visually rich virtual environment but use as the primary data transcripts of text chat, Stanko and Richter made a particular effort to collect extensive visual data. They took the equivalent of still and moving pictures using photo and machinima functionalities. These visual research methods greatly expand the forms and richness of their data. We could see some examples in this chapter. When the more-complete findings of the study are published, this aspect of the study will be instructive to future researchers who want to more fully capture the dynamics of research phenomena.

While they do not contribute data on their own experiences, their immersion in the study environment might indicate an emic stance, meaning as actors in the case, they saw and raised issues that emerged from within the case (Stake, 1995). As researchers, Stanko and

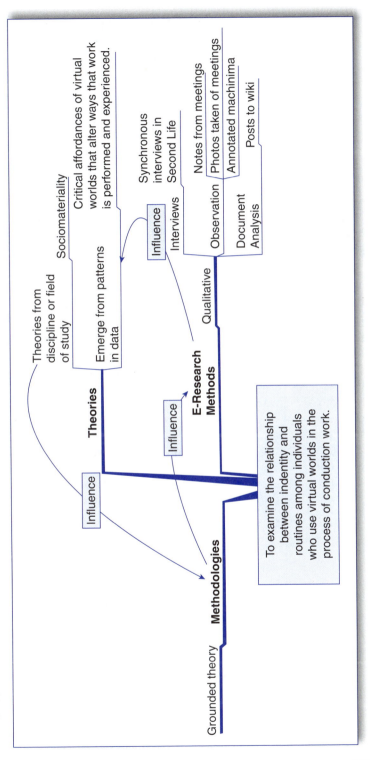

Figure 6.6 Research map for "Learning to Work In-World: Conducting Qualitative Research in Virtual Worlds Using In-Depth Interviews."

185

Richter experienced the virtual world as fellow *travelers* with each other and the research participants. The Collaboratory introduced in this study will undoubtedly offer new examples for—and challenges to—the concept of researcher as traveler since in this immersive environment, the researcher must travel with participants in the guise of an avatar. According to Kvale (2007; Kvale & Brinkman, 2009), the researcher as a *traveler* journeys with the participant to discover insights. Implications of the in-world "researcher-traveler" identity and experience offer fertile ground for future inquiry.

Table 6.1	Summary: Key Factors in the "Learning to Work In-World: Conducting Qualitative Research in Virtual Worlds Using In-Depth Interviews" Study			
Motivation for Choosing E-Research	**Sampling and Recruiting**	**Interview Style and Structure**	**Technology: Issues, Features, Lessons**	**Ethical Issues**
Stanko and Richter selected online research methods to study issues of online work and identity.	Purposeful, criterion-based sampling was used.	Semi-structured interviews were conducted in virtual worlds using voice and text chat	Richter and Stanko conducted interviews in Second Life and Open Wonderland environments created specifically for this study. Richter and Stanko complemented interview data with other observational and visual data.	Privacy issues in regard to photos in-world require ongoing negotiation to avoid inadvertent sharing of private information.

References

Kvale, S. (2007). *Doing interviews.* Thousand Oaks, CA: Sage.

Kvale, S., & Brinkman, S. (2009). *InterViews: Learning the craft of qualitative research interviewing* (2nd ed.). Thousand Oaks, CA: Sage.

Stake, R. E. (1995). *The art of case study research.* Thousand Oaks, CA: Sage.

Guides and Visitors

7

Capturing Stories in Virtual-World and Interactive Web Experiences

Patricia Wall, Jonas Karlsson, Zahra Langford, Tong Sun, and Wei Peng
Xerox Research Center Webster, NY, USA

Eric Bier
Palo Alto Research Center, Palo Alto, CA, USA

Christian Øverland, Mike Butman, Suzanne Fischer, and Lisa Korzetz
The Henry Ford Museum, Dearborn, MI, USA

Research Purpose and Questions

Document collections are an important aspect of institutional knowledge for many large companies and nonprofit organizations. An organization's ability to make effective use of the information contained in its collections requires preservation of the content and ways to search, navigate, and organize relevant collection content in order to make sense of it.

The work reported in this chapter began as a collaboration between Xerox Research and the Henry Ford Museum to explore ways for institutions to get more value from their document collections. The Henry Ford is an American history museum that has millions of artifacts, but only a fraction of them are available to view in the museum and online. The museum was interested in making more of its collections available online and to explore new kinds of interactions between visitors and museum staff and the collections. Xerox Research was interested in exploring ways to enable navigation, search, and collaboration around online collections via web-based and 3-D virtual-world immersive technologies.

This collaboration took shape as the Document Interactions Project. The project team consisted of members of the Henry Ford Museum staff located in Dearborn, Michigan, and a multidisciplinary team of computer scientists, ethnographers, and user-interface designers from the Palo Alto Research Center (PARC) in California and the Xerox Research Center Webster (XRCW) in New York. Due to the geographically distributed nature of the team, a combination of face-to-face workshops and weekly online meetings were used to establish and maintain team relationships. This enabled regular discussions, co-design sessions, and work-in-progress demonstrations with the team.

From our earliest interactions, the theme of "stories" emerged as salient in almost every discussion with the museum staff. The museum is a place where stories are told as a way to bring artifacts to life for visitors. A fundamental premise of the project was that people often make sense of the information in a collection by creating stories around it. If technology concepts were to be relevant to the museum, they would have to facilitate story creation and storytelling. Since a goal of this work was to enable visitors to interact around artifacts from an online historical collection, we felt that visitors should be able to select artifacts and weave them into a story, and if desired share the story with others, in the form of an online tour. To this end, we designed a web-based tool, Story Maker, which allows users to search a collection and create sequences of artifacts, called stories, from the artifacts they found. Users can save their stories to the repository and import them into the 3-D virtual world, where they can become the subject of virtual tours.

Research goals for Story Maker include investigating

- new forms of search that take advantage of connections between artifacts in a repository, entities mentioned in those artifacts, and the people who study them;

- new approaches for creating and using stories to find, organize, and interpret documents, images, and other artifacts; and

- new ways to extract metadata from artifacts to create richer connections between them.

To provide an environment for groups of people to explore and share stories, we created a 3-D Story Garden, providing an immersive, collaborative interface for experiencing stories. Research goals for the 3-D Virtual-World Story Garden included investigating

- how to support storytelling and interactions among a group of people relatively new to 3-D immersive environments, in a museum context;

- new approaches to capturing interactions during a storytelling session for replay in the environment at a later time; and

- the kinds of stories and interactions people have in this environment.

At the time we conducted our virtual tours, we had achieved all of these goals in whole or in part. We will discuss these results in a later section. First, we describe our technology prototypes.

Technology Prototype Design

STORY MAKER

The Story Maker component of our system helps users find documents and images related to a particular topic, such as a historical figure or technology, and then organize these materials into a story. It was designed and built as a web-user interface to artifacts from the Henry Ford Museum. The museum provided several collections of photographs, including images related to automobiles, American quilting, and President John F. Kennedy. In addition to the images, the Henry Ford provided manually curated metadata for each artifact including title, descriptive paragraphs, and a list of associated people, places, organizations, genres, and historical topics. Figure 7.1 shows the layout of Story Maker. The right-hand panel is a search tool, providing several ways to find and view materials. The left-hand panel is a story-editing region, showing a sequence of images, captions, and text paragraphs that represent a story.

| **Figure 7.1** | The Story Maker user interface, with story construction panel on the left and search panel on the right. |

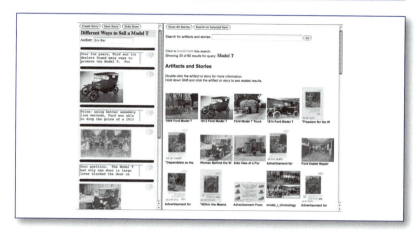

Story Maker can be understood by following the steps that anyone might use to construct a story. The process may begin by typing a key-word query into the search box shown near the upper right of Figure 7.1. The system returns an initial set of artifacts and stories. Each artifact is shown as a single thumbnail image. Each story is displayed as an array of images with blue borders. The user can double-click on the image of an artifact to view more information about it. Figure 7.2 shows the detailed view of an artifact, providing a title and a few descriptive paragraphs about the artifact.

The user can create a new blank story (e.g., by clicking the "Create Story" button shown in Figure 7.1), and can add new materials to a story (like the one shown in the left panel of Figure 7.1). For example, the user can click on a desired artifact in the search results pane and then indicate where the artifact should be placed in the story by clicking on the appropriate horizontal black line in the story pane. The user can add a caption for any story element, by clicking the black line under that element and typing.

The resulting story can then be viewed as a slide show by clicking on the "Slide Show" button. Figure 7.3 shows one slide from a slide show.

The user can save a story into the repository. The system indexes the story, so that it can be found using the search functions. It is indexed by several properties, including title, author, and the content of its captions, so users will be able to find it in multiple ways.

Story Maker also includes a search function that finds materials relevant to a particular artifact. For example, artifacts are considered

Figure 7.2 Story Maker shows the details of one artifact from the collection.

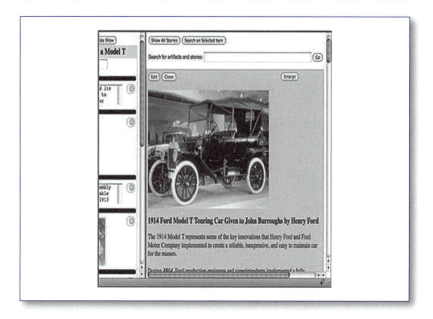

Figure 7.3 Slide show mode.

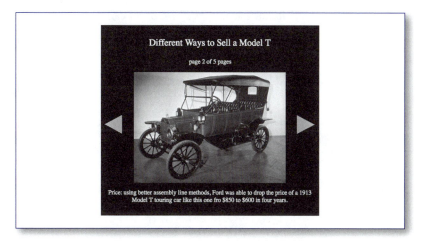

related if they are associated with the same person, company, city, topic, or genre. Users can also perform key-word searches on their own names to find stories they have written.

3-D VIRTUAL-WORLD STORY GARDEN

The 3-D Virtual-World Story Garden allows users to view stories created in Story Maker and interact with one another via virtual self-representation avatar in a 3-D immersive multi-user environment (Bartle, 2004; Churchill, Snowdon, & Munro, 2001).

A story garden is a 3-D "natural" environment, with grass, trees, and flowers, as shown in Figure 7.4. The sequence of artifacts in a story is displayed along a spiral path that extends to accommodate the length of the story. Users are also represented in the space by graphical avatars, as shown in Figure 7.5. Since the story garden is a shared space, all users currently using the system are visible.

When users first log in to the 3-D environment, they are placed in a "search tower" that provides an interface to the Story Maker search capability. Users enter key words and results are displayed as doors along the wall of the tower. A specific story is selected by clicking on the door, causing the user to be transported away from the tower, to a story garden. Other users selecting the same story from the search tower are transported to the same garden, enabling a synchronous, shared experience. Once in the garden, the story can be viewed sequentially, by following the spiral path. It is also possible to move off the path and go directly to an artifact that is of interest.

At each image or document in the story, users can add tags (single words or short phrases) or longer annotations that can be viewed by

Figure 7.4　A spiral story garden.

others. Users can also communicate with other nearby users via text chat. Each story element in the garden records the presence and text chat of nearby avatars. Users can click on a replay button to be transported to a replay space that displays a 3-D animation of previous visitors to that element and the conversations they had there (see Figure 7.6).

The Story Garden environment was built using the OpenSim platform (http://www.opensimulator.org). OpenSim is an open-source virtual-world server that provides basic capabilities for 3-D content creation, user management, and text-based communication.

Figure 7.5   Avatars around a story element.

Figure 7.6   Replay of interactions, observed by an avatar.

Research Design Overview

The research consisted of three parts: an ethnographic study of current museum and visitor practices, an evaluation of the Story Maker prototype, and an evaluation of the Story Garden prototype. The ethnographic study was conducted at the museum. The Story Maker and Story Garden evaluations took place online. Interviewing was an integral component of all three.

ETHNOGRAPHIC STUDY OF MUSEUM AND VISITOR PRACTICES

Given the exploratory nature of the project, we focused on capturing qualitative data to guide technology development. To establish a baseline understanding of museum practices, visitor experiences, and the role of stories, an ethnographic study was conducted early in the project. We shadowed a variety of visitors, including families, groups of friends, and school groups during their visit to the museum. We interviewed members of the museum staff, including curators, exhibit designers, and educators. The study led to a better understanding of the ways visitors interact with one another and the exhibits, what kinds of media and technologies are most effective, and how the visitors connect with and make sense of the experience. The ethnographic study provided a foundation for technology design.

The team took an iterative approach to design with frequent demonstrations and discussions of prototypes as they were being implemented to obtain feedback to guide further development. Once sufficient capabilities were implemented to test the Story Maker and Story Garden concepts, a set of training and evaluation sessions were scheduled with museum staff as the first evaluators. Figure 7.7 highlights the distinguishing aspects of the concept evaluations.

STORY MAKER EVALUATION

Five members of the Henry Ford Museum staff had their first opportunity to interact with the Story Maker application during a 30-minute group training session that was conducted using web

Figure 7.7	Overview of evaluation approaches for Story Maker and 3-D Story Garden.

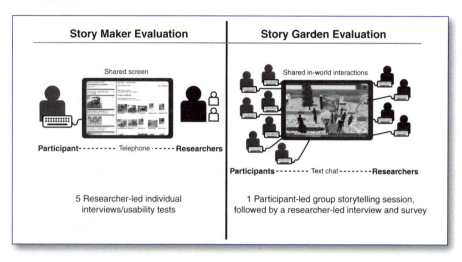

Story Maker Evaluation	**Story Garden Evaluation**
Shared screen	Shared in-world interactions
Participant - - - - - - - - Telephone - - - - - - Researchers	Participants - - - - - - - - Text chat - - - - - - - - Researchers
5 Researcher-led individual interviews/usability tests	1 Participant-led group storytelling session, followed by a researcher-led interview and survey

conferencing and a teleconference connection. This session included an overview of the application's interface and a review of the process of creating and editing a story, viewing a story in a slide show, and editing artifact metadata. The trainees performed these processes on their individual machines in the Henry Ford computer lab. They could ask questions throughout. The training was meant to help users become comfortable with the application, so they would give higher-quality feedback and be able to generate ideas about application extensions and future directions.

The next stage of the evaluation was part structured interview and part usability test, administered individually. The goal was to gather qualitative data in the context of performing progressively less-structured tasks in Story Maker. Each 90-minute session was conducted via web conferencing with a teleconference link to share the participant's view of Story Maker. The interview included demographic questions and then open-ended questions about stories and their meaning and application in the context of the subject's work at the museum. Participants were asked for their first impressions of the application. The next part of the interaction was a usability test with tasks. These were not timed and the participants were encouraged to think out loud. The first two (of four) tasks were very specific, designed to move users through all the major functionality in the application. The last two tasks were more open. Story Maker offers more than one way to create a story, and these tasks were presented to see which methods participants would naturally prefer. After the tasks were completed, the participants were asked a series of questions about their experience with the tasks, what they felt was missing or needed to change, and how they would envision using a tool like Story Maker in their work.

Each of the individual evaluations was attended by a minimum of two observers who took detailed notes. The notes from each session were consolidated and organized, reflecting positive and negative comments about the application and specific feature requests. Positive comments, negative comments, and feature requests were ranked by importance based on the number of participants who mentioned them. The development team retained the positive comments list to ensure that planned upgrades to the application did not eliminate the things users liked about it. Solutions to problems mentioned by more than one participant were shared with the development team. These solutions, along with feature requests were reviewed and prioritized by the application's stakeholders for phased implementation. A summary of the results was presented to the Henry Ford team for review and discussion.

3-D STORY GARDEN EVALUATION

The evaluation focused on the use of the Story Garden prototype to share and experience a story created in Story Maker. Seven members of the museum staff participated in the evaluation, including all five participants from the Story Maker evaluation plus two others. Four researchers were also present in-world as observers.

Two 60-minute, group training sessions were conducted. The first provided instructions and experience with basics of navigation and communication in the virtual world. In the second session, we described the specific capabilities of the search tower and story garden. Each training session was presented as a story in the story garden. The participants were given a homework assignment to customize their avatar and practice navigation skills.

One of the participants, a museum curator, volunteered to create a story in Story Maker for presentation to the other participants during the third session, a 60-minute storytelling session. The purpose of the third session was to observe curator and participant interactions during storytelling. At the end of the tour, the group was interviewed about their experience. Participants were asked about their favorite part of the story, avatar interactions, and navigation; desired capabilities for future iterations; and potential applications of the technology in museums.

A teleconference line was provided, as a means for dealing with any issues that could not be resolved using text chat. Participants were encouraged to use only the text chat for communication during the session, enabling a more realistic evaluation of the text chat capability. The museum participants were located in the same room during the session, and thus able to communicate directly with one another.

Data collection included recording the sessions using a screen recorder application (from the point of view of one of the researcher's avatars) for later analysis. In addition, the Story Garden application recorded the chat content and avatar interactions. The text chat was logged. Participants also completed a post-evaluation online survey. Session replays, chat logs, and survey responses were analyzed, providing positive and negative comments, identification of other applications for this technology, requests for new capabilities, and a summary of the kinds of participant interactions observed.

EVALUATION TECHNOLOGY CHOICES AND RATIONALE

Next, we focus on the technologies used to facilitate online interviews with study participants. The Story Maker evaluation used a web conferencing application, allowing researchers to observe prototype use. A teleconference connection enabled voice interactions. These technologies enabled multiple people—study participants, evaluation administrator, and researchers—to share the experience. Video recordings were made as a record for later analysis. One of the benefits of having researchers observe was that they could witness first-hand users' actions, feedback, and questions; this was an effective way to inform improvements in the technology.

The Story Garden prototype required that each study participant have access to a remote server with the OpenSim application. The museum information technology (IT) department set up PCs in their computer-training lab with access to our server and the OpenSim client installed. This allowed participants to be co-located in one room. A teleconference link was available for questions during the training sessions. It was used minimally during the storytelling session, as the participants relied primarily on text chat for discussion. Story Garden sessions were video recorded by a researcher in-world, so the recording captured the Story Garden perspective of the researcher's avatar. In addition, a web-based survey was used to collect additional feedback after the evaluation.

Ethical Issues and Approaches

Descriptions of the evaluation methodology were submitted to the PARC Human Subjects Review Board for approval. Study participants were asked to review and sign a consent form prior to each study. Consent forms contained a description of the evaluation methodology and request for permission to capture audio and video recordings of the sessions. Procedures and consent agreements were reviewed and verbally reconfirmed at the start of each evaluation.

As we concluded data analysis from each evaluation, we organized sessions to share and discuss the results with the participants and other members of the Henry Ford Museum staff. These sessions provided an opportunity for additional input from participants regarding their experiences, and a way to confirm priorities for improvements to the prototypes and other next steps.

INTERVIEW EXPERIENCE AND CHALLENGES

The evaluations combined use of the prototypes followed by interviews and discussion about their experiences. The Story Maker evaluation focused on individual users and their experiences building, editing, and viewing stories. The Story Garden evaluation focused on a curator-led group tour of a story created by the curator in Story Maker. In both cases, interviews were semi-structured so interesting threads could be pursued during the course of the interview.

Several of the study participants were members of our Document Interactions Project and had established working relationships with the Xerox researchers. Keep in mind that the entire project was coordinated virtually, uniting three separate physical locations (Palo Alto, Webster, Dearborn), so the team was already very comfortable using the conferencing technologies deployed for the evaluations. This may have had a positive impact on the candor of participants during the interviews. Future evaluations should include participants less familiar with the technology, such as museum visitors or staff from other museums.

In the Story Garden interviews, it was interesting to observe the very lively contributions to the discussion from all participants that were possible with text chat. These interactions became longer and livelier as the session progressed. This, of course, could have been influenced by the fact that the participants worked together and knew each other well.

The use of text chat was not without challenges. Since multiple threads or conversations could be going on simultaneously, various bits of conversations could be displayed in the middle of a new chat topic, requiring some effort to parse and make sense of the different chat threads. Participants commented that one of the things they liked about text chat was the ability to scroll to a previous part of the conversation to review parts they might have missed.

The mix of technologies used to enable communication and recording of interactions required significant coordination and set-up efforts, particularly in the configuration of participant machines by museum IT staff to enable the 3-D OpenSim application.

Research Findings

From a research standpoint, we hoped to answer several questions with the evaluation of Story Maker:

1. How usable was the current prototype and what should we improve in future versions?

2. How valuable are the experimental search and story-building capabilities?

3. Would museum staff members use this kind of tool in their work? If so, for what purposes?

4. Did they feel that this kind of tool would be useful in the hands of museum visitors?

The evaluation provided initial answers to all of these questions.

All of the participants reported finding the application interesting and were actively engaged in it. Most of them responded very positively to the search functionality, describing it, for example, as appealing, intuitive, useful, and powerful and noting that it allowed for different ways to find interesting artifacts.

Participants also provided a number of ideas for improving the user interface of Story Maker. For example, the prototype had a set of buttons at the top of the story-building panel for creating a new caption and for deleting an element from a story. As stories got longer, users had to do more and more scrolling to edit their stories. All participants reported frustration with this design. We repaired it in newer versions by making creation and deletion operations available throughout the length of a story.

Other ideas for improvement related to the treatment of duplicates, the stretching of images, and the number of search results displayed. Several participants reported confusion if the search results contained two images that looked identical or nearly identical. All of these ideas were valuable and many of them have already led to improvements to Story Maker.

Our participants also provided us a number of interesting requests for new features or behaviors. Four out of five asked for drag-and-drop capabilities, in-place editing of captions, and the ability to share stories via e-mail or documents. Three out of five asked for more ways to modify searches and to group related artifacts (such as connecting the photo of the front of a quilt to the photo of the back of the same quilt).

Participants had many interesting ideas about how Story Maker could be used in their daily work and also how it could be used in other museums and for museum visitors and potential visitors. The interview portion of the evaluation provided the opportunity for participants to share their ideas. The participants themselves thought they would use Story Maker as:

- a way to interact with museum visitors on the floor: Staff could access Story Maker to answer visitor questions and show them what is not on the museum floor. Staff could build a story on the fly and also have prepared stories for topics that visitors always ask about;

- an aid in the preliminary exhibit design process: The tool could be used to explore interesting connections between artifacts and provide a basic way to pull artifacts together to pass on to an exhibit designer;

- a discovery tool for exploring interesting connections, a starting point for a curator designing an exhibit;

- a way for marketing or exhibits staff to prepare presentations that communicate their ideas without needing someone else to look up each artifact for them; and

- a way to get information about which topics are most popular with users and then create exhibits on those topics if they do not already exist.

One unexpected suggestion was to use Story Maker as a way for another museum to put together a list of items that they want to borrow from the Henry Ford Museum. Participants also noted that it could be used as a way for smaller museums to put exhibits on the web, even if their staff has limited technical skills.

For visitors and potential visitors, our participants suggested these uses for Story Maker:

- a way for teachers to give meaningful assignments to students before and after a museum visit;
- a way for people to connect with objects before they see them in the museum;
- a way for people to do personal meaning making with things they have seen in the museum after a visit;
- a way for students and teachers to make their own slide shows of what they saw at the museum and then share it, so they don't have to try to take pictures of everything at the museum; and
- a way for history buffs to do research and learn about Henry Ford Museum artifacts.

Story Maker can already help create stories that can be used as the subject matter for a virtual tour or visit in a 3-D virtual world. We explored that functionality in our second evaluation, and those results are next.

The 3-D Story Garden evaluation was designed to gain insights related to several questions including:

1. How well does the Story Garden support storytelling and interactions among multiple avatars?

2. What improvements should be incorporated into future versions?

3. How did they envision this tool could be useful for museum staff and visitors?

In preparation for the Story Garden evaluation, a curator used Story Maker to create a story titled, "Hacking the Model T." The curator selected seven images showing examples of Model T modifications that transformed it to other special-use vehicles, including an ambulance, a hay wagon (truck), and two different tractors.

One of the themes that emerged from the initial ethnographic field study of visitors and museum staff was the importance of making new and interesting connections between museum artifacts and visitors' own life experiences. The curator's story inspired participants to make many connections to recent cultural phenomena, which were captured in the text chat exchange. For example, connections were made to terminology reflective of today's culture, such as:

- Jailbreaking, in reference to the Model T rather than Apple mobile devices ("Jailbreaking" involves unlocking the operating systems for iPad, iPod, and iPhone devices, so users can load unauthorized applications);
- DIY (do it yourself), in reference to the conversion kits people used to modify Model T's;
- mention of the television show *Pimp My Ride* as a present-day analogy for 19th-century Model T conversions.

Analysis of the text chat log revealed that the media enabled a rich and varied interplay of interactions during the evaluation. The following types of interaction were observed:

- *Instructions and questions* about navigating and using the Story Garden interface ("Are our computers set up to use the annotation feature?")
- *Social interactions*, for example, comments from one avatar regarding a change in appearance ("You changed your shirt.") of another avatar
- *Story interactions* that included guiding and confirming understanding ("Everyone following?")
- *Making connections* ("I remember a story about hooking a Model T up to a washing machine to power it.")

As with Story Maker, the participants made several suggestions for future capabilities and for improving the usability of the 3-D Story Garden. Some of the suggestions would impact Story Maker as well as the Story Garden, such as:

- enable other media formats (for example, use audio and video snippets in a story) and

- allow 3-D models of artifacts (in addition to two-dimensional documents, images, etc.).

In addition, the interview portion of the evaluation provided the study participants with the opportunity to share their thoughts for applications of 3-D Story Garden. It was suggested that it would be well used in classroom and educational contexts because avatars enable children to pretend they are someone or something else. They also thought that it would be less intimidating for children to present and interact with their avatars. The museum has an on-site academy that may be a good test bed for this application.

Overall, there were very few negative comments about the Story Garden experience; some people struggled with navigation and positioning their avatar to see around other avatars blocking their view of the story pictures. In addition, the Story Garden did not implement the display of image captions, causing some initial confusion. However, subsequent discussion turned this into a positive, as the participants remarked, "Captions would have made it feel more like PowerPoint and less like a conversation."

The team has incorporated many of the participants' suggestions from the evaluations into recent releases of the applications. We have also expanded our tool kit of methods to obtain insights from users based on real-time online interactions, observations, and interviews. One of the objectives of the study was to determine if the prototypes could successfully integrate museum collections and be used for story creation and sharing by a small number of relatively novice users. We are encouraged by our preliminary findings. While our initial work has focused on history museums and document repositories based on digitized versions of their collections, we believe story-based approaches to making sense of documents will apply broadly to many different kinds of organizations and document collections.

REACTION FROM THE HENRY FORD MUSEUM

As a partner in this project, the Henry Ford Museum staff provided feedback on our collaboration, stating that they gained new perspectives and learned new ways of prototyping potential visitor experiences. The platforms and processes used during the collaboration enhanced the team's ability to create and develop new ideas and approaches. In many instances, museum professionals are accustomed to working toward finished products rather than developing proto-types to test along the way. In fact, this project broke the museum staff's paradigm for how to create experiences, because it was based on (1) prototyping rather than perfecting, (2) new design processes, and (3) new technologies for learning.

The team found the collaborative model to be one of total respect, valuing opinions from all sources. Critical thinking and creativity were also hallmarks of the process. There were no political agendas to confront during the process, but the efforts were directed toward learning and imagining new experiences for visitors.

By the end of the project, the museum realized that it's a steep hill to climb to develop a virtual world that is ready for deployment on the floor of the museum today. In the shorter term, leveraging existing communities and virtual worlds would be a quicker way to offer this type of experience to guests rather than creating a virtual world from concept through deployment on the floor. Even so, the process of working on this project with its longer-term product development time horizons was invaluable to our colleagues at the museum.

Lessons Learned and Recommendations

Semi-structured online interviews were used as one of several methods in our evaluation of two prototype technologies. The interviews provided a valuable source of feedback and a way to give study participants a "voice" in the results that other methods don't. In our experience, given the opportunity, participants often bring up topics or make comments that lead to unanticipated insights or directions for further exploration. This was the case in this project, where participant suggestions for applications for the prototypes provided a range of interesting opportunities and potential next steps.

We used different technologies to facilitate online interviews. For the Story Maker evaluation, we relied on web conferencing so we could co-view the participants' view of the interface. Discussion took place over a conference telephone link. For the Story Garden evaluation, we relied primarily on observation of avatars in the 3-D environment and the text chat record. Participants provided lively and insightful conversation using text chat as the primary mode of communication. Based on comments from the participants during the interview phase, the visual cues provided by the avatars (e.g., their movement and location relative to the story elements and other avatars, the gestures and sounds of typing shown by an avatar as the participant typed into the chat window) played an important role in their anticipation of the next interaction and engaging their participation in the event.

Given the ethnographic orientation of the research team, we are inclined toward face-to-face interactions in participants' environments to collect observational and interview data. The continued growth in importance of online communities and social media in everyday life poses challenges to researchers who want to understand those communities and to develop innovative approaches to observe the experiences of community participants. It has been our experience that in-context interviews, ones that take place in the midst of the activity of interest for the interview, evoke a much richer set of responses from participants. In part, this is because objects relevant to the experience surround the participants, which adds to the richness of the recollections and responses they bring to the interview. In the case of online collaborative interactions, such as the 3-D Story Garden, conducting the group interview in-context in the 3-D environment enabled the participants to draw on each other and the cues in the environment to bear on their responses. It was interesting to observe that as the group moved through the story, they "warmed up" to the environment; interactions became quite insightful, often humorous and energetic. They made references to their experiences with each other and made many connections from the story to present-day culture. These interactions were not unlike many of those we observed while watching visitors at the museum, except these were taking place in an immersive environment.

 See the Appendix for suggested readings and resources on the software, methodologies, and methods discussed in this case.

 Find More Materials on the Study Site! See the book website for related resources, materials, discussion, and assignment ideas.

References

Bartle, R. A. (2004). *Designing virtual worlds.* Berkeley, CA: New Riders.
Churchill, E. F., Snowdon, D. N., & Munro, A. J. (2001). *Collaborative virtual environments.* London: Springer.

Sources Consulted

Brown, J. S., & Duguid, P. (2000). *The social life of information.* Cambridge, MA: Harvard Business School Publishing.
Casey, R. (2008). *The Model T: A centennial history.* Baltimore, MD: Johns Hopkins University Press.
Levine, A. (n.d.). *CogDogRoo: Story tools.* Retrieved from http://cogdogroo.wikispaces.com/StoryTools
Orr, J. E. (1996). *Talking about machines: An ethnography of a modern job.* Ithaca, NY: ILR Press/Cornell University Press.

CRITIQUE AND ANALYSIS OF WALL ET AL.'S "GUIDES AND VISITORS: CAPTURING STORIES IN VIRTUAL-WORLD AND INTERACTIVE WEB EXPERIENCES"

Jonathon Richter and Taryn Stanko

We have the distinct pleasure to review and comment on "Guides and Visitors: Capturing Stories in Virtual-World and Interactive Web Experiences," submitted by the Document Interactions Project. This study describes the collaborative effort between members of the Xerox Research Center Webster, the Palo Alto Research Center, and staff at the Henry Ford Museum to design and explore innovations in enhancing experiences of both online and visiting patrons in their interactions with museum artifacts. Using combinations of online search and artifact selection for narrative story development and subsequent display in social 3-D virtual environments, the project employed ethnographic methods to gather feedback useful for iterative designs to both determine and improve the effectiveness of the overall user experience. Their product designs, feedback processes, and content iteration stages appeared to work together very well in situated contexts to engage study participants. This real-time product development ecosystem was further complemented by the research method—a qualitative research design with all of the hallmarks of a well-planned design research experiment.

While the fascinating and extremely innovative research project described in the chapter has an abundance of great ideas, possible connections, and wonderful potentialities, our comments will focus primarily on two areas we hope are relevant to the discussion of online interview data collection and its alignment to the stated purpose of a particular study. First, we examine the use of sequential 2-D and 3-D media through carefully considered phases of the research to maximize the use of each medium; and second, we discuss the potential use of "patterns of actions" (Pentland & Feldman, 2005) associated with Henry Ford Museum artifacts as a possible means to add depth and context, and to enliven the participant stories as outcomes of this project.

2-D Compared to 3-D . . . and Both Together

It is interesting to consider the manner in which the web was used within the Document Interactions Project to collect data and meet research goals and compare that to ways in which the virtual world was employed. On the web, the participants searched and browsed, typed and tagged, and copied images to a timeline. In the virtual environment, participants were, by contrast, "transported away from the tower, to a story garden," where they walk about in the first person, chat with other visitors, walk along stories arranged in spirals, or wander freely from one artifact to another. One medium involves text and image manipulation, while the other is largely embodiment and experience. While reading this chapter, we found many parallels between our own study and theirs and make a number of comparisons between the two studies throughout this section.

First, for data collection, it is useful to consider the different means by which 2-D and 3-D media best present information sensible to the user and elicit their participation. Traditional two-dimensional (2-D) frames are appropriately well suited for asynchronously structuring and presenting narrative text for people to contribute and interact with, while three-dimensional (3-D) environments are arguably better than the web at providing immersive real-time social contexts with visually rich and meaningful cues within which to situate nontextual objects and signifiers. Words are better read in 2-D and objects, best beheld in 3-D. As in our own work, the Document Interactions Project team considered ways to structure and take advantage of these affordances and constraints in eliciting, capturing, and representing the respective phenomena under study. We believe others may find it of interest to compare and contrast the 2-D/3-D blending of media between the projects represented by our respective chapters, as the design patterns in both projects are rather telling of the nature of the research aims and purposes.

The Document Interactions Project team created a web interface to structure and present searchable collections of museum artifacts, helping users arrange their own selections in a sequence or story timeline through browsing interesting documents and images with associated metadata. The web is, of course, well suited for such a task and they appear to have adeptly designed their web-based phase of the project—the Story Maker component—as indicated by their own report of the user experience. For our study, we created a web interface, through use of a wiki, intended to meaningfully structure the analysis of findings that we, ourselves, encountered in the virtual world. Thus, in their study the participants used the web interface to structure and derive their own meaning; in ours, the web pages were used by the researchers, themselves, to structure and present their findings. Both projects, thus, used the web to create and structure narratives emergent through the course of the research.

Both projects also then, in turn, took the narratives constructed using the web and placed them within the context of the virtual environment designed specifically for the respective research project. The Document Interactions Project team used the results of the web participation for integration into the virtual world in the subsequent phase and we too placed the results of our web development in-world. While they used the virtual world to further enhance and provide new perspectives to participant experiences, our project sought to recontextualize data represented on the web into the virtual world—the native setting for the study, itself. Whether to provide participants with scaffolding with which to develop their own creative narrative (as in the case of the Document Interactions Project), or to situate the contexts and conditions of research results (as in our own Collaborative Virtual Work research), or for another purpose, embedding web pages within virtual environments as a means of adding appropriate narrative dimensionality as part of a research design pattern is potentially worthy of note to ethnographers and those looking to employ the use of virtual worlds in research, generally.

On the other hand, while the Document Interactions Project team used the web to *a priori* help their participants make sense of and structure selected artifacts from the museum and then used the virtual world to further enhance engagement, we sought out individuals who were already well versed in the virtual world, met them, and interviewed them—and then made use of the web to transcribe and structure the meaning that we made sense of out of those conversations. They made use of the web and then ventured into the virtual world, while we sampled from the virtual world and put the results on the web. In this way, thus, there is a conceptual inversion between the two projects' use of the media for data collection and integration as befits their differing research purposes.

The common principle is that both project teams made a conscious effort to capitalize on both the 2-D and the 3-D media formats in the design, development, and processing of their data and to recombine the results derived from these phases with respect to each medium's contribution to the context in such a way that the reintegration is potentially greater than that that may have been afforded by either the 2-D or 3-D, singularly. The designed entanglement of media in a situated research study thus appears to create potential for a pronounced effect that transforms—or at least offsets—the limitations of either. There is a holistic and systemic ideal sought after in data gathering and display with respect to the use of multiple media.

Patterns of Actions as Story Maker Potential

The Document Interactions Project chapter gave us second idea of possible relevance to the online researcher. It relates again to data collection and the Story Maker web interface. The chapter tells us that the included search function can be used to find artifacts as they "are associated with the same person, company, city, topic, or genre." We noted that these dimensions available to the user for associating artifacts within the museum web interface might be enhanced by connecting the verbs. The notion came to us that a potential method for making interesting associations and creative leaps for these stories might be to tag the artifacts with key words that may constitute "patterns of action" in narrative networks associated with each museum artifact. A car tire may "spin," "squeal," "burn rubber," or be "stuck in the mud"—and these phrases may, in turn, be associated with other artifacts and museum pieces that may not be associated by person, company, city, topic, or genre. By allowing user participants to view connections between museum collection pieces by virtue of their patterns of action, novelty may result—as well as connections that were nonintuitive, but nevertheless productive and rational once made.

In their analytic description of a potentially innovative and authentic method to assess organizational routines, Pentland and Feldman (2005) urge that researchers study both the ostensive, as well as the performative aspects of work routines that constitute patterns of actions to tell the story and pattern of use of particular artifacts. They rightly underscore the need to understand the thinking that undergirds enacted work routines in addition to the observable actions that center around a particular set of actions. Perhaps, borrowing these ideas for application and through historic analysis and interpretation, the Henry Ford Museum could provide key words that give clues to those interacting with Story Maker for not only the active verbs related to selected artifacts and images, but the thinking of those who once were involved in the creation of the respective museum pieces, too. These may be yet further grist for the development of story and enable the kinds of unique and valuable creative participation that the Documents Interaction Project already is well on the way to enabling.

Reference

Pentland, B. T., & Feldman, M. S. (2005). Designing routines: On the folly of designing artifacts, while hoping for patterns of action. *Information and Organization, 18,* 235–250.

CHAPTER 7
FRAMEWORK COMMENTARY: "GUIDES AND VISITORS: CAPTURING STORIES IN VIRTUAL-WORLD AND INTERACTIVE WEB EXPERIENCES"

Janet Salmons

In this ethnographic study, researchers and staff from the Xerox Research Center Webster, Palo Alto Research Center, and the Henry Ford Museum collaborated on a complex collaborative effort to evaluate and explore two prototype tools: Story Maker and Story Garden. They chose to conduct the interviews in the context of user trials of the tools using voice and text for discussion of the avatars' interactions in the online environments.

Visual elements were central to this study; given the nature of this study, visual data were used for evaluative purposes. Visual communication, elicitation, and generation (Salmons, 2010) were variously used to solicit responses to and uses of the prototypes. In addition to the navigation and interaction within virtual environments, online meeting tools and video recordings allowed researchers to collect detailed data about Story Maker and Story Garden.

As a research team, various members took different roles. Some could be described as travelers (Kvale, 2007; Kvale & Brinkman, 2009) who actually participated in the evaluation process, while others contributed from the gardener role (Salmons, 2010), seeding and supporting the growth of new ideas and interpretations. Similarly, members of the research and museum teams took both etic and emic stances, bringing to bear both in-case and external issues and experiences (Stake, 1995). This rich array of perspectives allowed for a comprehensive evaluation of Story Maker and Story Garden.

This chapter points to the value offered by collaborative research efforts that allows for input and participation from all key stakeholders. While this may be true generally, collaborative approaches seem particularly applicable to research in areas that involve broad rethinking of practices.

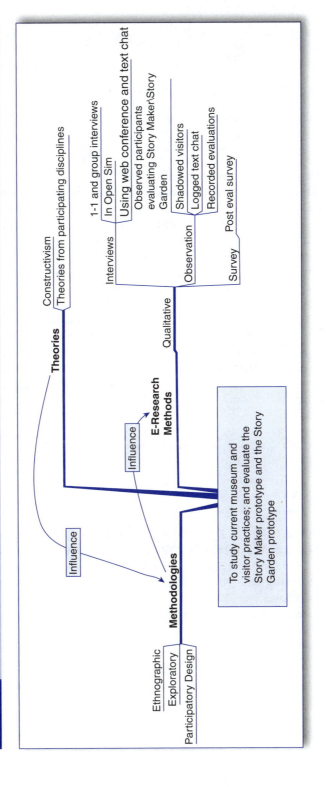

213

Table 7.1	Summary: Key Factors in the "Guides and Visitors: Capturing Stories in Virtual-World and Interactive Web Experiences" Study

Motivation for Choosing E-Research	Sampling and Recruiting	Interview Style and Structure	Technology: Issues, Features, Lessons	Ethical Issues
The Xerox Research Center Webster, Palo Alto Research Center, and the Henry Ford Museum selected online research methods to evaluate new approaches for using online tools: Story Maker and Story Garden.	Purposeful, criterion-based sampling was used. Participants were recruited by soliciting volunteers from the museum staff.	Structured and semi-structured individual and group interviews	Web conferencing, phone, text, and virtual-world interactions were used. Researchers complemented interview data with other observational, recorded, text, and visual data.	Museum staff and visitors who participated in the evaluation signed a consent form. Study results were shared with participants to encourage discussion and elaboration.

References

Kvale, S. (2007). *Doing interviews.* Thousand Oaks, CA: Sage.

Kvale, S., & Brinkman, S. (2009). *InterViews: Learning the craft of qualitative research interviewing* (2nd ed.). Thousand Oaks, CA: Sage.

Salmons, J. E. (2010). *Online interviews in real time.* Thousand Oaks, CA: Sage.

Stake, R. E. (1995). *The art of case study research.* Thousand Oaks, CA: Sage.

PART III

HYBRID ON- AND OFFLINE INTERVIEWS

Videoconference, Text, Meeting Tools, E-Mail, And Face-To-Face Interviews

The cases in this section describe varying combinations of synchronous and asynchronous approaches for online interviews. These studies, perhaps more than those in prior sections, focus on the preferences of research participants and availability of communications technologies that could be used for research interviews.

Electronic mail, popularly abbreviated as e-mail, continues to be the most widely used form of online communication. For research purposes, the interviewer can send questions one or two at a time, and allow the participant to answer before sending the next. This allows for a thoughtful, iterative asynchronous dialogue (Kitto & Barnett, 2007). Interviewer and interviewee can "explore and revisit insights . . . moving back and forth through their narratives, thinking about their responses, drafting and redrafting what they want to write, creating in effect, a form of enriched interview" (James & Busher, 2006, p. 406). Because the interview is in writing, an accurate transcript is immediately available with no loss or inaccuracy in transcription. Many researchers have found e-mail to be flexible, convenient, and productive for some kinds of studies. Others may use e-mail as part of the getting-acquainted process to prepare for a synchronous interview, or as follow-up to a synchronous interview.

For studies where immediate, visual communications are desired, videoconferencing allows researchers and participants to see each other in live, face-to-face interactions. Low-cost webcams and free online services mean one-to-one videoconferencing can be used on computers or mobile devices. Many free services allow for text chat and some file sharing as part of the system.

Multichannel online meeting tools are another option for interviews. These spaces are designed for one-to-one, one-to-many, or many-to-many online gatherings. Elluminate, Adobe Connect, DimDim and other such online meeting platforms allow for dialogue through VOIP two-way audio, text chat, and web camera desktop videoconferencing. They also allow researchers and participants to share applications, desktops, and whiteboards. These varied features allow researchers to keep meeting notes or use visual communication and collaboration within the interview (see Table 1.2 Typology of Online Visual Interview Methods).

ONLINE INTERVIEW PREPARATION FOR A MULTICHANNEL MEETING SPACE (SALMONS, 2010)

When using a multichannel meeting space for an interview, steps to prepare include the following:

- Check audio features. If the space allows for only one speaker at a time, determine protocols for turn taking in conversation and include in pre-interview run-through.
- Check recording/archiving features.
- Select or develop relevant diagrams, illustrations, examples, photographs, visual maps, and so on that can be used to show, rather than ask or tell the participant what you want to discuss. (See Chapter 8 for more discussion of visual methods in online interviews.)
- Some platforms allow for PowerPoint slides, others allow for shared documents. In addition to posing questions using audio, questions or key topics can be written out on the shared whiteboard. If this approach will be used, develop the slides and documents.
- Some platforms allow media, such as video clips, to be shown. If you are using media, make sure you can easily access, run, and close out of the media and back into the main discussion area.
- Review interactive features of platform; can any of them be used in the course of the interview? These could include asking participants to draw or diagram answers to some questions.

If conducting an interview with videoconferencing, consider the following questions and suggestions:

- Decide how you want to present yourself. Just as in a face-to-face, live interview, the background, your attire, and style all convey messages.
- Carefully review questions or interview guide so you can minimize need to look down at notes. Take the time, before looking down to read notes, to make the best "virtual eye contact" possible.
- Discuss options and parameters for participant's web camera. Is it acceptable for the participant to turn the camera off and use audio only?
- If using a facility where others (technicians, camera operators) will be present, determine policies for confidentiality. Depending on the setting and policies, you may decide to ask intimate questions in another way.
- Determine whether you want to use the webcam during all or part of the interview. For example, you could use the webcam to make contact in the introduction and then turn it off.
- Decide who gets to choose when and how to use the webcam. This decision may be one to discuss in advance of the interview.

References

James, N., & Busher, H. (2006). Credibility, authenticity and voice: Dilemmas in online interviewing. *Qualitative Research Journal, 6*(3), 403–420.

Kitto, R., & Barnett, J. (2007) Transcript analysis of e-mail interviews: A mixed-methods linguistics approach. *American Journal of Evaluation. 28*(3), 356–368.

Salmons, J. E. (2010). *Online interviews in real time.* Thousand Oaks, CA: Sage.

Transitioning From F2F to Online Instruction

8

Putting the Action Into Online Research

Wendy L. Kraglund-Gauthier
Xavier University, Antigonish,
Nova Scotia, Canada

As an instructional designer, it is my role to explore pedagogical meaning making in online classrooms, to create independence, and to empower users to use the tools to their advantage. As a doctoral student studying at a distance via online technologies and researching the pedagogical shifts professors make when moving to online classrooms, it was a logical choice to conduct the research itself via online, synchronous technologies. In this chapter, I present a detailed description of the action research project conducted via Elluminate Live! and add an additional insightful layer of how action research methodologies served as a vehicle to further support participants' own learning of online teaching tools and techniques. I also present an analysis of the interview process, including recommendations to address challenges and pitfalls that arose, and close with the lessons learned from my own experiences as an online researcher.

Research Purpose and Questions

Apart from the literature that seeks to explain how students coming to an online environment learn how to learn online, there is little in the literature about how teachers who are trained and experienced in face-to-face learning systems reorient themselves in their online classrooms. Dalziel (2008) has noted that one of our failures in open education (i.e., the movement to share freely educational best practices and knowledge over the Internet) is "our lack of progress on sharing 'pedagogical know-how' among educators. . . . We have not captured the teaching processes that expert educators use to bring learning alive in their e-learning courses" (p. 375). Furthermore, as Dalziel has argued, by conversing about educational processes and receiving advice on the online design of these processes, "then not only could a novice educator benefit from the work of experts, but all educators could collectively adapt and improve each other's work, leading to improved quality overall" (p. 376).

The central objective of this research was to gain an understanding of how Master of Education (MA Ed) professors transition from a traditional face-to-face classroom to an online environment that incorporates synchronous and asynchronous teaching tools. Based on the tenets of action research, the main thrust of inquiry emerged from the participants themselves (Noffke, 1994; Noffke & Somekh, 2009); however, the following questions served to guide me as a co-participant in their learning during the extension phases of their action research, and framed my own journaling of the research process:

1. Do MA Ed professors change perspectives (i.e., in values, beliefs, and practices) on teaching and learning when they move to an online teaching environment?

2. How do they negotiate identity and build community online?

3. Is it necessary for online professors to redefine teaching style to match the online learning environment?

Research Design Overview

In the following section, I discuss the design of the action research project. In order to address geographic, time, and financial constraints on both me and my participants, the underpinning methodology and methods of research design incorporated virtual technologies for data collection.

GUIDING THEORIES

In the 1930s, Bartlett (as cited in Good & Brophy, 1990) introduced the constructivist approach to social interaction and learning. Constructivists believe that learners construct and interpret reality based on how they perceive their experiences. Lincoln and Guba (1985) expanded the definition of constructivism and discussed the component of meaning making and the organization and reorganization of constructed reality. This ongoing reframing of reality prepares learners to resolve issues and to make meaning from ambiguous situations.

Qualitative research processes and outcomes emphasize the importance of seeing the world through participants' eyes (Bogdan & Biklen, 1998; Jackson & Verberg, 2007). As a means of discovering socially constructed realities, other authors (see Bogdan & Biklen, 1998; Creswell, 1998; Merriam & Simpson, 2000; van Manen, 1990) have further characterized qualitative research as an inductive process in which contextual meaning is explored. A naturalistic approach to investigation attends to the "unfolding multiple realities in interactions with respondents that will change both the investigators and the respondents over time" (Guba, 1981, p. 79). For these reasons and others, I designed my research study to address these tenets, specifically, to make space for constructivist learning in an online medium.

METHODOLOGY

The nature of the study and the purposes, assumptions, and significance were well suited to a qualitative method of exploration. In their text, Bogdan and Biklen (1998) have identified five key elements of qualitative research: (1) it is naturalistic, that is, based in real-world settings; (2) it incorporates rich, descriptive data; (3) it is process oriented; (4) it involves an exploration of how participants make meaning; and (5) it is inductive, that is, qualitative researchers seek to make conclusions about a particular phenomena based on what has been observed.

Action research is one form of qualitative research that enables researchers and practitioners to reflect on process and outcomes of inquiry (Newman, 2000; Schön, 1983). Specifically, I narrowed the context by evoking Corey's definition of action research as "research that is undertaken by educational practitioners because they believe that by so doing they can make better decisions and engage in better action" (as cited in Noffke, 1997, pp. 316–317). Much of the action research in educational contexts has centered on changes in curriculum theorizing, reflection, and pedagogy and is seen as a tool to bridge the gap between other forms of qualitative research and practice (Noffke, 1994). For Noffke, action research has the potential to move beyond the abstract, theoretical constructs of qualitative research and to ground teacher-researchers' awareness of self in the process and practice of teaching. Action research is also a way to draw teachers' professional knowledge into the research process (Carr & Kemmis, 1986).

Action research methods incorporate and encourage the participants' connections with what is being studied. As Newman (2000) has explained, through action research, participants (and researchers-as-participants) can gain an "expanded appreciation of the complexity of learning, of teaching, and a stronger sense of how external realities affect what we can really do" (para. 12). Action research is carried out by "'insiders,' by those engaged in and committed to the situation, not by outsiders" (Winter, 1998, p. 362). In my first individual interviews with participants, I asked that they consider the issue they would wish to explore as a group. In our first focus group meeting, participants decided that they wished to explore how they could build and maintain a sense of community in their online classes. I, as the researcher, was an integral member of this group, and we had opportunities to explore issues, identify successes and challenges, and work collaboratively to solve issues (Stringer, 2007) that impact online teaching practice.

SAMPLING

The research goal was not to make generalizations, but rather to gain rich descriptions of experience (Jackson & Verberg, 2007); therefore, participants were recruited via purposive sampling methods. Participants were full- or part-time (i.e., "sessional") professors employed at one Canadian university's (UniA, for the rest of this chapter) Faculty of Education's Master of Education program. They either had prior experience in teaching online using Elluminate Live! and/or BlackBoard, or they were new to the platforms. These criteria were chosen based on my anticipation that during focus group sessions, professors with prior experience would be able to describe their own learning process and reflect in such a way that professors who were new to online teaching could gain from their knowledge. Furthermore, all participants would be able to tap into each other's existing expertise—not just expertise in virtual modalities, but also in pedagogical constructs from face-to-face teaching—thus, incorporating the basic tenets of action research. From a pool of 32 potential participants, 10 volunteers met research criteria of teaching via Elluminate in the upcoming term. Ultimately, 6 of these 10 participated in the action research process.

DATA COLLECTION

I used a mixed-method approach to collect data. Specifically, five sources of data informed this research study and allowed for triangulation:

1. A survey questionnaire to collect background information on faculty members' teaching experience and self-assessed technological skills levels;

2. Transcripts of three focus group sessions with a total of 6 participants each—one held before classes commenced for the winter academic term, one held midterm, and one held after classes end for the term;

3. Transcripts of three one-to-one interviews with each participant;

4. Journals from professors, in which they tracked and reflected upon their thoughts about online learning and on the action research process throughout the academic term; and

5. My own field notes/journal, written as I worked with the participants throughout the academic term.

These data-generation tools enabled participants to explain and explore their experiences in relation to learning to teach online. Table 8.1 provides a visual display of the research phases in which these sources of information were collected. Through these phases, participants gained insight into real-life situations and experiences otherwise not allowed for in quantitative studies (Creswell, 1998).

Table 8.1	Sources of Research Data	

Pre-Action Research Phase	Action Research Phase	Post-Action Research Phase
• Professor's individualized professional development on online course design and Elluminate • Faculty survey on online teaching • Individual interviews with action research participants • My journaling	• First focus group session to determine action research issue to explore • Second focus group session • Individual interviews • Recordings of online classes • Journaling	• Third focus group session • Final individual interviews • Participants' presentation of action research outcomes • Journaling

Survey Questionnaire

The questions were designed to set context, to gather demographic data, and to identify current perceptions and opinions concerning online teaching and learning. I incorporated Likert-type scale questions to explore participants' comfort levels and motivations to engage in online teaching. As well, I included open-ended questions to enable participants to explicate responses further. Participants had the option to either complete the survey in paper copy or electronically with an online survey form via FluidSurveys. No surveys were received in paper copy; 22 of 32 (68.8%) potential participants responded electronically. As a tool from which to recruit participants for the core action research project, the questionnaire also served as a baseline from which to structure my initial conversation and questions as participants defined their action research issue.

Focus Groups

As the core element of this action research project, three semi-structured focus group sessions were held with 6 professors from the UniA Faculty of Education's Master of Education program. The focus group sessions were designed to extract information concerning participants' teaching philosophies and reflections on online teaching and technology. Participants were encouraged to identify the issues they wished to explore throughout the term. The first session was conducted before classes began, the second was midterm. The third session was conducted after the term had concluded and professors had submitted grades. This time frame was chosen in order to explore potential changes in perspective and opinion based on participants' experiences throughout the term and their analysis of student artifacts. Sessions were held via Elluminate and ranged from 75 to 90 minutes in length, during which I took handwritten notes. With permission from all participants, the sessions were also digitally recorded and the data were downloaded to a secure server and transcribed verbatim.

Interviews

Three semi-structured one-to-one interviews were carried out with the same 6 participants who were involved in the action research phase (one participant opted out of the final interview). Interview lengths ranged from 25 minutes to 78 minutes. Two of 17 individual interviews were conducted face-to-face at the request of participants. They both cited convenience as their rationale for meeting in person. The remaining interviews were conducted online via Elluminate. All interviews were digitally recorded and the data were downloaded to a secure server and transcribed verbatim.

Journaling and E-mails

As part of the action research process, I asked each participant to keep a journal throughout the term. My instructions were broad: Each week—ideally after classes, interviews, or focus group sessions—participants were to write their thoughts, ideas emerging from conversations or classes, questions, or "a-ha" moments. Participants could choose either to write this journal in the book I provided for each, or to maintain an electronic journal using a word processing program. At the end of the research collection phase, these journals were sent to me either via ground mail or electronically via e-mail. I, too, maintained a research log as I worked alongside faculty members in my own Faculty of Education and as I planned and facilitated each meeting with research participants. The participants struggled with this aspect of data collection. Many found the formal process of writing this journal at key points too time consuming and too labor intensive. A resolution naturally emerged for them: Some participants wrote their thoughts and sent them electronically via e-mail as they occurred. Others telephoned me and either left a voice mail or spoke with me directly. I transcribed these conversations and saved e-mail text, compiling an individual file under each participant's pseudonym.

DATA ANALYSIS

Results from these sources of research data were categorized into three distinct groupings: (1) professors' understandings, (2) instructional designers' understandings, and (3) key teaching moments. In the action research phase, the combination of individual and group discussions provided opportunities for participants to express individual perspectives and to explore these same perspectives in relation to those of others. Furthermore, 2 of the 6 participants met via their own Elluminate classroom space to discuss issues related to their online practice outside of the formalized research setting. Journaling added an additional space for individuals to reflect.

The data-generation techniques in this research yielded three discrete forms of communication: written, aural, and visual. Written responses were collected through the survey questionnaire, chat conversations with all participants during Elluminate sessions, journaling from participants, my field notes, and e-mail correspondence from participants. The interviews and focus group sessions hosted via Elluminate provided audio transcripts of data in which I could attend to participants' tones of voice, inflections, and pauses. In Elluminate, I set the system tools to allow only one microphone at a time; this was done to eliminate participants inadvertently talking over one another because of delays in data transfer. During a few interviews and focus group sessions, two participants decided to use their web cameras, but others opted out, citing a sense of self-consciousness. This removed the dimension of attendant body language to add meaning, but participants' use of Elluminate emoticons served to fill a visual void to a certain degree. Once I completed the transcription of the audio portions, I reviewed the session recording again and annotated the transcription to include participants' use of emoticons and text chat.

The journal writing component of the research data points to the challenges sometimes associated with participants finding the time or inclination to maintain a log faithfully throughout the research process. The immediacy afforded by electronic communication simplified the submission process for some participants. One participant reported that being able to "fire off thoughts and questions as they come" made her feel more engaged in the action research process. She also mentioned that the idea of journaling was awkward, citing the problems of locating the journal file between the three computers she accessed regularly throughout the term.

Technology Choices and Rationale

Because participants were located from one coast of Canada to the other, conducting traditional face-to-face interviews and focus group sessions was neither financially viable, nor timely. Even the traditional paper version of the survey seemed to be cumbersome to me; collecting mailing addresses of potential participants, mailing out a paper copy of the questionnaire, waiting for participants to mail back their responses, and then inputting the data manually would have necessitated more time and more steps. I decided e-mailing potential participants an electronic link to an online survey was much more efficient; however, I also indicated in my covering e-mail that I would provide a paper version to participants if they so chose. No one requested a paper version of the survey, and the response rate of 68.8% for the electronic survey points to the idea that participants found the mode of response suitable.

Time zones and time constraints during a busy academic term necessitated employing the most practical and efficient way to correspond and meet. Even scheduling the specific time of interview and focus group sessions was facilitated by online technology. After a few rounds of "e-mail-tag" to try to set an initial meeting time, I discovered an online software application called Doodle (see http://www .doodle.com). With this free web-based program, I was able to suggest a number of meeting days and times, e-mail the page link to participants, and they indicated their time preferences. Once all participants responded, we chose the first available time all participants selected.

Since I was researching how professors transitioned to synchronous online classrooms, it was a logical choice to collect interview and focus group session data via the same technologies we were exploring. Salmons (2010) noted the benefit of "communicating with the researcher in the comfort of a familiar environment" (p. 9); this was certainly the case in my context. Using Elluminate also afforded opportunities for participants to try new features "on the fly" and for me to model sound pedagogical practices, again, honoring the tenets of action research. In fact, my own journal notes are filled with "notes to self" to mention ideas and techniques to members of my own Faculty of Education Elluminate users.

Ethical Issues and Approaches

Research ethics approval was granted from my doctoral program at the University of South Australia and from UniA's Research Ethics Board without incident and without revisions. The lesson to learn in this case is to anticipate potential concerns and address them in the initial ethics application. I had to consider the ethical requirements of the University of South Australia and of my intended data collection site; as I wrote my application to University of South Australia, I addressed their requirements, too.

As part of my research ethics application to the University of South Australia's Research Ethics Board, I secured written support from UniA's Dean of Education and its Director of Continuing and Distance Education to conduct research that would involve their professors, students, and technology. They agreed to allow me access to individuals and technology, contingent upon receiving ethics clearance from both UniA and the University of South Australia. I reviewed UniA's ethics protocols, and conversations by telephone and e-mail with UniA's Research Ethics Board Chair clarified their common areas of concern, namely, data storage.

The nature and location of electronic data was an ethical consideration in terms of access to data transmitted over the Internet (Anderson & Kanuka, 2003). Generally, because of my Canadian context, and specifically because of my research location at a Canadian university, I was ethically bound to adhere to the host university's preference of Canadian-based electronic data storage locations. This protocol was designed to address potential concerns over data storage and privacy related to the United States of America Patriot Act. Questionnaire data were collected via FluidSurveys, an electronic survey software package, and stored on a secure server hosted in Canada. Elluminate session recordings were also hosted on Canadian-based servers.

Following the guidelines set forth by Anderson and Kanuka (2003), I advised participants in writing and verbally that I could not "absolutely guarantee that data would not be accessed, used, changed, or destroyed" (p. 62) by individuals with the authority to access the data (i.e., network administrators) or unauthorized personnel (i.e., hackers). Research participants did not appear to be concerned with the fact that their data were digital. As part of the research consent process, they signified awareness and agreement that I could not guarantee confidentiality and also that nothing professionally harmful would be described. To protect confidentiality, the geographic location of the research site was not revealed. Pseudonyms were used to protect the identity of all individuals interviewed and each individual was treated as a discrete unit. Furthermore, to respect participants' privacy, there were no references made to names of individuals during interviews and focus group sessions. Elluminate's recording function was set to remove individual names on playback, further addressing concerns over confidentiality. Once the raw data were collected and analyzed, it was transferred to a DVD, stored in a locked cabinet in my office, and removed from the external server.

During focus group sessions, the chat conversations themselves presented an interesting ethical issue: what to do with the messages sent privately to me as researcher in response to participant conversations. These comments were not captured automatically in the session recording yet were available to me to read during the session. I could also download the chat threads while still in the session, thus preserving their comments. These private conversations served as part of the conversation between a participant and me, yet other participants were not privy to them. This was an ethical concern that I did not anticipate. I decided in the first focus group session to send a private message back to the participant, either inviting him or her to share the comment or question with the group or to confirm whether the content was something he or she wished me to pursue as part of the group discussion. If the sender did not respond, I interpreted the lack of response as a refusal to share. I followed this same protocol for the remaining two focus group sessions.

Interview Experience and Challenges

A core component of this research was to provide a space for participants to interact freely with each other as they navigated their actionable plan of learning and practicing methods to create a sense of community within their online classes. In any research process, the researcher risks having participants feel uncomfortable or nervous with the mode of delivery; this is especially the case when using online technologies in research (Anderson & Kanuka, 2003; Salmons, 2010). Researchers must attend to these feelings and strive to develop and maintain a sense of trust with the researcher and the research process and between the research participants.

Because participants were all from the same Faculty of Education, most were known to each other; however, two participants were part-time, sessional instructors who had little to no virtual or physical contact with other participants. A portion of the first focus group session was dedicated to creating a sense of community with participants. One participant was in a supervisory role over the other five participants, so it was important for me to monitor for potential power issues that may have emerged and to ensure participants did not feel they were being supervised during the research. This did not emerge as an issue; faculty members were collegial and appeared to be comfortable sharing, criticizing constructively, and disagreeing. As well, individual interviews were opportunities to follow up privately on issues emerging from focus group sessions.

Technological glitches were rare throughout the research process. Only my first interview with one participant was affected by poor audio quality because of her Internet connection. My concern over data loss was mitigated by incorporating member checking—something I did with each participant. As well, during one focus group session, one participant could not get her audio to function for 30 minutes, but she communicated via the chat function until she was able to reset her hardware.

Lessons Learned and Recommendations

Elluminate lends itself to a potentially distracting environment; microphones, video windows, emoticons, back-channel chat conversations, text and images on the whiteboard, and so on—each add a layer of complexity during the actual research session and during data analysis. For the researcher to attend to all the dynamics happening during the session, comfort and skill with the platform itself is necessary. As well, because of unforeseen technological issues, researchers must be open to having to stop a session and reschedule or follow up via another means of communication. Sometimes, this may also require the researcher to have some technological trouble-shooting skills. The importance of selecting methods and data-collection tools that the researcher and participants are each familiar with cannot be emphasized enough.

Winter (1998) has characterized some universities as "warehouses" (p. 365), whose cultural authority leads them to separate knowledge from practical applications, and store that knowledge in libraries steeped in academic tradition. Like Winter, Dalziel (2008) has also noted that one of our failures in open education (i.e., the movement to share freely educational best practices and knowledge over the Internet) is "our lack of progress on sharing 'pedagogical know-how' among educators. . . . We have not captured the teaching processes that expert educators use to bring learning alive in their e-learning courses" (p. 375). Furthermore, by conversing about educational processes and receiving advice on the online design of these processes, "then not only could a novice educator benefit from the work of experts, but all educators could collectively adapt and improve each other's work, leading to improved quality overall" (Dalziel, p. 376).

As action research, this research project served to move participants farther along their learning journey toward creating community in their virtual Elluminate MA Ed classrooms. The multichannel meeting space enabled colleagues to work closely with their counterparts physically located some thousands of miles away, but connected through the same Faculty of Education. Participants had the tools at hand that they could use to demonstrate their own ideas and strategies to their colleagues and share ideas, concerns, and successes. By using the same virtual platform for our conversations as co-participants, we were able to explore together how to create a community of learners regardless of physical location. The modeling of effective virtual pedagogy and practice has indeed put the action in action research.

 See the Appendix for suggested readings and resources on the software, methodologies, and methods discussed in this case.

 Find More Materials on the Study Site! See the book website for related resources, materials, discussion, and assignment ideas.

References

Anderson, T., & Kanuka, H. (2003). *E-research: Methods, strategies, and issues.* Toronto, Canada: Pearson Educational.

Bogdan, R., & Biklen, S. (1998). *Qualitative research for education: An introduction to theory and methods.* Needham Heights, MA: Allyn & Bacon.

Carr, W., & Kemmis, S. (1986). *Becoming critical: Education, knowledge and action research.* Lewes, UK: Falmer.

Creswell, J. W. (1998). *Qualitative inquiry and research design: Choosing among five traditions.* Thousand Oaks, CA: Sage.

Dalziel, J. (2008). Learning design: Sharing pedagogical know-how. In T. Iiyoshi & M. S. V. Kumar (Eds.), *Opening up education: The collective advancement of education through open technology, open content, and open knowledge* (pp. 375–387). Cambridge: MIT Press. Retrieved from http://mitpress.mit.edu/catalog/item/default.asp?ttype=2&tid=11309

Good, T. L., & Brophy, J. E. (1990). *Educational psychology: A realistic approach* (4th ed.).White Plains, NY: Longman.

Guba, E. G. (1981). Criteria for assessing the trustworthiness of naturalistic inquiries. *Educational Communication and Technology, 29*(2), 75–91.

Jackson, W., & Verberg, N. (2007). *Methods: Doing social research* (4th ed.). Toronto: Pearson Education Canada.

Lincoln, Y., & Guba, E. (1985). *Naturalistic inquiry.* Thousand Oaks, CA: Sage.

Merriam, S. B., & Simpson, E. L. (2000). *A guide to research for educators and trainers of adults.* (2nd ed.). Malabar, FL: Krieger.

Newman, J. M. (2000). Action research: A brief overview. *Forum: Qualitative Social Research, 1*(1). Retrieved September 8, 2009, from http://www.qualitative-research.net/index.php/fqs/article/viewArticle/1127

Noffke, S. (1994). Action research: Towards the next generation. *Educational Action Research, 2*(1), 9–21. (doi: 10.1080/0965079940020102)

Noffke, S. E. (1997). Professional, personal, and political dimensions of action research. *Review of Research in Education, 22,* 305–343. (doi:10.3102 /0091732X022001305)

Noffke, S., & Somekh, B. (Eds.). (2009). *The Sage handbook of educational action research.* Thousand Oaks, CA: Sage.

Salmons, J. (2010). *Online interviews in real time.* Thousand Oaks, CA: Sage.

Schön, D. A. (1983). *The reflective practitioner.* New York: Basic Books.

Stringer, E. T. (2007). *Action research* (3rd ed.). Thousand Oaks, CA: Sage.

van Manen, M. (1990). *Researching lived experience.* London, Canada: Althouse.

Winter, R. (1998). Managers, spectators and citizens: Where does "theory" come from in action research? *Educational Action Research, 6*(3), 361–376.

CRITIQUE AND ANALYSIS OF KRAGLUND-GAUTHIER'S "TRANSITIONING FROM F2F TO ONLINE INSTRUCTION: PUTTING THE ACTION INTO ONLINE RESEARCH"

Lynn Wilson

In this case study, an instructional designer uses online interviewing to investigate how professors transition from face-to-face classroom teaching to online teaching. I believe that Kraglund-Gauthier's detailed descriptions of the process, technology choices, challenges, and choices make this case an appropriate instructional aid for researchers who use online interviewing as a qualitative research tool.

Kraglund-Gauthier presents a thorough introduction to the guiding theories and methodologies that support the study. Her explanation about the importance of being an "insider" in action research brings together the elements of her rationale for selecting the specific research methods. Beyond just being an insider, she understands the value of developing participant buy-in. She begins engaging participants in a virtual focus group by asking them to define the online teaching issue they will explore together. This activity helps build trust between researcher and subject as well as to strengthen group bonds. The participants elect to investigate better ways to create community in the classroom. That choice guides the methods selection and data-gathering approaches.

The stated research goal is rich description rather than generalization, making qualitative research methods appropriate for this study. It is clear that the research involves learning directly from the participant discussions in an open, rather than highly structured process. The topic choice, creating community, allows the experiential focus groups to serve as context for later online interviews during which the researcher more deeply explores individual participant perspectives. By modeling the synchronous experience in the focus group and using the same technologies for interviewing as for the group meeting, participation in the study is an enhanced learning experience for the subjects as well as a logical approach for the researcher.

The ethical issues encountered are not at all atypical when working with multiple institutions, especially from different countries. Data security and privacy issues are handled differently within national borders; international law is struggling to develop as quickly as technology demands, but what cross-border law does exist can be difficult to enforce. I find it ironic that data transmission over the Internet, something that enables broader research over wider geographies, becomes an ethical issue due to electronic data security concerns by individual nations and institutions. Some of those same issues are encountered in online research groups with which I participate, especially if they are conducted through universities in different countries such as in Kraglund-Gauthier's case study.

One way to minimize this problem is to conduct the online data exchange processes through third parties, especially if those parties have an established international presence. At one extreme would be studies conducted through the auspices of an IGO (intergovernmental organization) such as the United Nations; at the other extreme is an entrepreneurial approach through small businesses, NGOs (nongovernmental organization) or CBOs (community-based organization) that negotiate directly with the research participants rather than through host organizations. This is not to say that ethics and data security become any less important or less potentially litigious in these alternative settings. The ways in which such issues are approached are different, but can be just as rigorous as in any academic institution. What I am suggesting is that alternatives do exist to multiple university processes for research ethics approval. Costs, potential liabilities, ownership of the data and publications, as well as other rules governing a research study must be examined when considering less traditional options. While these approaches are not always practical, especially for novice researchers or graduate students who may not have contacts or access to outside organizations, cross-border institutional ethics issues can become so difficult that some researchers abandon the study altogether when other options may be available.

One of the key points of this case study is the interview participants' comfort and familiarity with the research tools. Many exciting and increasingly interactive options exist for today's online researcher. It can be tempting to use them in less-than-optimum circumstances, particularly if the researcher is intrigued by new and emerging technologies. For those of us in global work, new ways to interact and simulate face-to-face encounters is sometimes a lure that can lead us to use tools that intimidate or even alienate research subjects. In one of my online interview projects, I decided to use Skype instead of more intricate and potentially engaging tools such as Elluminate. As Kraglund-Gauthier found, Elluminate can be distracting in online research, especially interviews. She stresses that both methods and tools that are familiar to the participants are vital for successful online research. I agree, although incremental steps in bringing participants to new technologies can work *if* the technologies have relevance to the participants' own professional interests. For example, I find that scientists tend to be more willing to experiment with online technologies involving GIS (geographic information systems) than they are with tools like Elluminate that enhance communication. That makes sense; scientists are usually more interested and involved with data-rendering technologies than with communications.

Kraglund-Gauthier points out workable strategies while exposing pitfalls to avoid in online interviewing and associated online research. Even when, as in her study, technology performs well for the most part, the participants' comfort levels should be heavily considered in both research design and in the choice of data-collection tools. An early awareness of potential outside issues such as procuring ethics approval from multiple systems can also help guide researchers in their online research design choices. Anticipating potential issues and changes can also help a researcher to develop and engage the most appropriate partners in the early stages of the research, something that can save time, money, and a great deal of frustration for the researcher. While this case study is directed toward the novice researcher, it offers seasoned researchers good reminders about anticipating potential issues early in the process, and points out some of the new concerns that online interviewers and researchers face.

CHAPTER 8
FRAMEWORK COMMENTARY: "TRANSITIONING FROM F2F TO ONLINE INSTRUCTION: PUTTING THE ACTION INTO ONLINE RESEARCH"

Janet Salmons

In this action research study, Dr. Wendy Kraglund-Gauthier explored the use of Elluminate, a multichannel meeting tool, by professors transitioning from traditional to online instruction. She chose to conduct the interviews and focus groups in Elluminate. Using purposive sampling and an existing sample frame, she recruited educators from one university who were all at some stage of transition from face-to-face to online teaching.

Elluminate offers visual options, including use of a webcam, as well as text chat to complement the audio conversation. For this study, some participants used the webcam; others did not. The ones who opted out of being seen on screen sometimes chose to use emoticons to show moods and feelings. Kraglund-Gauthier acknowledged the visual content of her research and incorporated it into her findings. She viewed the use of emoticons as a surrogate for visual cues of body language (i.e., nodding acquiescence, down-thumbing disagreement, confusion) in face-to-face interviews. When reviewing recordings, she added the emoticon communication to the transcript (i.e., when one participant said something, she noted others' agreement via the happy face or the applause, or disagreement with the thumbs down).

As an instructional designer, Kraglund-Gauthier understands the value and application of online tools for teaching and learning. As a researcher, she experienced the study with research participants as a fellow traveler (Kvale, 2007; Kvale & Brinkman, 2009). But she also needed to take a gardener role (Salmons, 2010), seeding and supporting the growth of new ideas and interpretations through the series of interviews, focus groups, and reviews of educators' journals. Kraglund-Gauthier balanced etic and emic perspectives. While she states that she was a research "co-participant," and drew research questions from participants' issues, she also took an etic stance since she introduced concerns and questions different from what might have been evident to educators who were insiders in the case (Stake, 1995).

Figure 8.1 Research map for "Transitioning From F2F to Online Instruction: Putting the Action Into Online Research."

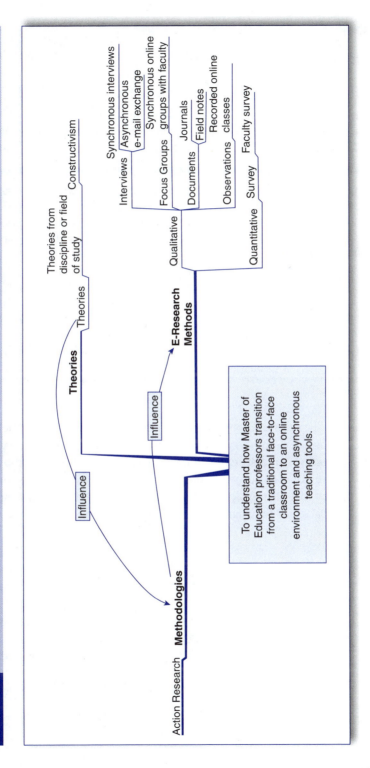

Table 8.2	Summary: Key Factors in the "Transitioning From F2F to Online Instruction: Putting the Action Into Online Research" Study

Motivation for Choosing E-Research	Sampling and Recruiting	Interview Style and Structure	Technology: Issues, Features, Lessons	Ethical Issues
Kraglund-Gauthier chose to conduct interviews with the same tool she was studying: Elluminate, a multichannel meeting space.	Purposeful, criterion-based sampling was used.\n\nParticipants were recruited online, through membership lists of established groups.	Semi-structured individual and group interviews	Web conferencing, and text interactions were used.\n\nResearcher complemented interview data with other reflective journal and survey data.	Primary question of review boards: data storage.

Kraglund-Gauthier points out some areas e-researchers need to consider. The array of possibilities for communication (visual, text, audio) can distract or offer more cause for confusion, if participants are not accustomed to the environment. Still, she shows the potential for collecting rich and varied data using multichannel meeting spaces for focus groups as well as one-on-one interviews.

References

Kvale, S. (2007). *Doing interviews.* Thousand Oaks, CA: Sage.

Kvale, S., & Brinkman, S. (2009). *InterViews: Learning the craft of qualitative research interviewing* (2nd ed.). Thousand Oaks, CA: Sage.

Salmons, J. E. (2010). *Online interviews in real time.* Thousand Oaks, CA: Sage.

Stake, R. E. (1995). *The art of case study research.* Thousand Oaks, CA: Sage.

Integrated Interdisciplinary Online Interviews in Science and Health

9

The Climate and Health Literacy Project

Lynn Wilson

SeaTrust Institute, Olympia, Washington,
and Kaplan University, USA

Introduction

Climate and health scientists are increasingly being called upon to work together to address both adaptation and mitigation aspects of climate change in the global environment. Differences in focus, methods, language, and even approach have made this an often uneasy alliance with less than optimum results. When "climate and health literacy" are looked at together, climate change issues are framed in terms relevant to health professionals' work and health issues. Important relationships between climate and health are integrated more directly into climate science discussions enabling a larger role for health in climate change decisions.

The online interview component of this ongoing research study demonstrates how collaboratively constructing research with interview subjects may modify the research process and decisions, resulting in a product that is directly influenced by the subjects who are representatives of the target audience. This particular type of e-research collaboration differs from designs in which predetermined rules, premises, or organizational directives more strictly define and bound the research. Process and content are constantly negotiated while navigating the intercultural, systemic, communications, political, ethical, and trust-related pitfalls inherent in all e-collaborative efforts.

Technologies used for conducting the semi-structured interviews vary as appropriate for the needs of the interviewee. These include videoconference, video calls, audio-only VOIP, and multichannel meeting tools. Only rarely is the telephone used for interviewing. Experiences in identifying and recruiting the most valuable interview subjects for specific types of online interviews, especially from among scholars and practitioners in the medical and scientific communities, illuminate the value of professional relationship building at all stages of the interview process.

The case presented in this chapter is an example of the "fundamental, use-inspired research" that is called for by current interdisciplinary climate change adaptation and mitigation scientific teams and science-informed policy processes (National Academy of Sciences, 2010, pp. 115–116). In demonstrating multiple theories and methods that inform the research purpose and design, this study acknowledges the multidimensional, topical, interpersonal, interorganizational, and societal complexities inherent in global social issues, such as climate change and human health. Complex knowledge creation remains at its heart a social process, amenable to the impacts of the current Web 2.0 and other emerging technologies.

Research and the Climate and Health Literacy Project

Environment and population health are inextricably linked. At the nexus of these issues it becomes apparent that both health and climate scientists can benefit from aligning their knowledge, messages, and approaches to forge a stronger relationship so that they can act as a unified catalyst for meaningful action at local, regional, national, and global scales. This study is part of a larger, ongoing

Climate and Health Literacy Project. Key components rely on online research interviews with health practitioners, climate scientists, and public policy actors who engage with both climate science and human health. Climate and health science information methods and goals are integrated in this publication to better facilitate working relationships between these two sets of critical expert actors in adaptation and mitigation strategies to address global climate change.

Many earlier studies using interviewing to investigate different knowledge bases in climate change issues were regionally or sectorally focused. They typically relied on face-to-face or telephone interaction rather than employing newer technologies. Rapid developmental changes in the interdisciplinary content fields of climate science and health mean researchers need access to informants in multiple locations. At the same time, changing technologies and access require the researcher to make dynamic changes in interview content, style, and methods throughout the process to collect the most time-critical data. Achieving this balance requires considerable flexibility in interview style, approach, technologies, and even content while remaining within epistemological, methodological, and ethical boundaries that guide the research.

This study is conducted by an independent nongovernmental organization (NGO), so agility and flexibility are more practical than in projects that are sponsored, funded, or otherwise influenced by more formal, structured entities. It is also an interdisciplinary study and as such is not constrained by the respective research parameters common to the fields of science and health. While the research acknowledges specific considerations and requirements—such as those instituted by regional and organizational governing bodies—the overall purpose of this research is independent of these influences and thus allows for mid-course corrections in online interview design.

Research Purpose and Questions

The Climate and Health Literacy Project originated while framing the Consortium on Climate Change and Population Health, an investigatory project led by SeaTrust Institute and its globally dispersed health and climate sector partners. The project aims to integrate knowledge, methods, and perspectives on critical human health issues related to climate change. Impetus for formalizing the Climate and Health Literacy Project came from requests made by health professionals during the scoping phase of the consortium development; potential consortium participants and supporters in the health community requested a climate literacy text specifically directed toward health scholars and practitioners. Both clinical and public health professionals suggested that a climate literacy text specifically oriented to medical research and clinical interests would help them more effectively contribute to collaborative efforts involving multiple scientific disciplinary experts. The same information need arose during SeaTrust Institute's participation in incubating an interdisciplinary coalition of health and climate science professionals at the United Nations Climate Meetings in Copenhagen in 2009 and continuing at the 2010 Cancun meetings. With the fledgling health coalition's central purpose being to bring health to the forefront of global climate change discussions and decisions, health professionals participating in the international policy meetings also expressed the need for climate science information that was relevant to, and directly linked with, health issues, practices, and professional orientations.

During the research design phase, climate-related health categories were initially identified through the literature from a variety of disciplines related to climate change and human health, especially noting the instances of emerging climate and health linkages in governmental and academic reports. The health categories were vetted with representative working health practitioners and scholars from different health sectors through informal discussions and e-mail interchanges. Most of these health scholars were directly referred to the researcher by environmental health NGOs to which these experts belong and contribute. Categories agreed upon by these trusted experts form the backbone of a taxonomy of climate change and health issues; this categorization in the scoping phase of the research project preceded but closely mirrors those delineated in a 2010 National Institutes of Health report on research needs across health and climate change issues (Portier, 2010, p. 85).

Within each category, the research questions relate to three key elements: (1) specific health issues or symptoms within the category, (2) potential causes or indicators for that health issue, and (3) relevant climate factors for the geographical locations where the specified health issues are changing or increasing. To explore the interrelationship of the key elements above, interviews focus on

1. The degree of uncertainty surrounding the relationship of climate change to the health issue, other factors affecting the issue;

2. Variability by geographic region including patterns of dependency on extreme weather events, observation systems, and surveillance processes;

3. Identification and information about the most vulnerable populations;

4. Cultural and political considerations;

5. Existing and preferable health impact assessment tools, methods, planning, and models;

6. Additional stressors;

7. Professional policies and ethics; and

8. Interconnected complexities such as ecosystem services and indirect or derivative outcomes.

Research Design Overview

This research design is informed by the pragmatic considerations of relevance to the target audience: health professionals. Following a review of literature, interviews with a variety of types of experts are purposeful and managed within the design parameters. To aid an iterative design through feedback from the target group of experts, the research is conducted in tiers, with each increasingly intricate level of interview questions being informed by the information gathered at the previous broader level. For example, if a clinical physician is working with children's health issues in sub-Saharan Africa, the question focus tightens to that population, to critical diseases like malaria and fresh water maintenance issues that impact new adaptation strategies, and to the related effects on food supply and security related to children's health rather than to international policies that can affect global tropical diseases. Because of the dynamic nature of the topics impacting climate change and human health, new studies are continuously monitored and appropriate reports integrated into the interview and analyses processes.

GUIDING THEORIES

For the purpose of this chapter, the primary emphasis is on one-on-one discourse across geographical distances that engages the subject in research decisions (see the examples in Table 9.1).

Informed by systems thinking, collaborative learning, and conflict theories, prepared interview discussion guidelines are used by the

Table 9.1 Theories That Influence Virtual Interview Decisions and Practice

Theories	Dominant Theoretical Aspects and Applications Within Expert Interviews
Discourse and Networks	• Cognitive hierarchy preferences expert knowledge: health and climate science experts • Expert knowledge primacy is elaborated upon through peer and some public discourse to achieve information consensus. New ideas build on previous expert testimony during interviews. • Networks within and across disciplines serve to vet opinions and knowledge through integration while preserving key norms, methods, and identities. Suggestions are confirmed or elaborated upon by other experts and publics.
Systems and Adaptation	• Complex systems generate new features from interaction among system parts. • Counterintuitive outcomes of complex systems may preference choices.
Collaborative Learning and Behavior	• Learning occurs on both sides of the interview. • "Frames" help participants navigate complex situations. Incompatible frames inhibit communication and create barriers to developing knowledge. • Values drive belief systems (subjective norms) and attitudes, which manifest in the priority of knowledge claims by a particular expert.
Collaboration and Conflict	• Strength of power structures and assumed hierarchies in scientific and expert systems must be honored yet managed to encourage appropriate contributions from interview subjects. • Interdisciplinary processes often require negotiating methods. Data and analytic assumptions are among interview subjects' contributions.

researcher to encourage expert content input while respecting the unique characteristics and potential additional contributions of each participant. This type of less-rigid yet rules-informed discussion proves effective in negotiating values, methods, and data between interview subjects' contributions and between researcher and subject. Remaining open and conversational while still being goal-directed provides the researcher with a framework through which to make iterative modifications of questions so that they incorporate the new knowledge and perspectives while addressing the research outcomes.

This juxtaposition of object and subject orientation appeals to the intuitive alongside, not instead of, communicative process rationality in keeping with constructivist epistemic processes (Dreyfus, 1988). The distinctions made between analytical/rational expertise and intuition, context, judgment, and common sense to transcend the *solely* rational perspective is consistent with the positions held by Foucault, Nietzsche, and others who challenge rationality as the dominant paradigm in relation to process, power, and what is counted as knowledge. At the same time, rational communicative processes are also consciously used. As a practical matter, many of the interview subjects are trained in the scientific method and actively look for evidence of its application as a signal of legitimacy in research that relates to their areas of expertise.

This pragmatic process mixes methods in an abductive reasoning approach that leverages the inductive/deductive and subjective/objective dichotomies rather than selecting a single methodological "camp" that would necessarily constrain the inquiry. While more difficult to execute, this combined and iterative approach is preferable for this study because the goal is to explicitly explore new ways of knowing rather than to test bounded hypotheses.

Broader inclusion and respect for a variety of values and viewpoints is an example of effective communication in which we see "appreciation" in action; we change not only one another's views of the situations we share, but we change one another and ourselves as well. Educating through discourse is basic to the practice of creating consensus. Knowledge that affects action across climate science, health, and public policy requires not only new information and methods, but also a significant degree of consensus.

Experts, like other groups, come in many flavors and in this case represent various sides of environmental and health arguments. Sometimes a particular idea introduction is a political, esthetic, cultural, or religious issue rather than a peer-supported scientific one, an idea illuminated by the debates surrounding approaches to discourse (Alario, 2001; Skollerhorn, 1998). These theories generally contend that solutions to most environmental problems, while they may focus on scientific, technological, and economic issues, are appropriately dependent on value-laden human behavior. By purposefully creating knowledge *with* the interview subject experts, the door to values and attitudes swings wide; but a balance must be maintained by the researcher between the rational and social aspects of the expert, particularly in analyzing the data.

METHODOLOGY

A combined approach to data collection using empirical phenomenological research and situational analysis guides the interviews. This allows subjects the freedom to explore meanings and concepts of health effects from climate change events while examining social ramifications of theirs and others' scientific endeavors. A grounded theory approach of iterative data analysis allows concepts emerging from the collected data to be worked out during the study.

In keeping with the goal that these interviews define and affirm relevant methods for presenting climate science and health information as well as emerging new knowledge among the relevant disciplines, the continuum of methods the researcher uses is modified to best accommodate the professional norms of the subject. Although flexible in the order and use of research methods, the study progresses within the conceptual framework defined for the Consortium; the researcher makes measureable movements toward defining the interconnected issues and goals of health and climate scientists, developing a common language through which to explore these issues and creating spaces for collaborating on research projects, practical adaptation solutions, and mutual learning. Contributing new information and knowledge about each of the 12 identified topical areas challenges subjects to consider their current framework in a new way in terms of scientific and human factors, and encourages subjects to consider ways in which they might collaborate with scientists in the other disciplines that impinge on their work at the nexus of climate change and health.

INTERVIEW SUBJECT SELECTION

Participants in this study are primarily referred from other colleagues in an effort to build on related trusted networks. A nominated approach has proven to be the most effective method through which the researcher in this study gains access to experts who would have been otherwise inaccessible. Cascading or snowball referrals across networks lead to other, often less well-known experts who also hold vital content information. In a few cases, subjects have found the researcher through participation in online and in-person activities related to the Consortium and international meetings such as the webinar held by the researcher following the 2009 Copenhagen Climate Change Meetings. Although referrals have proven the most effective sampling technique to date, the planned addition of emergent, opportunistic, and politically important recruiting methods will be implemented as the study moves into the climate scientist and policy maker components, particularly through opportunities for face-to-face interviews and for setting up post-event virtual interviews through personal interactions during the 2010 UN Climate Change Meetings in Cancun, Mexico.

Recruiting the most valuable interview subjects for expert online interviews, especially in the medical and scientific communities, requires an understanding of perceived barriers by these professionals. Referral from a trusted colleague or network is the most effective way to quell concerns. Another deterrent can be the subject's perception that they are not sufficiently expert in the specific area of inquiry to warrant their time in participating in the interview, even if their interest in the general subject matter is high. If approached respectfully and if requested, follow-up with information from the study is made by the researcher. Contact with nonparticipant experts of this type can be turned into an opportunity for building enduring professional relationships whether or not they participate in the online interviews. These professionals have high expectations. They see their time as valuable and expect the researcher to be conversant in their specializations and aware of the expert's particular contributions. Successful interactions with medical and scientific experts include being well prepared, and presenting succinct project background notes and information requests *in the form requested by the expert.* In this study, that means that the researcher may create materials specific to the interests of a single potential participant if their input is sufficiently valuable to the study. It also means that personal contact by e-mail and sometimes a phone or video call prior to the interview may be required to establish credibility and to assure the subject that their expertise is a valid contribution to the study.

INTERVIEW APPROACH AND ANALYSIS CONSIDERATIONS

Although the interviews are conducted by a primary researcher, the integration of subject involvement provides the potential for a durable and pervasive relationship and common mission (Mattessich, Murray-Close, & Monsey, 2001) reliant on negotiation and knowledge sharing, trust, and communication within the virtual research environment. Boundary organizations such as NGOs have shown particular promise as precipitators of trust, a key element in interdisciplinary collaborative efforts (Olaniran, 2008).

While the research design calls for synchronous one-on-one semi-structured interviews, some of these later morph into unstructured co-constructed narratives as subjects suggest new directions based on their experiences or offer new information that was unknown to the interviewer prior to the exchange. For some subjects, the defined questions in the design are not appropriate and for others a conversational approach unlocks new ideas better than following patterned questions and responses. Some focus-type group interviews may take place later in the process as basic knowledge and structure in each of the categories is more clearly articulated and affirmed by experts in those fields.

Because this is an ongoing study, iterative analyses are interwoven into the fabric of continuing interviews. Following the initial round of health professional interviews, climate scientists will be interviewed with special topical interviews reserved for exploring discrepancies, ambiguities, or new areas of possible knowledge creation unveiled during the process.

Technologies

In addition to the fluidity of subjects and categories of interview topics, the degree and types of technologies used in the study vary widely from Web 2.0 and mobile technologies to face-to-face interviews. Choices are made based on geographic proximity, technological capabilities, comfort and access of the participants, the perceived need for additional cues from in-person interactions, participant time constraints, and accepted professional norms. Participant and researcher capabilities rather than specific products drive technology decisions; while a wide range of Web 2.0 products are currently and will continue to be used in the e-research aspects of this study, all levels of available technology will be used when needed to accommodate appropriate subjects.

Most communication used to initiate the interviews is written. Referrals from peers or colleagues primarily begin through e-mail, although some telephone communication is used for these introductions. First researcher-to-subject contact is also commonly by e-mail through which mutually acceptable times, technologies and methods, ethics, confidentiality, and other expectations for interviews are established.

The interviews may be conducted using a variety of technologies. Most subjects are geographically separated from the researcher. When such a subject has access to video conferencing, synchronous interviews of 30 minutes to up to 2 hours are held using that technology. Subjects widely report satisfaction with this method, except in cases of lost connections or degraded sound quality. Audio interviews using VOIP technology are used when video conferencing is not practical but synchronous communication is agreed upon. In only one instance did an interview subject request using a telephone instead of a computer-based technology.

Text interviews are usually a backup for instances in which the participant cannot access video conferencing. Text interviews may be conducted by e-mail or, increasingly, through mobile devices. Because of the global nature of this study, participants in remote locations and in countries with limited technology infrastructure or in disaster zones can more likely access mobile technology than computer-based communications tools. Text interviews are also used for very short interviews in which the subject is responding to one or a very few specific questions.

In a few cases, text or video call interviews are continued in a multichannel environment so that the participant can dynamically respond to visual images and text of other subjects' points of view in their own words. It is expected that this will become a more frequent method of interaction, particularly as interview subjects move into related areas of the larger project as collaborative researchers in the Consortium on Climate Change and Population Health, which includes a semi-interactive GIS (geographic information system) and the generation of climate- and health adaptation-related applications for mobile technologies for use by global health practitioners. For these interviews, video calls prove to be the most effective with the majority of interview participants. Multichannel meetings, while offering the capacity for rich interchange, are less fruitful at this stage and with individuals who may not be part of later collaborative work.

Research Findings

Emerging patterns point to areas of climate information that are of special interest to health professionals. Climate change information and data need to inform:

- Preparedness plans
- Early warnings: health indicators
- Health Surveillance Information for inclusion in federal and global databases
- Clinical implications and public health imperatives
- Advocacy and education

Of the eight research questions, numbers 2 (variability by geographic region including patterns of dependency on extreme weather events, observation systems, and surveillance processes), 3 (identification and information about the most vulnerable populations), and 7 (professional policies and ethics) appear particularly useful in linking information about the current states, perceived needs, and identified gaps in data or knowledge that address issues most emphasized by interview participants.

For each of the twelve categories of geographic variability, relationship to extreme weather events, most vulnerable populations, and professional policies, smart practices, and potential actions are being compiled, reflectively considered, and combined. Each category addresses a specific health topic, the relevance and focus of which was confirmed by vetting with key health professionals at the start of the study. The interview data provide information, new ways of considering problems, and we hope it will help those working in the field to consider new collaborative approaches to adapting to human health ramifications from a changing global climate.

Conclusions and Future Directions

This case study highlights elements and effects of an online interview process with health professionals in the Climate and Health Literacy Project. Because of the wide geographic distribution and types of practices and research, different research strategies are used to most efficiently and appropriately elicit the information needed. Ensuring that climate science topics and information are arranged and presented to the subjects in health-related categories, using familiar professional terms and examples, and in ways that are meaningful to clinicians, medical researchers, and public health officials is critical. The language and respective terminology of health and medicine is respected and incorporated along with that of climate science. Every effort is made to integrate rather than assign primacy to one discipline, language, or process over others, yet focus communication on the relevant audience for each part of the publication. Practical steps related to the information are relevant, actionable, and do not add undue stress on the already overburdened health professional.

As has been stated throughout the chapter, this is an ongoing study. While any conclusions are really interim reports, some valuable lessons have already emerged. Some interviews have proven more successful than others in terms of information accessibility, flow, and in developing ongoing relationships. The last point is vital in measuring the success of this study. Practical outcomes of the research include engaging the professional scientific and health communities in ongoing dialogue and collaboration on climate change and human health. And it is by those criteria that the long-term success of this project will be measured. Some interviews may yield less useful information or reduced input due to time or other considerations but those aspects may be offset by involving a higher-profile individual whose participation elevates the profile of the study and therefore of the global issues.

Some online interview technologies have been more useful than others. Videoconferencing provides the most personal and professional interactivity across geographic boundaries. Yet mobile technologies allow participants in remote locations who are dynamically engaged with the health emergencies from climate change events to add invaluable testimony. Another value of text-based interviews is the ability to incorporate input from individuals who cannot (or choose not to) commit time to a complete interview, yet who are considered leaders in the field. Including their expertise on key topical elements related to their areas of expertise further validates the results for their professional colleagues. This validation increases the perceived value of the climate and literacy book, the training courses, and materials on climate and health literacy, and it provides additional rationale for involvement in the research project, the

Consortium on Climate Change and Population Health, and the global Health Coalition emerging through the UN Climate Change meetings.

Interviews may be expanded after the initial round of synchronous expert interviews to include asynchronous responses and an increasing use of social networking sites and multichannel meeting spaces. These methods may provide introductions and contexts for collaborations that may develop into more formal research among interview participants, other scholars and students, and other interested publics such as NGOs and communities facing challenges from climate change and global health concerns. Other possibilities include a short online survey of those who either were not approached or did not participate in the interviews to test whether experts' opinions reflect the larger group they were selected to represent, especially on complex, controversial issues.

Ongoing assessments will be conducted based on the principles of adaptive risk management—iteratively updating as the learning progresses. By integrating the interview results for the Climate and Health Literacy Project with its sister initiatives described in this chapter, a portfolio of approaches can emerge that are both interdisciplinary and integrative.

See the Appendix for suggested readings and resources on the software, methodologies, and methods discussed in this case.

Find More Materials on the Study Site! See the book website for related resources, materials, discussion, and assignment ideas.

References

Alario, M. (2001). A turn to scientific analysis and democratic deliberation in environmental policy: Political risk, legitimation crisis or policy imperative? *Theory and Science, 2*(2). Retrieved from http://theoryandscience .icaap.org/content/vol002.002/alario.html

Dreyfus, H. L. (1988). *The power of human intuition and expertise in the era of the computer.* New York: Free Press.

Mattessich, P., Murray-Close, M., & Monsey, B. R. (2001). *Collaboration: What makes it work* (2nd ed.). St. Paul: Wilder Publishing Center.

National Academy of Sciences. (2010). *Advancing the science of climate change.* Washington, DC: National Academies Press.

Olaniran, B. (2008). A proposition for developing trust and relational synergy in international e-collaborative groups. In J. Salmons & L.Wilson (Eds.), *Handbook of research in electronic collaboration and organizational synergy* (pp. 472–486). Hershey, PA: Information Science Reference.

Portier, C. J., et al. (2010). *A human health perspective on climate change: A report outlining the research needs of the human health effects of climate change.* Research Triangle Park, NC: Environmental Health Perspectives/National Institute of Environmental Health Sciences.

Skollerhorn, E. (1998). Habermas and nature: The theory of communication action for studying environmental policy. *Journal of Environmental Planning and Management, 41*(5), 555–573.

CRITIQUE AND ANALYSIS OF WILSON'S
"INTEGRATED INTERDISCIPLINARY ONLINE
INTERVIEWS IN SCIENCE AND HEALTH:
THE CLIMATE AND HEALTH LITERACY PROJECT"

Sally Dowling

This is an interesting case and the discussion of it here contains much that will be useful to other researchers. The subject matter, research design, and methods used are very different from those used in my research, discussed in Chapter 11. There are however some points of approach in common. These and other aspects may be of particular interest to other researchers. The focus here will be on discussing the online elements of the research, but I will also briefly outline other issues of interest.

The main points I would like to highlight relate to the benefits of collaboration, flexibility, and responsiveness and how, in this research project, these are particularly related to the use of the Internet. These strong themes recur throughout the discussion and, while their use in research design and conduct are not new, Wilson demonstrates here the specific ways that using the Internet increased both collaboration and flexibility in her project and enabled her to be responsive on a number of levels. Other researchers might be able to learn from this. Of particular value is the way in which this case illustrates the potential to be inclusive and adaptable in both research design and execution. While this approach might possibly appear, to the novice qualitative researcher, to contain many uncertainties, it provides a good example of the benefits of choosing a nonrigid approach to research design. The flexible approach to the use of technologies in this case may be particularly instructive to those who might believe that methods are chosen early in research design and applied consistently through data collection.

Collaboration with research participants allowed for modification of both processes and decisions as the research progressed. While some might find this unsettling, Wilson says that it improved the "product," because those who would benefit from the results of the research had influence over its conduct and content. The choice of technology was varied according both to participants' professional role and geographical situation. Being able to interview people geographically far apart is often cited as an advantage of Internet research. I particularly liked the way in which Wilson demonstrated the benefits of using technology for qualitative interviewing through the example of the participation of those involved in work in disaster zones. Interviewing via the medium of mobile technology enabled valuable input to the project that might have been impossible if the focus had been on more traditional forms of interviewing, or even more conventional uses of technology. Wilson demonstrates how interviewing geographically disparate people whose views are important to your project requires both flexibility of approach and methods, and shows how this can increase the effectiveness of the work.

Another example of collaboration/flexibility that comes across particularly strongly in this study relates to the researcher's beliefs about, and respect for, the expertise of her participants. Throughout, Wilson talks about the importance given to understanding the perspective of the professionals involved—in terms of how they see her and the research project and in how they perceive their involvement. Materials are tailored specifically and technological choices made to fit in with the participants working lives, their perceptions of research conduct, and/or the norms of their profession. The choice and use of technologies are driven by researcher and participant situations and capabilities—again, I liked how responsiveness and flexibility are emphasized. I think that some researchers—perhaps particularly novices—might find this anxiety provoking and difficult; Wilson demonstrates the real advantages of being able to take this approach and this is a key learning point from this case.

Technologies used are chosen in part because of the geographical distance between researcher and participants and include videoconferencing, audio interviews using VOIP technology, and, occasionally, the telephone. E-mail is sometimes used in the pre-interview phase and e-mail and mobile devices are used for text interviews if necessary. Wilson talks about the use of Web 2.0 and mobile technologies and, as a researcher whose use of the Internet has been at its most basic level, I would have liked more detail about what this actually means. Reading Wilson's chapter made me realize that although I am someone who is comfortable with technology and interested in Internet-based research, my understanding of the use and potential of some technologies is limited. Feeling that this might be true for other researchers too, I contacted Wilson (via e-mail) for clarification (see transcript below). I found her response interesting and helpful, although do not agree (see the discussion in my chapter) that e-mail interviews are necessarily "less personal" or less rich.

Although this chapter is primarily about the use of synchronous interviewing using the Internet, Wilson demonstrates the need to adapt and develop approaches. Synchronous interviews sometimes lead to further interaction ("morph into unstructured co-constructed narratives"). As this is an ongoing project, she allows for future flexibility too, with the suggestion of possible focus groups or further interviews. This future adaptability also allows for differing uses of technology with the suggestion of other potential developments occurring during the life of this ongoing project (as noted in our discussion below).

> SD: You talk about the use of Web 2.0 and mobile devices...for other readers like me who may not be entirely sure what this means, could you explain further? Text interviews conducted through mobile devices are contrasted with those conducted via e-mail – do you mean you used text messaging?
>
> LW: Mobile technology for the interviews themselves are more often related to those, skype or other, for online interviewing using mobile devices rather than text messaging for this set of interviews, but rather mobile connectivity to web communications tools.
>
> SD: Were the interviews conducted using mobile technology shorter than those using other means? Or substantially different in any other way?
>
> LW: No difference in time whether mobile devices were involved or not.
>
> SD: Could you say more about what you mean by 'a wide range of Web 2.0 products are currently and will continue to be used'? I think it will help others to have some examples.
>
> LW: Mobile technology is moving fast. Streaming capabilities need to be leveraged for interviewing as well as for video and other channels. These lines between channels are becoming blurred as people with new mobile technologies can stream voice and live video for interviews. This contrasts with the less personal interactivity of e-mail interviews and gives a richness not available through text only media.

I was interested in Wilson's comment (on the inclusion/respect aspects of her research design) that "we change not only one another's views of the situations we share, but we change one another and ourselves as well." This clear example of researcher reflexivity provides a learning point for others—conducting qualitative research offers opportunities for the personal (or other) development of both researcher and participants. Recognition of this is important and necessary in a research paradigm that values researcher openness and honesty. For her, this was perhaps facilitated by the collaborative nature of her inquiry; for me it was through the co-construction of data facilitated by a shared experience. For both of us, the Internet provided a medium in which this was made more possible.

Wilson has a pragmatic stance to mixing methods, and although this can be seen as beneficial in this context, it is not unique to Internet research. Neither is the use of flexibility of style within interviews— "remaining open and conversational whilst still being goal directed" will be familiar to many qualitative interviewers. I tried to use this approach in my interviews, seeing it in my context as a specific tactic in relationship forming. It might be particularly important for those using Internet technologies where a range of nonverbal cues is not available, although, as Wilson demonstrates, using voice and live video through newly available technological choices opens up different possibilities.

This flexibility in research design also allowed Wilson to respond to changes, both in appropriate technologies for interviewing and in climate science. This might be a particularly attractive technique for other researchers working in rapidly changing fields. It illustrates how it is possible, as Wilson comments, to both remain true to the original research design (sometimes associated with boundaries or restraints) and to be flexible and responsive.

The discussion of this case raises some questions for me. A more reflexive style, using the first person, might have led to more clarity. For example, it is not clear whether the author conducted all interviews herself (I found out later that she did), and what the implications would be for her project if she did not. The emphasis on respect/deference to experts, acknowledgment of what's important to them, and consequent prioritization of research styles/methods is fairly uncritical. More explanation of why "trusted experts" were viewed as such would have been helpful. However, there are many ways in which the discussion of this case will be extremely valuable to other researchers; discussing it has been thought provoking and useful to me.

CHAPTER 9
FRAMEWORK COMMENTARY:
"INTEGRATED INTERDISCIPLINARY ONLINE INTERVIEWS IN SCIENCE AND HEALTH: THE CLIMATE AND HEALTH LITERACY PROJECT"

Janet Salmons

In this ongoing exploratory study, Dr. Lynn Wilson explores intersections of climate science and health in the context of changing conditions resulting from climate change. The motivation to use online communications is quite obviously due to the wide geographic dispersion of participants. Also obvious is the very real-world nature of the research problem. In the global context of this study, participants have uneven access to communications technologies. As a result, Wilson cannot realistically select one type of tool, online environment, or technology to use across the study. While images may be important to a given participant's report of conditions, problems or options, she cannot rely on multichannel or visual forms of communication. She needs to adapt the selection of the technology and to some extent the style and format of the interview, to the participant. She must take advantage of whatever opportunity the participant has to give input, and accept inherent limitations.

Purposeful sampling strategies are similarly flexible, using nominated and snowball strategies. So, while some recruitment may occur online, the referral process ensures that participants' identities are authentic; and that the sample represents the breadth of knowledge in the expanding interdisciplinary field of study. The study is based on input from high-level expert participants with specific types of experiences. An open call for participants would not align with the research purpose.

Because the study is with high-level expert participants, establishing trust online quickly was a very important part of this e-research. Busy, distracted participants did not give Wilson much time to do that. She had to establish credibility through e-mail to get the interview and trust within the first few questions and moments of online personal interaction whether or not they could make visual contact though a webcam connection.

As a researcher, Wilson is both traveler and gardener. She experiences the interview as a participant in the dialogue. Kvale (2007;

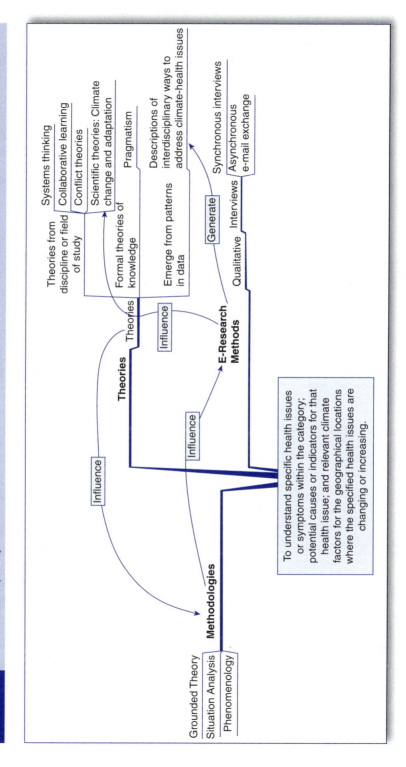

259

Kvale & Brinkman, 2009) describes the interviewer as a traveler when the interview is a journey undertaken together to discover insights. In an emerging, rapidly changing field where the ramifications are potentially dire and widespread, the researcher appropriately jumps aboard the moving train. At the same time, Wilson must take a gardener role (Salmons, 2010), seeding and supporting the growth and cross-fertilization of new ideas and understandings that emerge from respective disciplines or across disciplines. As an actor in the case, she takes an emic stance to identify issues and questions (Stake, 1995).

Wilson's work demonstrates the value of e-research as an approach for building collaborative approaches and discovering new solutions to widespread problems.

Table 9.2	Summary: Key Factors in the "Integrated Interdisciplinary Online Interviews in Science and Health: The Climate and Health Literacy Project" Study			
Motivation for Choosing E-Research	Sampling and Recruiting	Interview Style and Structure	Technology: Issues, Features, Lessons	Ethical Issues
Wilson chooses online communication to reach geographically dispersed experts.	Snowball sampling is used. Participants are recruited through referrals and professional networking.	Semi-structured and unstructured interviews	Wilson chooses whatever communications technology is accessible or preferable to the participants in this ongoing study.	Privacy and confidentiality, as appropriate for participant.

References

Kvale, S. (2007). *Doing interviews.* Thousand Oaks, CA: Sage.

Kvale, S., & Brinkman, S. (2009). *InterViews: Learning the craft of qualitative research interviewing* (2nd ed.). Thousand Oaks, CA: Sage.

Salmons, J. E. (2010). *Online interviews in real time.* Thousand Oaks, CA: Sage.

Stake, R. E. (1995). *The art of case study research.* Thousand Oaks, CA: Sage.

Implementing Technology in Blended Learning Courses

10

Nellie Deutsch

Integrating Technology for Active Lifelong Learning (IT4ALL), Toronto, Canada, and Universidad Autónoma de Aguascalientes, Mexico

I conducted a qualitative phenomenological research study to better understand how instructors felt about the technology they were using in blended learning courses. Blended learning may be appealing to instructors in higher education because the combination of the face-to-face and online components allows instructors to continue teaching in the traditional brick-and-mortar classroom and also include elements of e-learning technologies.

In a blended learning modality, instructors and students meet in a face-to-face class for lectures or lab work, but continue interacting with the content, peers, and the instructor in an online learning environment. E-learning technologies such as blogs and wikis or course management systems such as Moodle and Blackboard provide instructors with an online learning environment where they can add lectures, engage students in discussion forums, and post multimedia. Flexible learning environments may facilitate learning because students can continue accessing class lectures and engaging in discussions about the content after the class has ended.

Research Design Overview

The study's purpose was to learn how instructors felt about using technology to complement face-to-face instruction, and what instructional techniques they used to support their students' efforts to bridge the face-to-face live classroom and online learning. Interviews focused on 23 instructors' experiences when implementing technology in blended learning courses in campus-based institutions of higher education in seven countries. Interviews were conducted online using Skype audio and instant messaging system. Online interviews were an appropriate method since research participants use online communications to teach, so they had the skills to access and use the tools needed to participate in the interview.

A qualitative phenomenological study provided a systematic means of developing the interviews, collecting and analyzing the data, and reporting the experiences (Moustakas, 1994). Moustakas's phenomenological approach to gathering and analyzing the data included (1) Epoche, (2) Reduction, (3) Imaginative Variation, and (4) Synthesis (Moustakas, 1994). The Epoche step meant clearing my mind of any of my own experiences or bias in using technology in blended learning courses. Next, I had to make sure the interviewees stayed on the topic, but expressed themselves as freely as possible. The remaining two steps, Imaginative Variation and Synthesis, refer to the manner used for data analysis and interpretive summaries of the information.

ISSUES RAISED IN THE LITERATURE

One of the benefits of blended learning courses is that they can transform the way teachers teach and students learn (Garrison & Vaughn, 2008; Vaughn, 2010). Vaughn (2010) discovered that faculty members who used blended learning benefited in ways that changed the way they taught. Faculty claimed that teaching blended learning courses allowed them to experiment with technology. The process of experimenting with the tools caused the transformation in their teaching (Vaughn, 2010). In contrast, Zhen, Garthwait, and Pratt (2008) found faculty chose to teach online only and spend time learning and experimenting with technology only if they felt it would benefit their students.

A common-sense assumption is that blended learning courses require effective implementation of technology to succeed. In blended learning courses, faculty members may need to use technology in the form of course management systems such as Moodle or Blackboard, live online classes such as Blackboard Collaborate or WiZiQ, or tools such as screen sharing, and audio or video to deliver lessons, clarify assignments, or give feedback. Learning to use such technologies requires time.

Faculty members who teach blended learning courses may face technical, pedagogical, organizational, and personal challenges that may affect their motivation or ability to implement and use technological tools effectively. For example, Vaughn (2010) identified time and compensation for time spent in preparing online courses as a factor that determined whether faculty would adopt technology or not. Yet, a study on faculty adoption of e-learning by Zhen et al. (2008) showed that time was not a factor in determining faculty use of technology in online courses. Given these research findings, interview questions were crafted to elicit interviewees' experiences with benefits and challenges of blended learning, and ways faculty development contributed, or not, to their sense of success with a blended model of instruction.

SAMPLING APPROACH

In purposeful sampling, participant selection is dependent on the participant's abilities to provide information required to learn about the phenomenon. Purposeful sampling was appropriate because of the subjective nature of study in exploring instructors' experiences with integrating technology in blended learning courses. Selected participants were instructors in campus-based institutions of higher education who had taught at least three blended learning courses and had a postgraduate degree status. Only instructors with experience using technology in at least three blended learning courses had the depth of information required to answer the research questions.

Participants were recruited online for this study. The International Human Subjects Research Requirements and guidelines set by the university review board were used to protect the identities and rights of the subjects. I created an online questionnaire on Google Documents to recruit targeted blended learning instructors for the study. The questionnaire was published on two online social networks, Facebook and Ning, in e-learning and blended learning groups of over 2,000 members. The questionnaire included explanations of the purpose, voluntary nature, and confidentiality of the study. Of the 42 respondents who filled in the forms and showed interest in the study, 23 were invited to participate.

Selected participants received a formal invitation to participate in the study. The letter outlined the nature, purpose, and potential risks and benefits of the study; assurance of participant anonymity; and confidentiality of information as well as criteria for participation. The online form provided the initial screening of (1) demographics and (2) teaching experience with and without technology in blended learning programs. These materials also provided participants with an assurance of anonymity and the options for abstaining from participating or answering any of the questions or for withdrawing from the study at any time without penalty or loss of benefit. Research participants provided written permission to record the online interviews with the understanding that none of the information would reveal their identities. All 23 of invited participants contributed data to the study.

INTERVIEW STYLE AND DATA COLLECTION APPROACH

I recruited and interviewed participants online to resolve geographic challenges with international participants and provide them with a familiar and relaxed atmosphere by using technologies similar to those used for instructional purposes. Data were collected by interviewing the participants online through Skype, using audio and video. Text chatting complemented audiovisual communication when the participants wished to add information, such as links to websites or e-mail addresses.

During the recruitment phase, I communicated with the participants through e-mail, and instant messaging via Google chat and Skype. Within 11 days, 45 candidates had completed the online questionnaire. Eight candidates did not fit the criteria because they had not taught at least three blended learning courses in institutions of higher learning. The remaining 37 received e-mails with individualized consent forms with the candidates' full names and the researcher's signature. I selected the first 22 candidates who returned the signed consent forms. I then made appointments via e-mail to discuss the time and choice of instant messaging system for the personal interviews.

I had developed the questions and created an interview guide beforehand. The interview guide helped me organize the questions, ensure uniformity, and determine (1) the sequence, (2) the wording, and (3) the need for clarifications. This pre-interview planning process ensured that questions were crafted in a way that encouraged the respondents to converse freely about the experiences of implementing technology in blended learning courses in higher education.

Participants received a definition of blended learning and a list of questions before the interview. My working definition of blended learning for the purpose of this study was, "teaching a course using face-to-face and an online environment through a course management system." The interview questions participants received beforehand are presented below.

INTERVIEW QUESTIONS

1. How do you feel about technology? Describe your experiences with technology.
2. What do you think of blended learning courses? Tell me about your experiences with blended learning courses.
3. How do you blend the instruction? How much time do you devote to face-to-face and to online instruction? How do you feel about the blend? What feelings or thoughts were generated by the experience of teaching a blended learning course?
4. What kind of technology do you use in your blended learning courses? What experiences have you had implementing technology in blended learning courses?
5. How did the experiences with blended learning affect you or others in your life? How has implementing technology affected you and those in your life? Have you shared your experiences with implementing technology with others?
6. Is there anything else you would like to share about your experiences with technology and blended learning?

Individual interviews followed a semi-structured conversational format to encourage the research participants to share their experiences freely without guidance from the interviewer. The duration of the interviews was approximately 60 minutes each, with follow-ups by e-mail for further inquiry, clarifications, and participant approvals.

Data collection involved personal interviews using the Skype instant messaging (IM) system. Prior to the interview, the respondents received the interview questions as attachments through Skype and were reminded about (1) the recording of the interview, (2) the protection of their anonymity, (3) the storage of the data for 3 years before its deletion, and (4) their right to withdraw from the study at any time. The semi-structured interviews began as social conversations that helped build trust. During the interview, participants were able to use the chat box to send links or websites and to clarify any names that may not have been heard correctly. This helped me later on with the transcriptions because I was able to correctly spell any names or organizations mentioned in the interview.

Interviewing online with the same tools they use to teach provided the instructors with a comfortable way to discuss their teaching practice in general and blended learning courses with technology in particular. Interviewees had the option of using a webcam. Some of the participants asked to use their webcams so I could see them and asked me to do the same. These participants felt the visual exchange helped relieve any tension and helped researcher and participant to get acquainted. Others did not want to turn on their webcams because they felt the webcam would expose them to the very things that would distract them in a face-to-face interview. The participants seemed to have felt very much at ease because they wanted to continue talking even after they answered the last question.

DATA ANALYSIS

With the approval of the participants, I recorded the online interviews using TipCam screen recording software. I transcribed the recordings without changing the words to avoid bias. ATLAS.ti 6.0 computer software provided storage and helped in the coding of recorded interview transcriptions. After listening to the interviews and reading the text transcriptions numerous times, I analyzed the textual data from two perspectives for the purpose of triangulation (Patton, 2002). The first step involved analyzing the data from the perspective of the respondents and the second from the perspective of the interview questions.

Transcriptions of the interviews were analyzed using a process of scanning, coding, and categorization for recurring themes using a modification of the Van Kaam method of analysis of phenomenological data (Moustakas, 1994). The process as prescribed by Moustakas (1994) consisted of seven steps:

1. Horizonalization, or making sure that each statement related to the question asked,

2. Reduction and Elimination or removing information that was not relevant,

3. Clustering and Thematizing the Invariant Constituents, or listing common elements into categories,

4. Final Identification of the Invariant Constituents, or identifying the themes,

5. Relevant, Validated Variant Constituents and Themes, or making a list of the themes,

6. Individual Structural Description, or summarizing each of the responses by relating them to the themes, and

7. Textural-Structural Descriptions, or summarizing the themes.

The phenomenological data analysis process was long, but I was able to understand the whole picture from the individual research participants' descriptions of their experiences. Key themes included participants' perspectives of facilitating instruction and learning and the factors that made blended learning frustrating, satisfying, rewarding, and/or socially connecting.

Interview Experience and Challenges

Phenomenological researchers practice *epoche* in order to listen actively to each interviewee, be attentive to their words, and thus avoid misinterpretations. Epoche means to "stay away from or abstain" from judging things and instead observe things as if for the first time without preconceived ideas (Moustakas, 1994, p. 85). According to Finlay (2008), engaging in epoche prepares the researcher "to be open to whatever may emerge rather than prejudging or prestructuring one's findings" (p. 4). The challenge is to sustain a focus on the phenomenon and on the respondents' experiences and not on the researcher's preconceived notions.

I underwent *epoche* to prepare for each interview. I attempted to reach the state of epoche by practicing "mindfulness meditation" (van Manen, 2002) and "reflection and self-dialogue" (Moustakas, 1994, p. 90) before and during the interviews. I found epoche very useful because it aligned with my experiences with the practice of mindfulness meditation and the Alexander technique.

In a phenomenological research study, interviews focus on people's innermost feelings and viewpoints concerning a phenomenon. I followed the suggestion made by Moustakas (1994) to view the participants as research partners who share and discuss the experience of the phenomenon. The interview questions allowed me to engage in open dialogues but also provided me with a framework. Listening carefully meant each answer was a springboard to further probing questions built on those spelled out in the interview guide.

Research Findings

Analysis of the transcripts of the responses to the interview questions yielded 35 invariant constituents, meaning the words used to describe the experiences. The invariant constituents were clustered into four themes that describe respondents' experiences with implementing technology in blended learning courses:

- The *Facilitating Instruction and Learning* theme encompassed findings that blended approaches help instructors teach and students learn.

- The *Frustrating* theme encompassed findings about instructors' negative feelings about the time it takes to learn to use the tools and manage the face-to-face and online sessions.

- The *Satisfying and Rewarding* theme encompassed findings about instructors' positive feelings toward teaching in a blended learning environment.

- The *Socially Connecting* theme encompassed findings about instructors' perceptions about the use of technology to connect faculty and students online in ways they could not in the face-to-face class.

Thus, it appears that implementing technology into blended learning can be both rewarding and frustrating for the teacher and student. The results of the study indicated that instructors spent a lot of time learning about technology and ways of implementing technology into instruction as well as learning to engage students in the face-to-face and online components of blended learning courses. Still, the instructors were very enthusiastic about technology. This suggests that the same results might be found in a study of fully online courses.

References

Finlay, L. (2008). A dance between the reduction and reflexivity: Explicating the "phenomenological psychological attitude." *Journal of Phenomenological Psychology, 39*(1), 1–32.

Garrison, D. R., & Vaughn, N. D. (2008). *Blended learning in higher education: Framework, principles, and guidelines.* San Francisco: Jossey-Bass.

Moustakas, C. (1994). *Phenomenological research methods.* Thousand Oaks, CA: Sage.

Patton, M. (2002). *Qualitative research and evaluation methods* (3rd ed.). Thousand Oaks, CA: Sage.

van Manen, M. (2002). *Writing in the dark: Phenomenological studies in interpretive inquiry.* Winnipeg, Manitoba, Canada: Hignell.

Vaughn, N. D. (2010). A blended community of inquiry approach: Linking student engagement and course redesign. *Internet and Higher Education, 13*(1–2), 60–65.

Zhen, Y., Garthwait, A., & Pratt, P. (2008). Factors affecting faculty members' decision to teach or not to teach online in higher education. *Online Journal of Distance Learning Administration, 11*(3), 1–16.

CRITIQUE AND ANALYSIS OF DEUTSCH'S "IMPLEMENTING TECHNOLOGY IN BLENDED LEARNING COURSES"

Wendy L. Kraglund-Gauthier

In a qualitative research paradigm, hypothesis testing and replicating results—that is, reliability and validity (Golafshani, 2003)—are not as germane as understanding the research context and identifying the themes that emerge from the data. Furthermore, as Mitchell (as cited in Merriam & Simpson, 2000) argued, "Quantification has no magical property to confer accuracy on the data: if the basic observations are inaccurate or incomplete, statistics derived from them will assuredly also reflect those weaknesses" (pp. 108–109). When using either qualitative or quantitative research methods, or a combination of the two, researchers must take care to design the project properly. In qualitative research, to ensure the trustworthiness, rigor, and quality of results, researchers must have a concise understanding of what is to be studied and know how to accurately implement research methods to collect and interpret data. Nellie Deutsch's conscious, informed decision to approach her data collection and analysis through a qualitative, phenomenological lens is well suited to the nature of her inquiry.

In her research design, Deutsch focused specifically on identifying how instructors in higher education settings integrate technology in their blended learning courses. By framing her research design with constructivist and experiential theoretical approaches, Deutsch was able to emulate the very processes under study. In this case, the interview data has—as Deutsch reports—the potential to reveal participants' innermost feelings and viewpoints when approached with a phenomenological lens. Online interviewing has the potential to capture the experiences of diverse interviewees; the data emerging from the conversations of participants across vast geographical spaces can be rich and revealing.

The immediacy of online interviews in comparison to e-mail and other written forms of communication, coupled with the almost limitless physical boundaries of the Internet translates into an efficient and cost-effective method of collecting data. The challenge may be in balancing the desire for a broad subject pool with the ability to effectively identify and isolate the variables affecting responses and to sift through the volumes of data. In particular, when studying the application of technology in educational processes, a purposeful sampling technique is an important approach. Deutsch's decision to screen individuals based on the number of blended courses taught at the post-secondary level speaks to degree of experience she thought would produce informed interviews. To allow the researcher to guide meaningful conversations, participants must possess prior knowledge of and experience with the phenomenon under study.

As Deutsch intended, interviews can supplement questionnaires and provide a more in-depth sense of participants' interpretation of questions (Ouimet, Bunnage, Carini, Kuh, & Kennedy, 2004). Semistructured interviews allow researchers and participants to explore themes that emerge during interactions. During these interviews, participants have an opportunity to verbalize their comments and concerns about the issue under examination; however, the onus is on the researcher to interpret participant responses accurately and without bias.

In their guidelines for researchers to follow when collecting data from oral interviews, Merriam and Simpson (2000) advised that an electronic recording of the session is a more reliable means of data collection, because handwritten notes can be inaccurate or incomplete. With electronic recordings, researchers can repeatedly review the original information. Deutsch's careful data analysis speaks to the necessity for researchers to set sufficient and adequate time and place aside for their review and interpretation of data. It is only with multiple passes that key themes can emerge clearly from the data. I would also advise the process of "member checking," in which participants review the transcripts to confirm their interview responses match the intent of their words and meanings. As well, it is important to report on any technical problems that may have emerged when connecting with participants; this detail will inform future researchers' planning, preparation, and implementation of online research.

In reading and constructing my commentary for this chapter, I was struck by the parallels between Deutsch's experience in conducting research and my own. Although she focused on blended classrooms and used Skype for interviews, and I focused on fully online classes and used Elluminate for interviews, we were both interested in learning more about instructor experiences. Either platform has the power to reduce the sense of disconnect participants in a less sensoryrich environment may have with the interview or the teaching and learning process. The issue of the "faceless" participant is a concern for many instructors of online courses (Kraglund-Gauthier, Chareka, Murray Orr, & Foran, 2010) and has led to the emergence of blended options for learning. It follows that researchers would also be concerned with creating a social connection with participants at a distance. The emergence of webcams has, quite literally, changed the face of conducting research at a distance. If participants are willing, interviews previously conducted via telephone or e-mail can now be held using instant messaging, voice-over technologies, and visual feeds. As Deutsch discovered in her research, technological tools enable learners "to engage in social communication."

I would have liked more detail on how Deutsch collected the written consent forms. In surveys—online or not—the participant's action of returning the questionnaire signifies consent to participate. As Carini, Hayek, Kuh, Kennedy, and Ouimet (2003) noted in a comparison of web- and paper-based questionnaires, mode does not appear to matter in terms of the depth and breadth of responses. There is, however, a dearth of research on the actual process of conducting research in temporal spaces such as the Internet. As a researcher, I wonder about the extent to which participants and interviewers are affected by the mode of delivery. At what point does technology impact negatively on the process itself? How does a familiarity with the online platform serve to support the sense of comfort and connection required for effective interviews?

Blended learning courses require instructors to balance face-to-face interactions with virtual classroom time. They also require instructors to be comfortable with the mode of content delivery and maintain a constant state of awareness of teaching and learning processes. Both new and experienced blended learning instructors, along with instructional designers (as in my perspective) and program administrators can benefit from such reflective action, following from Lindeman's (1926/1961) statement that "increased inventiveness [is] required to discover the kind of education which will most effectively meet the needs of varying capacities" (p. 18).

Teaching is a personal experience—one that changes with each new group of students. Qualitative research is also a personal experience, conducted in real-world settings. Researchers seek "illumination, understanding, and extrapolation to similar situations" (Golafshani, 2003, p. 600). From Deutsch's perspective of a phenomenological researcher, she has had a glimpse at the blended learning classroom design of her participants, but, equally important, she has had a glimpse at the private teaching moments and experiences of those same participants. By researching and reporting on those experiences, others—instructors and researchers alike—can take up the lessons learned and advance the field of blended and online learning and research.

References

Carini, R. M., Hayek, J. C., Kuh, G. D., Kennedy, J. M., & Ouimet, J. A. (2003). College student responses to web and paper surveys: Does mode matter? *Research in Higher Education, 44*(1), 1–19.

Golafshani, N. (2003). Understanding reliability and validity in qualitative research. *The Qualitative Report, 8*(4), 597–607.

Kraglund-Gauthier, W. L., Chareka, O., Murray Orr, A., & Foran, A. (2010). Teacher education in online classrooms: An inquiry into instructors' lived experiences. *The Canadian Journal for the Scholarship of Teaching and Learning, 1*(2).

Lindeman, E. (1961). *The meaning of adult education.* Montreal, Quebec, Canada: Harvest House. (Original work published 1926)

Merriam, S. B., & Simpson, E. L. (2000). *A guide to research for educators and trainers of adults* (2nd ed.). Malabar, FL: Krieger.

Ouimet, J. A., Bunnage, J. C., Carini, R. M., Kuh, G. D., & Kennedy, J. (2004). Using focus groups, expert advice, and cognitive interviews to establish the validity of a college student survey. *Research in Higher Education, 45*(3), 233–250.

Patton, M. Q. (2002). *Qualitative research & evaluation methods* (3rd ed.). Thousand Oaks, CA: Sage.

CHAPTER 10
FRAMEWORK COMMENTARY:
"IMPLEMENTING TECHNOLOGY
IN BLENDED LEARNING COURSES"

Janet Salmons

In this phenomenological study, Dr. Nellie Deutsch explored the perceptions of blended learning in interviews conducted using Skype. Using purposive sampling, she recruited educators from seven countries who had a common base of experience in blended learning. She chose to conduct interviews online because the participants were geographically dispersed and given the nature of the participants' work she could be assured of their ability to engage in online discussions.

Skype offers visual options with use of a webcam, as well as text chat to complement the audio conversation. For this study, most of the participants did not use the webcam and she did not collect visual data.

As an online and blended learning educator herself, Deutsch understands the use of varied online tools for teaching and learning. As a phenomenological researcher, she was careful to practice epoche, which means she intentionally cleared her mind of preconceptions before each interview. Thus, she experienced the study with research participants as a gardener role (Salmons, 2010), seeding and supporting the growth of conversation in the interview, but taking an *emic*, external perspective (Stake, 1995).

Deutsch found that while the instructors experienced some challenges when they had to learn a new tool, most of the instructors were very positive about the use of technology and seemed to prefer the online side of the blended learning experience.

Figure 10.1 Research map for "Implementing Technology in Blended Learning Courses."

Theories from discipline or field of study

Contructivism

Experiential learning

Theories

Theories

Influence

Influence

Methodologies

Phenomenological

E-Research Methods

Qualitative

Interviews

Synchronous interviews

Questionnaire

Demogaphic and background info

To explore the experiences instructors had implementing technology in blended learning courses in campus-based institutions of higher education.

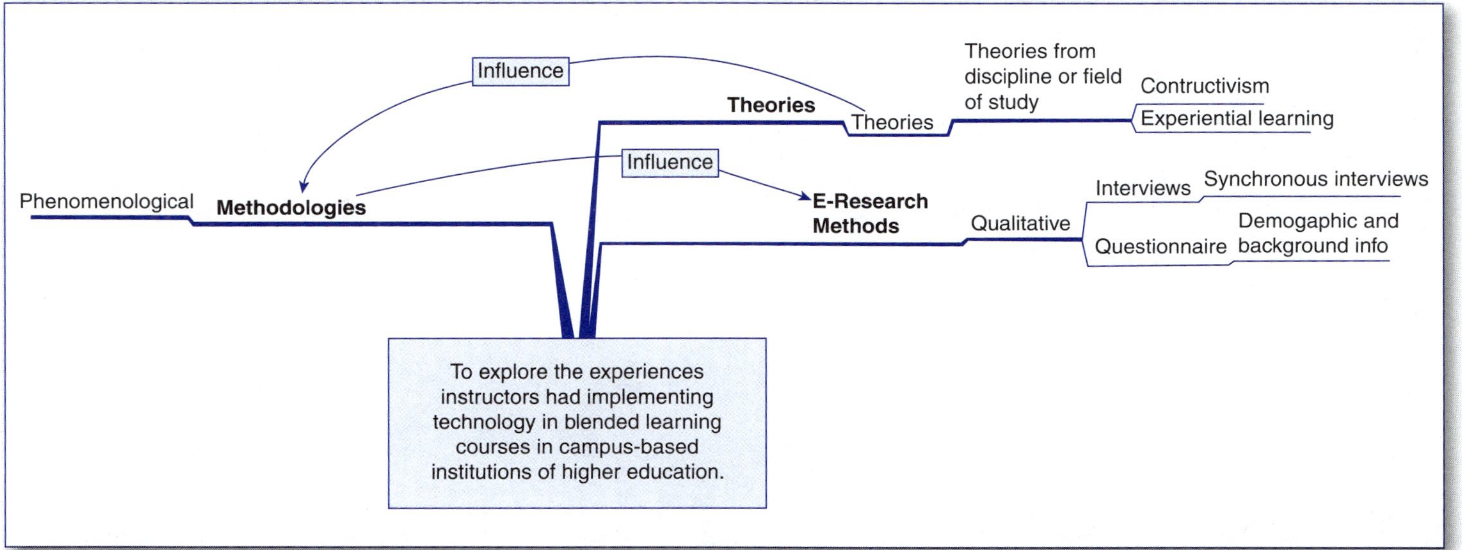

Table 10.1	Summary: Key Factors in the "Implementing Technology in Blended Learning Courses" Study

Motivation for Choosing E-Research	Sampling and Recruiting	Interview Style and Structure	Technology: Issues, Features, Lessons	Ethical Issues
Deutsch chose to conduct interviews in Skype, a free, easy-to-use means to communicate, with an international sample.	Purposeful, criterion-based sampling was used. Participants were recruited online, through membership lists of established groups.	Semi-structured individual interviews	Audio and text interactions were used.	No risks to participants were evident.

References

Salmons, J. E. (2010). *Online interviews in real time*. Thousand Oaks, CA: Sage.
Stake, R. E. (1995). *The art of case study research*. Thousand Oaks, CA: Sage.

Online Asynchronous and Face-to-Face Interviewing

11

Comparing Methods for Exploring Women's Experiences of Breastfeeding Long Term

Sally Dowling
University of the West of England, Bristol, UK

The use of combined methods to understand more about experiences is established in qualitative research (Flick, 2009). Traditionally, ethnographers have used participant observation, in-depth interviews, and other face-to-face (F2F) methods to further understanding about the people and groups they study (Hammersley & Atkinson, 2007). Increasingly, researchers from many disciplines have used the Internet as a research tool to investigate diverse topics. The discussion here concerns a comparison between two of the three methods used in a recent study: face-to-face synchronous and online asynchronous interviews. A small body of work has compared their use (see, for example, Curasi, 2001; Meho, 2006); this chapter aims to contribute further by considering a number of issues, related both to the method and to the subject matter.

Discussion and comparison of the use of different types of interviewing will highlight some advantages and disadvantages of each.

277

The relational aspects of the two methods will be particularly considered. Questions asked included the following: Can online interviews create as good a relationship as those conducted F2F? Is the online method more appropriate, or even better, for researching sensitive subjects and conducting insider research? Or are the two interchangeable, the online interview simply another way of conducting an in-depth focused research exchange? I question whether I would conduct the research differently another time and talk about the experience of using these two methods in this situation.

Early work on the use of the Internet in qualitative research rarely focused specifically on the use of the online asynchronous interview, discussing it with other methods of computer-mediated communication (CMC) such as online surveys, focus groups, or participant observation in virtual communities (Kanayama, 2003; Meho, 2006). Some discussed asynchronous and synchronous methods alongside each other (Mann & Stewart, 2000), with others making a clearer distinction between those methods relating to participants in "real" time (if not space) and those in which there is no temporal relationship (James & Busher, 2009). Variously called e-interviews (Bampton & Cowton, 2002), e-mail interviews (Hamilton & Bowers, 2006; Kivits, 2006; Meho, 2006; Murray & Sixsmith, 1998), online interviews (Mann & Stewart, 2000; Salmons, 2010), correspondence (Kralik, Koch, & Brady, 2000), and e-mail correspondence (Dowling, 2009a; Orgad, 2005), the technique of conducting extended interviews using e-mail is increasingly used. In contrast to the work discussed in the present study, in other examples of online interviewing the Internet has been both the subject of the research, the medium for recruiting participants, and the primary method used to communicate with participants (Kanayama, 2003; Kivits, 2005).

Asynchronous online interviewing does not necessarily use e-mail; interviews can take place via a research website, where participants log in to receive or send messages (James & Busher, 2009), threaded discussion forums, or text messaging programs that deliver a message the next time the user logs in (Salmons, 2010). There are a number of key differences, both from other methods using the Internet and from F2F interviews. These have been summarized by others (Bampton & Cowton, 2002; Meho, 2006; Murray & Sixsmith, 1998) and will be explored further in the context of this discussion. In brief, distinctions unique to e-mail interviewing include the way it involves multiple private exchanges between the interviewer and interviewee. These exchanges are not usually shared with other participants. Also, the e-mail exchanges between researcher and participant might take place over some considerable period of time. E-mail interviews allow for participation at the interviewee's convenience; participants do not need to be in the same place (or even the same country); the interview can take place at the pace of the respondent; and it is possible (although this requires forethought) to be truly anonymous (particularly advantageous to participants in research addressing sensitive or possibly illegal behavior). The medium also allows for the revision of responses and for participants to have a greater ownership of the narrative (James & Busher, 2009).

Research Purpose and Questions

Interviews took place in the context of a study with the primary aim of exploring the experiences of women who breastfeed long term in the United Kingdom (UK). Participant observation in breastfeeding support groups and face-to-face and asynchronous online interviews with breastfeeding women were used over a period of 14 months. "Long-term breastfeeding" was defined as longer than 6 months; less than 25% of women in the UK breastfeed for this length of time (Bolling, Grant, Hamlyn, & Thornton, 2007) in comparison with 43% in the United States (Centers for Disease Control and Prevention, 2010). The recommendation from the World Health Organization (WHO) is that all children, after being exclusively breastfed for 6 months, receive their mother's milk alongside complementary foods up to the age of 2 years or beyond (World Health Organization & UNICEF, 2003). Good research evidence confirms the benefits of breastfeeding for babies, children, and mothers.[1]

My interest in conducting this research arose both from my own experience as a long-term breastfeeder and from my background in public health. Thus, the research was conducted from an insider perspective, as I was breastfeeding throughout research design, data collection, and analysis. I was interested in increasing understanding of the experience of women who continue to breastfeed after most around them have stopped. Long-term breastfeeding is misunderstood and censured in many Western cultures (Smale, 2001), with the result that it is often carried out in secret or in limited settings (Battersby, 2007; Britton, 2003). It can thus be seen as a sensitive issue, as discussed by Renzetti and Lee (1993). Theoretical issues of liminality, stigma, and taboo were used to think about the experience of long-term breastfeeding; however, this chapter will focus primarily on the methods used to collect data.

Research Design Overview

GUIDING THEORIES AND METHODOLOGY

This work was underpinned by specific beliefs about research, the appropriateness of methods and conduct, and how findings are used and disseminated; thus, feminist approaches influenced choices of methodology and methods. Feminist research has emphasized the importance of exploring women's (often otherwise invisible) experiences and using this knowledge to challenge positivist claims about knowledge (Brooks & Hesse-Biber, 2007). Ethnographic research has been said to be the most suitable approach for exploring breastfeeding women's experiences (Cricco-Lizza, 2007), with a "phenomenological approach informed from feminist methodologies" proposed as the most appropriate (Spencer, 2008, p. 1823). Madge & O'Connor (2005) also suggest that the Internet is a particularly suitable site for exploring feelings about motherhood.

The use of methods (usually in-depth F2F interviews) that recognize both the importance of the participants' and the researcher's experience (most notably discussed by Oakley, 1981) is often highlighted in feminist research (Hesse-Biber, 2007). The researcher is encouraged to be open about, and use, her own perspective in the research (Brooks & Hesse-Biber, 2007). These were important considerations as my experience was central to research design, data collection, and analysis. Using a grounded theory approach, the iterative nature of data collection and analysis allowed thematic categories to arise from the data as the research progressed. These were later used as a lens through which to view the data in subsequent analysis and writing phases.

SAMPLING AND RECRUITMENT

The original research design did not include the intention to interview via e-mail; I became aware of this method after participant recruitment had begun. A growing understanding of the potential of correspondence (Kralik et al., 2000), and how this might be conducted via the medium of an online interview (Kivits, 2005), opened up the possibility of also using e-mail to extend the interview opportunity to more participants. In particular, I was attracted to the idea of creating a "critical reflective conversation" (Kralik et al., 2000, p. 911) and to the way in which the method was built on ideas of reflexivity and collaboration. Three women who had offered to take part in F2F interviews were asked to participate instead in what I then referred to as e-mail correspondence (after Kralik et al., 2000) but have come to think of as in-depth online asynchronous interviews.

Women were recruited using purposive and snowball sampling. A letter describing the project was posted in the e-newsletter of the local La Leche League (LLL) group[2] to give information about participant observation I would conduct in meetings and to recruit participants for interviews. The Internet was not used in any other way to recruit participants in this project, mostly because the intention was to conduct small-scale work and local recruitment was considered adequate. Five women contacted me as a result of this letter (two were interviewed F2F; three online); two women were contacted by other interviewees (one interviewed F2F; one online); and two women were recruited for F2F interviews via the participant observation groups and one further woman (F2F interview) was recruited using personal networks. A total of six women were interviewed F2F and four online; this data complements that gained through contact with more than 80 women via participant observation in three breastfeeding support groups on 21 occasions over 14 months (Dowling, 2009b).

All participants were anonymized, all interviews digitally recorded and fully transcribed, and all e-mails copied into Word documents. All documents, transcripts, and field notes were imported into NVivo for data management and to facilitate thematic analysis.

The Participants

Participants included women in heterosexual and lesbian relationships, single parents, those in full- and part-time work, and full-time mothers. The two interview groups were similar although with some differences. Those interviewed online had higher educational qualifications (three had doctorates, one a first degree; two out of four were in paid work), compared with those interviewed F2F (three out of six were educated to first-degree level; only one was in paid work). Online interviewees had breastfed for between 14 months and

6 1/2 years and had only one child each. Those interviewed F2F had breastfed 11 children for between 18 months and 4 1/2 years; some also had experience of breastfeeding during pregnancy and of tandem nursing.[3] Online interviewees were older (35 to 47, mean age 40) compared to F2F (27 to 42, mean age 33). At the time of data collection, I was breastfeeding my 3-year-old daughter and was closest in age to those interviewed online. I had very brief previous contact with one of the online interviewees (although we had not spoken), and I had never met the other three. In contrast, I had met all but one of the F2F interviewees before (in breastfeeding support groups). Most interviewees lived in the same city as I did; two lived elsewhere but in the same geographical area.

DATA COLLECTION

Online Interviews

Four online interviews were carried out for between 3 and 6 months (February to August 2008). The intention was to allow the participants to explore with me their breastfeeding experience during an open-ended period, my e-mails also contributing to the final body of data. All the women were sent the same opening e-mail in which I told them a little about myself and my breastfeeding experience and invited them to respond with some information about themselves. I tried to use this e-mail to establish an open and friendly rapport:

> I'm anticipating that we might do this for a few months but we can review it as we go along and I'd like it if you could tell me if you are finding it too onerous or feel that you need to stop for any other reason. . . . Please don't feel that you have to answer all this at once, or even at all. Tell me what you feel comfortable with and we can take it from there. (Sally, e-mail to all, January 28, 2008)

After this introductory e-mail, the relationship with each woman developed at a different pace; some responded very quickly while others took more time.

Principles Underlying the Online Work

Adapting the work of Kralik et al. (2000), I developed a set of underlying principles with which to approach interviews. It was felt particularly important to respond in a timely, respectful, and thoughtful manner, which in practice meant that I tried to reply within 24 hours. I told participants when I was not going to be able to do this and gave them some idea of when to expect a response. I also tried not to respond too hastily, considering their e-mails and formulating a response that both recognized and built on what they had said. I embarked on the process with a belief that it was impor-tant that I too talked about my experience as a long-term breast-feeder (and so did this where it felt appropriate), feeling that this was an element of the reciprocal and reflexive nature of the data genera-tion (Kralik et al., 2000). I took care also to forewarn the participants of the ending of the research relationship. The interviews appeared to be drawing to a conclusion at a time when I was about to take a planned summer break; I ended each interview gradually but left the possibility open for further contact if necessary.

F2F Interviews

Six F2F interviews were carried out over a period of 7 months (November 2008 to June 2009). These took place in the interviewees' homes at times and on dates agreed to by them. Five interviews were arranged via e-mail; one by telephone. Five out of six interviewees e-mailed beforehand introducing themselves and their breastfeeding experience; this information was used to open the interviews and establish rapport. E-mail was thus used with both groups as a way of introducing the research aims and objectives as well as to establish relationships and set the scene for what was to follow. Interviews took between 50 and 70 minutes, often taking place with children present and were carried out using an interview guide.

Technology Choices and Rationale

Asynchronous online interviews were chosen for a number of rea-sons. The method was seen as particularly attractive for women with young children: While the F2F interviewees were often dis-tracted (as was I) by the presence of their children and others, online interviewees could respond at suitable times and at their own pace (and often commented on how they were writing late at night, or while a child napped). The use of e-mail rather than F2F interaction allowed for more thoughtful and considered responses than were possible in the sometimes distracting interview settings. In the same way, I was also able to consider my questions and comments differently as well as being able to fit my participation more comfortably into a busy life.

In some ways, this can be seen as the most elementary use of technology (see other contributions to this volume for examples of more advanced applications), but it does require participants to have some skill with CMC and with e-mail (Mann & Stewart, 2000). Although its use has been criticized as excluding those without this familiarity, this is felt to be increasingly less of an issue with more pervasive use of e-mail for social and family communications. The participants and I were all confident in using e-mail and in expressing ourselves via text. Using text-based CMC for interviewing requires consideration of the precise form that this may take: Mann and Stewart note the need to be aware of the use and meaning of electronic paralanguage (such as "hehehe" and "lol") as well as conventions such as the use of capitals or underlining to indicate emphasis (2000, pp. 134–135). Emoticons are used in multiple forms of text-based communication, and the Internet researcher may need to be sensitive to their use in interviews and adapt their style to suit that of the interviewee. Mine did not use anything other than conventional English; where terms or abbreviations with which I was unfamiliar were used, I asked for clarification.

Online interviewing is cheap—although it was far more time-consuming than I had anticipated. Its use eliminates the need to transcribe documents and thus also reduces both time and costs.

Ethical Issues and Approaches

Ethical approval was obtained from the Research Ethics Committee (REC) of my university before data collection commenced. The use of online interviews had not been considered initially, and so I reapplied to the committee to ask for approval to add this to data collection. The use of e-mail appeared to be seen as less problematic than other forms of Internet research; proposals to the same committee at other times in relation to using discussion groups and other online settings have not been approved, or approval has had restrictive conditions attached. Approval was granted and information sheets and consent forms altered to take account of the change. All F2F interviewees were given written information about the project and signed a consent form in my presence; online interviewees were sent the information sheet along with an explanatory e-mail. Consent forms were returned via e-mail in three cases and a physical copy posted in the fourth. E-mailed consent forms were printed (including the senders e-mail address) and kept with all research documentation in a locked file cabinet.

Gaining informed consent can raise specific issues in online research. These include the opportunity for participants to deceive researchers through changing their identity or even assuming multiple identities (James & Busher, 2009). The freedom of participants to choose when they participate, particularly in asynchronous interviews, can also leave the researcher unsure if consent has been withdrawn (Hodgson, 2004, cited in James & Busher, 2009, p. 64).

Internet research frequently uses online methods to recruit participants. This can raise important questions in relation to consent; often, a number of contacts have taken place *before* the consent form is signed, or a "consent e-mail" received. Personal information may have been exchanged and all parties need to be clear when the project (and therefore the consent) has begun. While early e-mail exchanges in this project allowed for development of rapport, data were not collected before consent was signed. Information gathered in this phase could be seen to have contributed to my understanding of each woman's experience; in future research projects I will consider addressing this during the process of gaining consent.

A well-designed research project should protect both participants *and* researcher from harm. Miller and Boulton (2007) suggest that researchers may not always consider what they *themselves* are consenting to when they embark on a research relationship. The confidentiality of the researcher's views or personal information may not be considered beforehand. In this project, I revealed personal information to the online interviewees (to a far greater extent than I did in FTF interviews or in participant observation). I did not discuss with participants what they might do with this information, but at no stage judged this to be a problem (although I would consider this further in future projects).

Interview Experience and Challenges

I did not consider interviewing the same participants both FTF and online although others have done this and found it beneficial. Orgad interviewed informants online and then face-to-face, considering that the latter method enabled stories to be told in "greater depth" (2005, p. 57). I considered them different but complementary methods; reflecting on them during the writing of this chapter has enabled me to think more about this complementarity than I did during the process.

CHALLENGES IN F2F INTERVIEWS

In all but one of the F2F interviews, there were other people present for at least some of the time. This is perhaps inevitable when interviewing women with babies and young children, but it was distracting. Judging each situation and deciding how to maximize the chances of getting a "good" interview meant that I often had to work hard at concentrating and maintaining the interaction and flow.

Putting participants at their ease and creating rapport happens in a relatively short space of time with a F2F interview. Factors such as body language, tone of voice, and eye contact are extremely important in relationship building. This was aided by the fact that I had met four of the interviewees previously and that we had exchanged pre-interview e-mails. All women knew beforehand that I was also a breastfeeding mother. This common bond helped with establishing the interview relationship although I was also aware that it could potentially lead to assumptions about participants' beliefs and parenting practices—which would fall outside the scope of this study.

As a mother of young children, I frequently found that factors like fatigue affected my ability to carry out the interviews. I sometimes found it hard to concentrate and to listen fully. In particular, it was difficult when I thought of something I wanted to ask and then forgot it when the opportunity arose later to ask it! Listening to the recordings and reading the transcripts, I realized that I did not always pick up on interesting points. I could have requested follow-up interviews but decided not to, mainly because I had also heard most of the women talk about their breastfeeding experiences in support groups during participant observation and used this to help build up a fuller picture of their experiences.

It was sometimes difficult to judge how much disclosure was appropriate. Carrying out insider research carries with it both benefits and difficulties in relation to data collection (Chavez, 2008). Drawing on my interest in feminist approaches to qualitative methods, I made an early decision that I would never hide my own identity as a long-term breastfeeder and that, whenever it felt appropriate, I would share my experiences (Oakley, 1981). My breastfeeding experience arose in all interviews but more as a common interest and less as part of the data generation (as it had been in the online interviews). It felt more awkward in the FTF interviews, perhaps because of the time and other constraints and, interestingly, open and honest disclosure felt easier in online interviews. There is no doubt that my insider status facilitated access; however, I tried to minimize the risk of bias through reflexive writing, doctoral supervision, and honesty with participants (Dowling, 2009b).

CHALLENGES IN ONLINE INTERVIEWS

Carrying out the online interviews was very different from the experience of carrying out the F2F interviews. Establishing a relationship took more time, although with e-mail interviews there is (usually) plenty of time to allow this to develop (James & Busher, 2009). Lack of physical cues and the necessity of adapting one's personal style to each participant can lengthen the process. Keeping each one interested in the research and engaged with the process is also important and considerable time was invested in this. Responding to personal information given, acknowledging the time involved, and using encouraging words and phrases all helped to sustain the research relationships. With one participant, this was harder than with the others, as contact was sporadic and she found it difficult to find time to be involved, working full-time, with a young child and a second pregnancy:

> I'm sorry it has taken so long to reply about your research. I really do want to do it, I've just been tired with this pregnancy and to be honest I keep forgetting about it. (Judith, e-mail to Sally, March 1, 2008)

We each responded to e-mails in our own time (no parameters were set, although this would be a consideration for future work), and there were advantages in this to both researcher and participants. The asynchronous nature of the communication gave time to reflect on my responses and for the women to fit participation into their daily lives. In contrast to the FTF interviews, women were able to find space to be alone and have time to think. E-mail enabled participants to start a reply, save it, and return to it before sending it (as could I), sometimes days after it was started. For example,

> I am starting this e-mail at 10 at night, while waiting for John to get to a point in his computer game that he can leave and go to bed. So I will probably finish it tomorrow. (note, it is now the day after tomorrow!) (Christine, e-mail to Sally, March 12, 2008)

As I result of using this strategy myself to reduce the effect of my fatigue, I think I was more fully present in these e-mail interviews than the FTF ones, and that this is reflected in the nature of the data obtained.

Kivits (2005) points out that asynchronous communication is particularly suited to the reflective process and thus to the qualitative research project; James and Busher (2006) also comment on this, noting that the reflexivity of the online interview helps to ensure rigor. The nature of the interaction meant that we could revisit what had been said before, either to change or comment further. Some participants did this more than others. E-mail also allows for documents to be attached in addition to the body text sent (Kivits, 2005), and I received letters, articles written for publication, and web links. These were also copied into NVivo and used as part of the data set.

Kivits has also described the process of carrying out e-mail interviews as an "unusual, even sometimes troubling, research relationship" (2005, p. 35). I found this to be true in a number of specific ways. Kivits noted the difficulty in interpreting e-mail "silences," or nonresponses, in the context of qualitative interviews, as have others (Hodgson, 2004, cited in James & Busher, 2009, p. 64; Kivits, 2005). I found this aspect of the process difficult, particularly when a respondent who had previously replied promptly did not do so. I was often torn between wanting to send a reminder and a desire to respect a participant's right to take part or not on whatever terms suited them. I tried to strike a balance, sometimes sending a gentle prompt if a response had taken longer than usual, while trying not to exert pressure. It was hard to manage my feelings about nonresponses. As a novice to this method, I worried that I might have alienated a participant in some way by what I had written, that I was asking for too much, or was in some way "doing it wrong."

Another difficult aspect was the way in which some interviewees appeared sometimes to be using the process almost as therapy. This was not an issue in the FTF interviews, possibly because the prolonged relationship-building aspects of the online interviews facilitated a much more intimate exchange. Boundary blurring has been noted as a potential risk when carrying out qualitative interviews, particularly on sensitive issues and where the participant may have had no other outlet for talking about the topic (Dickson-Swift, James, Kippen, & Liamputtong, 2007, 2009). One interviewee noted this herself:

> This whole process has been very interesting for me. We started our correspondence at a time when I was reaching a breaking point and felt that something had to change. Writing about my experience was quite therapeutic. . . . It has helped me that I don't know you. . . . I probably would have edited myself if I had known you. I have been very open and sometimes it strikes me that you know more about my breastfeeding experience and how I have felt about it than any other person! I started out being open because I wanted you to have the information and data you would need and then I think it took a turn as I started working through my breastfeeding relationship. (Sarah, e-mail to Sally, July 29, 2008)

There were other times when I, perhaps naively, was surprised by aspects of the process. Intending to correspond with my participants in an open-ended and reciprocal way, with ideas about the co-creation of data, I thought that participants would see it in the same way— and, of course, this was not always so. One participant fully entered into the relationship in the way I anticipated, with long e-mails reflecting honestly and openly on her experience, raising issues as well as responding to points that I had made. Two others responded at times like this but sometimes as if they were taking part in a more structured interview than was intended, responding to a question and then waiting for another to be posed. The fourth interviewee also had elements of both styles but was very brief. The extended period of the asynchronous online interview can lead to an easier/ freer disclosure of personal information (Kivits, 2005), but I learned that this was something that needed to be worked on and to a certain extent depended on interviewees perceptions of what was required. This remained throughout, however much I worked at trying to change the way individual interviews developed.

The group of women interviewed online were highly educated. Two were currently working as academic researchers and were very keen to provide me with "good" data:

> As I really am not able to get much academic work done I am quite happy to participate in someone else's research. . . .
> I just write everything I can think of hoping that within it there will be something of use to you. I work on literary texts primarily and think of my e-mails as providing you with a text. (Sarah, e-mails to Sally, January 30, and February 27, 2008)

While this was beneficial, contributing to the fullness of some responses, the insight into the research process may also have been restraining.

Research Findings

In brief, findings from this research have furthered knowledge about what it is like to breastfeed long term in a culture that is unsupportive of this practice. Although I had not anticipated this, the fullest and richest data were obtained from the online interviews. Many of the same topics were addressed by F2F and online interviewees, but the prolonged nature of the contact with the latter meant that issues were explored in more depth, returned to over time, and explored through the relationship with the interviewer. It also seemed that women interviewed online felt more able to be critical or negative about their experiences than women interviewed F2F.

Participants found a variety of sources of support, including partners and friends, although the greatest was from belonging to groups of other, like-minded women. For most, these were F2F sources of support (LLL and other groups), but for some, support from online communities was very important. Many women appeared to belong to supportive subcultures, where their decision to breastfeed long term was one of a number of out-of-the-mainstream parenting practices adopted, such as co-sleeping or home educating. Some expressed shock or disappointment that health professionals were especially unsupportive of their parenting choices, including long-term breastfeeding. Many talked about how lack of support, even hostility, came from extended families (especially in-laws).

Online interviewees were generally more open about the difficulties they had with long-term breastfeeding, particularly where they felt strongly that they had made the "right" choice (to breastfeed long term), but when it conflicted with their own needs (for personal space or with a desire to work, for example), FTF interviewees were less likely to talk about difficulties overtly. Many, however, talked about an awareness of others' censure and described a range of strategies they used to manage this. Strategies were particularly employed around breastfeeding in public, although "public" was variously interpreted and included breastfeeding in front of relatives in the home (Dowling, Naidoo, & Pontin, in press).

Lessons Learned and Recommendations

The experience of using both asynchronous online and F2F interviews has been interesting and fruitful. Although others have not always been so successful (Hodkinson, 1999, quoted in Mann & Stewart, 2000, p. 131), in this case richer and fuller data were generated through online interviews. This could be because of the prolonged nature of the contact, leading to the exchange of more personal information such as details of everyday lives and feelings in addition to material specifically focused around the research topic, and thus creating overall a more intimate exchange (Kivits, 2005). Relationships in the online interviews felt more equal; with FTF interviews there was a power differential (despite intentions to the contrary). With online interviewees, some of the exchanges felt more akin to friendship; I recognize that this could be because their lives were very similar to mine and we had multiple points of contact. My lack of experience may have negatively influenced the FTF interviews, whereas with the online exchanges I had time to learn and to refine my practice. In retrospect, I feel that I should have returned to the F2F interviewees and undertaken additional interviews—or followed up the contacts with e-mails to clarify issues. In most cases, our contact was simply not long enough. Interesting data were collected, but without the richness and depth of that from the online interviews.

The embodied nature of the topic was, interestingly, explored to the greatest extent using the disembodied medium of e-mail. In F2F interviewing, there is a reliance on an ability to put people at ease relatively quickly, to interpret social cues, and to use one's own skills with language (verbal and nonverbal) to create a situation that will facilitate the exchange of useful information (Flick, 2009; Hesse-Biber, 2007). In online interviews, the ability to use text is relied on to create the right conditions in which people will want to confide details of their lives. The former uses the body as an essential element; the latter privileges the mind and the ability to use words, with the physical body absent from the exchange. In online interviews more than in FTF interviews, however, I made greater use of information about my own body, with more disclosure about my own experiences and day-to-day life as a breastfeeding woman. This may have been one important factor in increasing the value of these interviews.

Exploring issues related to the experience of the milk in their bodies and of nurturing and nourishing their children, as well as the relationship of their bodies to those around them both in private and in public thus appeared easier for the women using text-based communication. Other successful Internet-based projects have also focused on issues of and about the body, such as experiences of using Internet support groups for breast cancer, Alzheimer's disease, colorectal cancer, or eating disorders (Eysenbach & Till, 2001), or exploring gay men's use of the Internet to seek sex (Davis, Bolding, Hart, Sherr, & Elford, 2004). This experience confirms that the Internet may be a particularly good medium for conducting research into sensitive topics (Mann & Stewart, 2000).

Experience gained from carrying out this project would lead me to proceed differently in future online work. These points may be of value to other researchers. Carrying out an interview online is a temporally uncertain undertaking and this can be hard to manage (James & Busher, 2006; Kivits, 2005). I would be more prepared for this in the future. Discussing with participants how they might use the information they receive as well as what will happen to the information they give is also an important and easily neglected consideration, along with other issues of consent.

Interviewing F2F might feel more familiar and possibly "safer," but interviewing online can provide valuable data on experiences and feelings and allow for fruitful research relationships to develop. I would argue that the creation of deeper, more personal relationships is possible through e-mail interviewing and that this is an appropriate method for exploring issues of a sensitive or personal nature. Used in conjunction with, or instead of FTF interviews, asynchronous online interviewing is a valuable tool for qualitative researchers.

See the Appendix for suggested readings and resources on the software, methodologies, and methods discussed in this case.

Find More Materials on the Study Site! See the book website for related resources, materials, discussion, and assignment ideas.

Notes

1. Breastfeeding is an important public health issue; two recent reviews summarize the evidence for the long-term health benefits of breastfeeding (Horta, Bahl, Martines, & Victora, 2007) and for breastfeeding in developed

countries (Ip et al., 2007). Artificially fed babies are more at risk of gastro-intestinal infection, respiratory infections, necrotizing enterocolitis, urinary tract infections, ear infections, allergic disease (eczema and wheezing), insulin-dependent diabetes mellitus, sudden infant death syndrome, and childhood leukemia (McNeil, Labbok, & Abrahams, 2010; UNICEF, 2010). Breastfeeding also has health benefits for mothers, with good evidence that it reduces the risk of premenopausal breast cancer (Collaborative Group on Hormonal Factors in Breast Cancer, 2002), ovarian cancer, hip fractures, and loss of bone density (UNICEF, 2010). Other benefits for babies and mothers are also hypothesized with more research needed in these areas (UNICEF, 2010). In many places, encouraging women to breastfeed is less of a problem than supporting and enabling them to carry on; thus initiation rates are often high but fall off very quickly (Bolling et al., 2007; Centers for Disease Control and Prevention, 2010).

   2. La Leche League (http://www.llli.org/), established more than 50 years ago, is the world's foremost breastfeeding support organization. With its focus on "mother-to-mother support" and child-led weaning, it is an attractive community to many women who choose to breastfeed their children "long term."

   3. Tandem feeding/nursing is when a mother breastfeeds two children at once—usually a baby and an older child—having breastfed throughout the pregnancy of the youngest and then continuing to breastfeed both (see Flower, 2003).

References

Bampton, R., & Cowton, C. J. (2002). The e-interview. *Forum Qualitative Sozialforschung/Forum: Qualitative Social Research, 3*(2). Retrieved October 10, 2010, from http://www.qualitative-research.net/index.php/fqs/article/view/848/1843

Battersby, S. (2007). Not in public please: Breastfeeding as dirty work in the UK. In M. Kirkham (Ed.), *Exploring the dirty side of women's health* (pp. 101–114). London: Routledge.

Bolling, K., Grant, C., Hamlyn, B., & Thornton, A. (2007). *Infant feeding survey 2005.* Retrieved March 2, 2010, from http://www.ic.nhs.uk/webfiles/publications/ifs06/2005%20Infant%20Feeding%20Survey%20%28final%20version%29.pdf

Britton, C. (2003). Breastfeeding: A natural phenomenon or a cultural construct? In C. Squire (Ed.), *The social context of birth* (pp. 305–317). Abingdon, UK: Radcliffe Medical Press.

Brooks, A., & Hesse-Biber, S. N. (2007). An invitation to feminist research. In S. N. Hesse-Biber & P. L. Leavy (Eds.), *Feminist research practice: A primer* (pp. 1–24). Thousand Oaks, CA: Sage.

Centers for Disease Control and Prevention. (2010). *Breastfeeding report card—United States, 2010.* Retrieved October 13, 2010, from http://www.cdc.gov/breastfeeding/data/reportcard.htm

Chavez, C. (2008). Conceptualising from the inside: Advantages, complications and demands on insider positionality. *The Qualitative Report, 13*(3), 474–494.

Collaborative Group on Hormonal Factors in Breast Cancer. (2002). Breast cancer and breastfeeding: Collaborative reanalysis of individual data from 47 epidemiological studies in 30 countries, including 50302 women with breast cancer and 96973 women without the disease. *Lancet, 360,* 187–195.

Cricco-Lizza, R. (2007). Ethnography and the generation of trust in breast-feeding disparities research. *Applied Nursing Research, 20*(4), 200–204.

Curasi, C. F. (2001). A critical exploration of face-to-face interviewing vs. computer-mediated interviewing. *International Journal of Market Research, 43*(4), 361–375.

Davis, M., Bolding, G., Hart, G., Sherr, L., & Elford, J. (2004). Reflecting on the experience of interviewing online: Perspectives from the Internet and HIV study in London. *AIDS Care, 16*(8), 944–952.

Dickson-Swift, V., James, E. L., Kippen, S., & Liamputtong, P. (2007). Blurring boundaries in qualitative research on sensitive topics. *Qualitative Health Research, 16*(6), 853–871.

Dickson-Swift, V., James, E. L., Kippen, S., & Liamputtong, P. (2009). Researching sensitive topics: Qualitative research as emotion work. *Qualitative Research, 9*(1), 61–79.

Dowling, S. (2009a). Inside information: Researching long-term breastfeeding. *The Practising Midwife, 12*(11), 22–26.

Dowling, S. (2009b). Women's experiences of long-term breastfeeding. *The Practising Midwife, 12*(10), 22–25.

Dowling, S., Naidoo, J., & Pontin, D. (in press). Breastfeeding in public: Women's bodies, women's milk. In P. L. Smith, B. Hausman, & M. Labbok (Eds.), *Beyond health, beyond choice: Breastfeeding constraints and realities.* New Brunswick, NJ: Rutgers University Press.

Eysenbach, G., & Till, J. E. (2001). Ethical issues in qualitative research. *British Medical Journal, 323,* 1103–1105.

Flick, U. (2009). *An introduction to qualitative research* (4th ed.). Thousand Oaks, CA: Sage.

Flower, H. (2003). *Adventures in tandem nursing: Breastfeeding during pregnancy and* beyond. Schaumberg, IL: La Leche League International.

Hamilton, R. J., & Bowers, B. J. (2006). Internet recruitment and e-mail interviews in qualitative studies. *Qualitative Health Research, 16*(6), 821–835.

Hammersley, M., & Atkinson, P. (Eds.). (2007). *Ethnography: Principles in practice* (3rd ed.). London: Routledge.

Hesse-Biber, S. N. (2007). The practice of feminist in-depth interviewing. In S. N. Hesse-Biber & P. L. Leavy (Eds.), *Feminist research practice: A primer* (pp. 111–148). Thousand Oaks, CA: Sage.

Horta, B. L., Bahl, R., Martines, J. C., & Victora, C. G. (2007). *Evidence on the long-term effects of breastfeeding: Systematic reviews and meta-analyses.* Geneva: World Health Organization.

Ip, S., Chung, M., Raman, G., Chew, P., Magula, N., DeVine, D., et al. (2007). *Breastfeeding and maternal and infant health outcomes in developed countries.* Retrieved June 7, 2010, from http://www.ahrq.gov/downloads/pub/evidence/pdf/brfout/brfout.pdf

James, N., & Busher, H. (2006). Credibility, authenticity and voice: Dilemmas in online interviewing. *Qualitative Research, 6*(3), 403–420.

James, N., & Busher, H. (2009). *Online interviewing.* Thousand Oaks, CA: Sage.

Kanayama, T. (2003). Ethnographic research on the experience of Japanese elderly people online. *New Media and Society, 5*(2), 267–288.

Kivits, J. (2005). Online interviewing and the research relationship. In C. Hine (Ed.), *Virtual methods: Issues in social research on the Internet* (pp. 35–49). Oxford, UK: Berg.

Kivits, J. (2006). Informed patients and the Internet: A meditated context for consultations with health professionals. *Journal of Health Psychology, 11*(2), 269–282.

Kralik, D., Koch, T., & Brady, B. M. (2000). Pen pals: Correspondence as a method for data generation in qualitative research. *Journal of Advanced Nursing, 31*(4), 909–917.

Madge, C., & O'Connor, H. (2005). Mothers in the making? Exploring liminality in cyber/space. *Transactions of the Institute of British Geographers, 30*(1), 83–97.

Mann, C., & Stewart, F. (2000). *Internet communication and qualitative research: A handbook for researching online.* London: Sage.

McNeil, M. E., Labbok, M. H., & Abrahams, S. W. (2010). What are the risks associated with formula feeding? A re-analysis and review. *Birth, 37*(1), 50–58.

Meho, L. I. (2006). E-mail interviewing in qualitative research: A methodological discussion. *Journal of the American Society for Information Science and Technology, 57*(10), 1284–1295.

Miller, T., & Boulton, M. (2007). Changing constructions of informed consent: Qualitative research and complex social worlds. *Social Science and Medicine, 65*(11), 2199–2211.

Murray, C. D., & Sixsmith, J. (1998). E-mail: A qualitative research medium for interviewing? *International Journal of Research Methodology, 1*(2), 103–121.

Oakley, A. (1981). Interviewing women. In H. Roberts (Ed.), *Doing feminist research* (pp. 30–61). London: Routledge.

Orgad, S. (2005). From online to offline and back: Moving from online to offline relationships with research informants. In C. Hine (Ed.), *Virtual methods: Issues in social research on the Internet* (pp. 51–65). Oxford, UK: Berg.

Renzetti, C. M., & Lee, R. M. (1993). *Researching sensitive topics.* Newbury Park, CA: Sage.

Salmons, J. E. (2010). *Online interviews in real time.* Thousand Oaks, CA: Sage.

Smale, M. (2001). The stigmatisation of breastfeeding. In T. Mason, C. Carlisle, C. Watkins, & E. Whitehead (Eds.), *Stigma and social exclusion in healthcare* (pp. 234–245). London: Routledge.

Spencer, R. (2008). Research methodologies to investigate the experience of breastfeeding: A discussion paper. *International Journal of Nursing Studies, 45*(12), 1823–1830.

UNICEF (United Nations Children Fund). (2010). *The health benefits of breastfeeding.* Retrieved July 19, 2010, from http://www.babyfriendly.org.uk/page.asp?page=20

World Health Organization & UNICEF. (2003). *Global strategy for infant and young child feeding.* Geneva: Author.

CRITIQUE AND ANALYSIS OF DOWLING'S "ONLINE ASYNCHRONOUS AND FACE-TO-FACE INTERVIEWING: COMPARING METHODS FOR EXPLORING WOMEN'S EXPERIENCES OF BREASTFEEDING LONG TERM"

Nellie Deutsch

Breastfeeding always seemed natural to me because it was accepted in my family. However, the subject of prolonged breastfeeding or even breastfeeding itself is a sensitive subject for most women. Some women feel that breastfeeding should not be out in the open and perhaps hidden from the public eye. In West Auckland, New Zealand, mothers staged a "breastfeeding protest" (Wade & Irvine, 2010) after a mother was asked to stop breastfeeding in a restaurant because some of the customers complained to the owner.

Discussing personal experiences is not easy for many people, but discussing a controversial subject such as breastfeeding long term must be difficult for most women. Although breastfeeding is a natural and healthy process, disclosing information about the subject is not as easy as one may think.

Sally Dowling conducted a research study involving long-term breastfeeding. She compared women's experiences of the phenomenon as they described it in face-to-face and online asynchronous interviews. In her study, Dowling considered the advantages and disadvantages of online versus face-to-face interviews. The author interviewed 10 women who had experiences with long-term breastfeeding. Six women were interviewed face-to-face and four were interviewed by e-mail. In addition, Dowling had observed over 80 women for a period of over 14 months. According to Dowling (2009), the findings from the observations correlated with what the women had said in the interviews.

As I read the case study, I understood the importance of connecting with research participants to gain trust. Having the participants trust the researcher is of paramount importance because it allows participants to be open to sharing personal experiences. In addition, the fact that the researcher was also breastfeeding must have facilitated the process and helped her gain the trust of the women in the study.

The case study provides valuable information about the benefits of both the face-to-face and asynchronous online interviews. Dowling mentions that there were noticeable distractions in the face-to-face interviews, while in the online asynchronous e-mail interviews there were not. Perhaps the subjects were distracted, but the researcher was not there to help them refocus on their responses.

In reading the case study, I deduced that there is a great deal of pressure on the interviewer to be focused in the face-to-face interaction, but perhaps less so in the asynchronous meetings where time and place are not relevant. There is no need to set a specific time for the e-mail, but appointments are required for the face-to-face interviews. The interviewer needs to be more spontaneous in the face-to-face meeting because the respondent's answers are not predictable and there is need to pay careful attention to the questions and answers. It's not always possible to plan all the questions. There is more time to think, for both researcher and participants, in the asynchronous interviews.

Ethical issues may be the hardest to overcome in online interviews. I had a difficult time convincing my committee to approve the online meetings. One of the questions I was asked was whether I would recognize who was speaking and whether their identity would be real. In addition, I had to ensure that nothing could be manipulated with technology. In other words, I had to prove that the recordings were just as authentic as they would be in a face-to-face recording. In Dowling's case, approval was granted quite easily.

Dowling raises excellent points in her discussion on online recruiting. In my doctoral dissertation on instructor experiences with implementing technology in blended learning courses, I also had issues with online recruiting. My research committee asked me to prove that the participants signed a consent form before the online interviews. I had to add the consent agreement to the online forms for the participants to sign. Dowling also mentions the importance of signing the consent form before any information is passed on to the researcher. Dowling's online forms for recruiting participants asked for information from the participants. Would it be ethical to ask for information about the participants' demographics before the participants signed the consent forms?

According to Dowling, personal information provided from both the subjects and the researcher should be protected. The researcher provided personal information about prolonged breastfeeding practices. Sharing such information publicly takes a great deal of courage, but I believe it also has many benefits. For one, the participants feel more at ease sharing their experiences on a sensitive topic if they know the interviewer has undergone or is undergoing the same experiences. Knowing that the researcher is involved and understands encourages more than openness and trust, it also has the potential to be educational if it brings the topic to public attention. Perhaps long-term breastfeeding will be discussed more publicly if qualitative studies are conducted on the topic and more women speak openly about it.

On the other hand, being involved personally in any research topic may cause the researcher to be biased. To gain insights with less risk of researcher bias, future research on the topic should include studies by external researchers.

One way of gaining a close and open discussion and reducing researcher bias is through online interviews by means of e-mail. Unlike the synchronous online or face-to-face interviews, where the interviewer can use probing or leading questions, the e-mail exchange process can distance the interviewer and allow both researcher and participant time to think more carefully about the questions and answers. As Dowling mentions, "E-mail enabled participants to start a reply, save it, and return to it before sending it (as I could), sometimes days after it was started." The author concludes that the "fullest and richest data were obtained from the online interviews." From my doctoral research study, I also found that online interviews were very open, created friendships, and were therapeutic for both the interviewer and interviewee.

References

Dowling, S. (2009). Women's experiences of long-term breastfeeding. *The Practising Midwife, 12*(10), 22–25.

Wade, A., & Irvine, K. (2010, December 4). Mums stage breastfeeding protest. *New Zealand Herald.* Retrieved from http://www.nzherald.co.nz/amelia-wade/news/article.cfm?a_id=693&objectid=10691982

CHAPTER 11
FRAMEWORK COMMENTARY: "ONLINE ASYNCHRONOUS AND FACE-TO-FACE INTERVIEWING: COMPARING METHODS FOR EXPLORING WOMEN'S EXPERIENCES OF BREASTFEEDING LONG TERM"

Janet Salmons

In this grounded theory study, Sally Dowling explored experiences of nursing mothers and compared methods of data collection by either face-to-face or e-mailed interviews. She chose to try e-mail exchanges with participants after reading several published studies that described the value of thoughtful reflection between question and response. She used purposive and snowball sampling and recruited participants within the established sample frame of a local chapter of an organization that serves the target population. So while she used online recruitment for the study, e-mail was sent only to members and friends of the La Leche organization. A determination of whether the participant was interviewed online or F2F was made based on the participant's availability and preferences.

Participants, given the nature of the study, are mothers of small children, so convenience and timing of the interview were critical. E-mail interview answers could be given any time, and that proved to be beneficial to this study.

As a researcher and nursing mother, Dowling was immersed in the research phenomenon. She could raise issues and questions only someone within the case might identify. She joined the study from the emic stance and as a fellow traveler (Kvale, 2007; Kvale & Brinkman, 2009; Stake, 1995). She openly describes the study as "insider research" and felt comfortable revealing information about her own experiences to participants, but did not directly contribute data to the study.

Neither group of participants (online or F2F) presented, generated, or shared visual data; visual exchange was apparently not part of this study. Dowling did note that "lack of physical cues and the necessity of adapting one's personal style to each participant can lengthen the process." However, the lengthier process may have ultimately been its strength. These points are interesting in the context of Media Richness Theory (Daft & Lengel, 1986), since this study

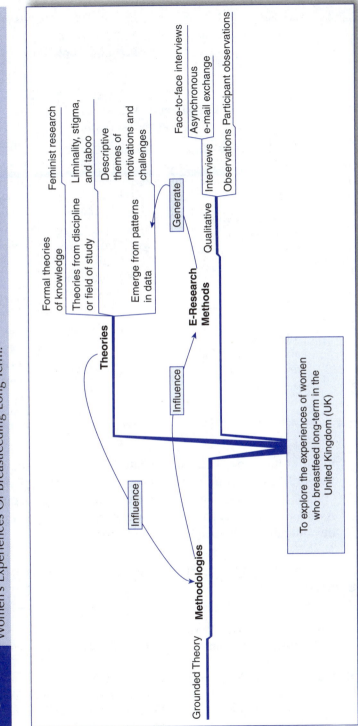

Formal theories of knowledge

Feminist research

Theories from discipline or field of study

Liminality, stigma, and taboo

Descriptive themes of motivations and challenges

Emerge from patterns in data

Theories

E-Research Methods

Generate

Influence

Qualitative

Face-to-face interviews

Asynchronous e-mail exchange

Interviews

Observations Participant observations

Influence

Methodologies

Grounded Theory

To explore the experiences of women who breastfeed long-term in the United Kingdom (UK)

Table 11.1	Summary: Key Factors in the "Online Asynchronous and Face-To-Face Interviewing: Comparing Methods for Exploring Women's Experiences Of Breastfeeding Long Term" Study

Motivation for Choosing E-Research	Sampling and Recruiting	Interview Style and Structure	Technology: Issues, Features, Lessons	Ethical Issues
Dowling chose to conduct interviews online for the convenience of research participants.	Purposive and snowball sampling were used. Participants were recruited online, through membership lists of established groups. Online interviewing allowed for wider recruitment of participants.	Semi-structured individual and group interviews	E-mail interviews were used to complement face-to-face interviews and participant observation.	Research Ethics Committee did not see e-mail as problematic in terms of human subjects. Online interviewees were sent the information sheet along with an explanatory e-mail, and consent forms were returned by e-mail.

includes both the "rich," immediate F2F exchange and the "lean," text-only asynchronous exchange; yet Dowling reports that the "fullest and richest data were obtained from the online interviews." As she notes, this is particularly intriguing in research that focused on a literally "embodied" research phenomenon.

References

Daft, R. L., & Lengel, R. H. (1986). Organizational information requirements, media richness and structural design. *Management Science, 32*(5), 554–571.

Kvale, S. (2007). *Doing interviews.* Thousand Oaks, CA: Sage.

Kvale, S., & Brinkman, S. (2009). *InterViews: Learning the craft of qualitative research interviewing* (2nd ed.). Thousand Oaks, CA: Sage.

Stake, R. E. (1995). *The art of case study research.* Thousand Oaks, CA: Sage.

PART IV

REFLECTIONS ON E-INTERVIEW RESEARCH

Building the Bike While Riding It **12**

Creating E-Interview Methods While Conducting Research
A Meta-Synthesis of the Cases

Janet Salmons

The 10 cases presented in this book apply e-interview techniques in a multiplicity of ways to achieve each researcher's unique purpose. Contributors were selected using an approach akin to theoretical sampling. They were each chosen to represent a particular e-interview research construct or approach (Miles & Huberman, 1994; Patton, 2002). Rather than choose a number of similar exemplars that used the same kinds of technologies or methodologies, contributions were selected on the basis of "maximum variation sampling" to purposefully locate alternatives that have emerged as researchers have adapted to varied and changing conditions (Miles & Huberman, 1994; Patton, 2002). Since selection criteria related to the data collection methods without regard to research purpose, the resulting collection of chapters spans disciplines including psychology, education, health, science, and business. A collective analysis of these 10 cases is offered here to draw instructive lessons from the plans, challenges, and outcomes from e-interview approaches used to collect data for these diverse studies.

Naturally, these researchers did not set out to study e-interview research; they set out to study some problem or phenomenon with data collected from interviews they chose for their own reasons to conduct online. Once selected, each contributor was invited to create a case study about his or her research, using a template provided by the editor.

A Meta-Synthesis of the Cases

Quantitative researchers use meta-analysis to synthesize and reanalyze the data or findings from multiple studies. Qualitative researchers sometimes encounter a similar need, but reject statistical analysis as inappropriate for a study of qualitative research. McCormick and colleagues stake a position on the potential for qualitative meta-analysis.

> We take the position that, rather than providing a means to greater "truth," qualitative meta-analysis is another "reading" of data, an opportunity to reflect on the data in new ways. It does not necessarily provide more accurate or truthful accounts by virtue of having more data, collected by multiple researchers in different settings. Nevertheless, there are significant advantages in being able to draw on qualitative data across a number of studies that, we believe, cannot be realized in single studies. (McCormick, Rodney, & Varcoe, 2004, p. 936)

Weed proposes "development of a *meta-interpretation* approach to the interpretive synthesis of qualitative research." He observes that "the value of a synthesis can perhaps be determined by the extent to which it is synergistic, the extent to which it produces insights that are more than the sum of the parts" (Weed, 2005). Walsh discusses the use of the term "qualitative meta-synthesis," coined by Stern and Harris (Stern & Harris, 1985), to describe amalgamation of a group of qualitative studies:

> Their aim was the development of an explanatory theory or model which could explain the findings of a group of similar qualitative studies. This highlights one of the key differences between this method and meta-analysis of quantitative studies. The latter aims to increase certainty in cause and effect conclusions in a particular area, while the former is more hermeneutic, seeking to understand and explain phenomena. (Walsh, 2005, p. 204)

This chapter draws from the qualitative meta-analysis, meta-interpretation, and meta-synthesis styles described by these authors. The E-Interview Research Framework (see Figure 12.1) is used here to organize a comparative analysis and synthesis of the 10 cases collected in this book.

Framework for
Understanding E-Interview Research

Figure 12.1 Organization of the E-Interview Research Framework.

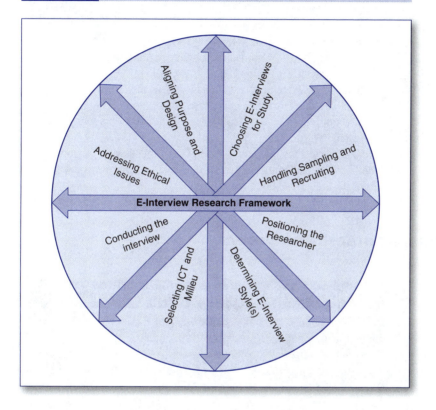

TEN STUDIES BASED ON DATA
COLLECTED FROM E-INTERVIEWS

- "Blog Like An Egyptian" by Sally Bishai
- "Stranger in a Strange Land: The Challenges and Benefits of Online Interviews in the Social Networking Space" by Allison Deegan
- "Interviewing in Virtual Worlds: An Application of Best Practices" by Jonathan Cabiria
- "Beneficial Interview Effects in Virtual Worlds" by Ann Randall

(Continued)

(Continued)

- "Learning to Work In-World: Conducting Qualitative Research in Virtual Worlds Using In-Depth Interviews" by Taryn Stanko and Jonathon Richter
- "Guides and Visitors: Capturing Stories in Virtual-World and Interactive Web Experiences" by Patricia Wall, Jonas Karlsson, Zahra Langford, Tong Sun, Wei Peng, Eric Bier, Christian Overland, Mike Butman, Suzanne Fischer, and Lisa Korzetz
- "Transitioning From F2F to Online Instruction: Putting the Action into Online Research" by Wendy L. Kraglund-Gauthier
- "Integrated Interdisciplinary Online Interviews in Science and Health: The Climate and Health Literacy Project" by Lynn Wilson
- "Implementing Technology in Blended Learning Courses" by Nellie Deutsch
- "Online Asynchronous and Face-To-Face Interviewing: Comparing Methods for Exploring Women's Experiences of Breastfeeding Long Term" by Sally Dowling

Aligning Purpose and Design

KEY QUESTIONS: ALIGNING PURPOSE & DESIGN

- Are research purpose, theories and epistemologies, methodologies and methods clearly aligned?
- How will the data collected from e-interviews relate to theories? Does the researcher want to explore, prove, or generate theory?
- Does the researcher offer a compelling rationale for using e-interviews to achieve the research purpose?

Contributing authors provide a glimpse of the range of qualitative methodologies that can frame studies that are carried out using online interview data. Respective chapters represent ethnography, phenomenology, case study, feminist, and action research. Given the book's focus on the data collection methods and limitations on chapter length, contributors did not provide details on all aspects of the research design. However, information offered shows that researchers went through full approval procedures at their respective institutions and were successful at providing a rationale that explained how and why online interviews aligned with their research purpose and methodologies.

Three studies used grounded theory methodologies and were designed to generate new theory. Of these, two developed theoretical constructs related to online, specifically, virtual-world behaviors (see Figures 12.2 and 12.3). Both of these studies, in addition to generating constructs related to the researchers' fields of study (psychology, virtual work), also generated theoretical constructs on the nature of identity and relationships between humans and avatars, generally, and as research participants, particularly.

A third case to propose new theory focused on behaviors in the real world (see Figure 12.4). Bishai proposed a theory to explain the negative dialogical state people experience when dealing with acculturation.

Choosing E-Interviews as a Data Collection Method for the Study

KEY QUESTIONS: CHOOSING E-INTERVIEWS

- Does the researcher provide a compelling reason for using data collected from online interviews? Is the rationale aligned with methodologies, research purpose, and questions?
- Are online interviews chosen to investigate real-world phenomena?
- Are online interviews chosen to investigate online phenomena?

The researchers represented in this book chose e-interviews instead of face-to-face or telephone interviews for various reasons. Some of the issues involved in this choice are summarized in Figure 12.5. Six chose to conduct interviews in the environment where the behaviors or phenomena of interest occur. Two (Cabiria and Randall) were interested specifically in online research, so reflexively explored the methods they were using. Two (Kraglund-Gauthier and Deutsch) were interested in online learning; one (Kraglund-Gauthier) conducted the research in the same environment used for e-learning classes.

Four contributing researchers chose to conduct interviews online to discuss behaviors that occur offline. They chose e-interviews to bridge geographic distances (Bishai and Wilson), to ease participation for busy mothers (Dowling), or to accommodate participants' preference to spend free time in social networking communities (Deegan).

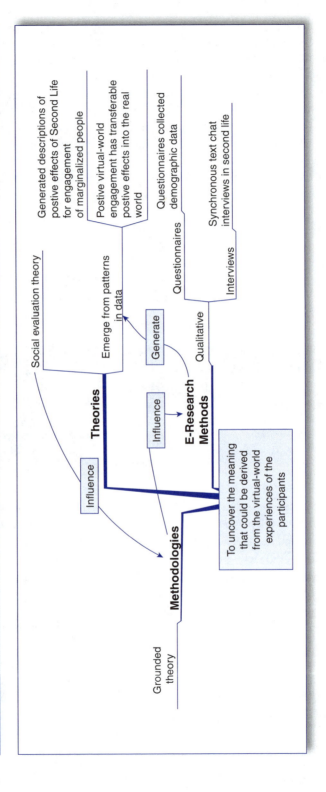

Figure 12.2 Design map for "Interviewing in Virtual Worlds: An Application of Best Practices" by Jonathan Cabiria.

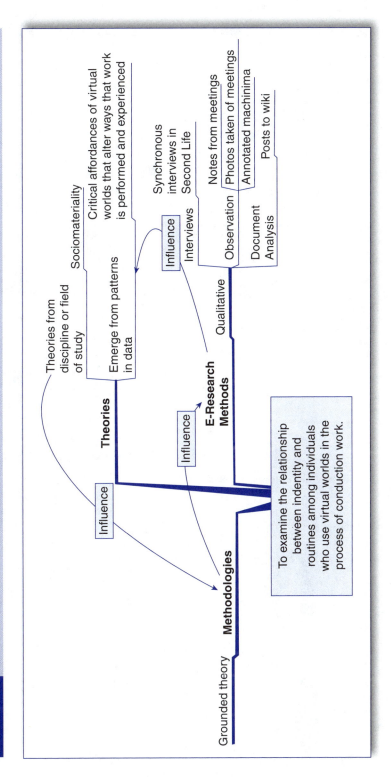

Theories from
discipline or field
of study

Sociomateriality

Critical affordances of virtual
worlds that alter ways that work
is performed and experienced

Emerge from patterns
in data

Theories

Influence

Synchronous
interviews in
Second Life

Influence

Interviews

Notes from meetings

Photos taken of meetings

Annotated machinima

Posts to wiki

Observation

Document
Analysis

Qualitative

**E-Research
Methods**

Influence

Influence

Methodologies

Grounded theory

To examine the relationship
between indentity and
routines among individuals
who use virtual worlds in the
process of conduction work.

Figure 12.4 Design map for "Blog Like An Egyptian" by Sally Bishai.

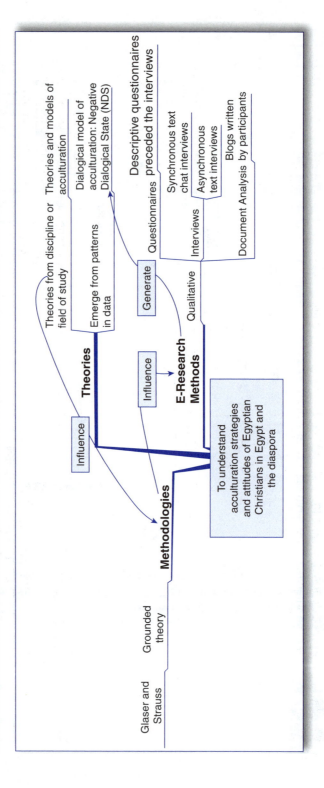

Figure 12.5 Additional questions to consider before choosing e-interviews as a data collection method.

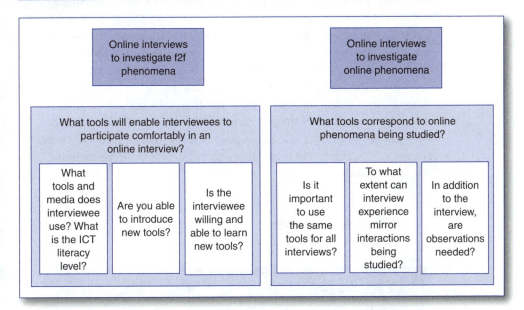

Handling Sampling and Recruiting

KEY QUESTIONS: HANDLING SAMPLING & RECRUITING

- What sampling approaches are appropriate given the purpose of the study and e-interview approach?
- How will the researcher assess whether the target population has access to the interview technology and the capability and willingness to use it as a research participant?
- How can the researcher locate credible research participants? How will the researcher verify the identity and age (or other relevant criteria) of research participants recruited online?
- How will online recruitment be carried out?

Existing sample frames in the manner of lists or access to formal or informal group memberships or affiliations were used widely for participant recruitment. Five researchers (Bishai, Wilson, Deegan, Dowling, Wall et al.) had face-to-face contact with at least some of their research participants prior to online interviews. As a result, authenticity of participants was not in question. Four more (Randall, Deutsch, Kraglund-Gauthier, Wall et al.) recruited participants from programs, projects, or groups or e-mail lists for professional organizations. Again, authenticity of participants was not a concern. Cabiria, while using extant lists of professional educators, was skeptical of volunteers' credibility, and so instituted a triangulation approach to allow for cross-verification of demographic data.

One of the dangers in online interviewing is the ease of withdrawal using a simple click to close the interview conversation window. However, none of the researchers reported significant problems with no-shows or dropouts. This point speaks to the success of these researchers' recruitment approaches and efforts to build participants' commitment to the study.

Positioning the Researcher

KEY QUESTIONS: POSITIONING THE RESEARCHER

- Is the researcher positioned as an insider, as one of the actors in the case? Is the researcher looking at *emic* issues, revealed by actors in the case (Stake, 1995)?
- Is the researcher positioned as an outsider who brings questions in from outside the case, looking at *etic* issues (Stake, 1995)?
- Can the researcher's role be described as miner, traveler (Kvale, 2007; Kvale & Brinkman, 2009), or gardener (Salmons, 2010)?

None of the researchers took a fully outsider, etic stance. This may be a characteristic of qualitative research generally, but all of the researchers indicated at least some degree of insider perspective. At the far end of the spectrum three researchers self-identified as actors in the case being researched. As insiders they used social capital, networks, and specialized knowledge of the research phenomena and context to not only recruit willing participants but to engage them (see Figure 12.6).

Some members of the Wall team contributed data as research participants while others did not. Six of the researchers (or research teams) noted that they shared characteristics and some level of insider knowledge, but they did not contribute data and made efforts to bracket pre-research knowledge.

Given the slant toward insider, or emic perspectives in this collection of studies, it is probably not surprising that the researchers

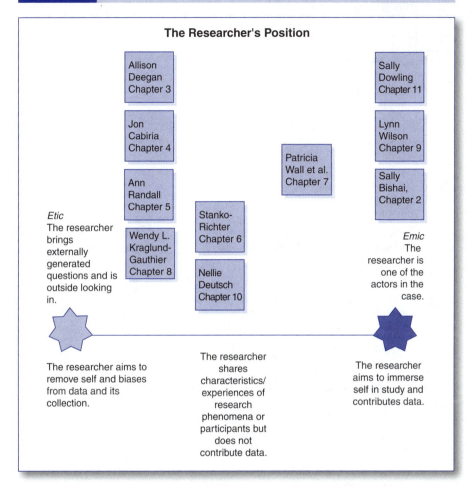

Figure 12.6   Insider/outsider position of the researchers.

chose to travel with or garden with research participants (see Figure 12.7). In all of the cases, to conduct online interviews the researchers had to learn about, join, and become immersed in the online communications medium in order to converse with participants. Bishai, Wilson, and Dowling all made choices about information and communications technologies (ICTs) and interview protocols based on preferences and convenience of participants. The four researchers or research teams studying virtual worlds (Cabiria, Stanko and Richter, Randall, Wall et al.) had to create an avatar and build virtual spaces or travel into the virtual world inhabited by participants.

As travelers, researchers could see and surface issues from actors within the case. As gardeners, many of the researchers cultivated

| Figure 12.7 | Positioning of the researchers as travelers, gardeners, or miners. |

- Stanko-Richter, Chapter 6
- Wall et al. Chapter 7
- Wendy L. Kraglund-Gauthier, Chapter 8
- Lynn Wilson, Chapter 9
- Sally Dowling, Chapter 11

• Sally Bishai, Chapter 2 • Jon Cabiria, Chapter 4 • Ann Randall, Chapter 5	• Allison Deegan, Chapter 3 • Nellie Deutsch, Chapter 10	
Metaphor: Travel with . . .	**Metaphor: Garden with . . .**	**Metaphor: Excavate from . . .**
The researcher as a *traveler* who journeys with the participant to discover insights.	The researcher as a *gardener,* who plants the seeds of the interaction with a question, and cultivates a response with follow-ups, prompts, and encouragement.	The researcher as a miner who digs out facts and feelings from research participants.

relationships that extended beyond a single interview interaction. It could be said that overall this collection of studies bridged etic and emic. By traveling with and gardening with participants, researchers gained new perspectives on issues, concerns, and priorities from the view of actors in the cases. At the same time, researchers brought in external, disciplinary questions and needs for new knowledge about or understanding of the phenomena at the center of inquiry.

Determining E-Interview Style(s)

KEY QUESTIONS: DETERMINING E-INTERVIEW STYLE(S)

- Does the researcher plan to use *structured, semi-structured, unstructured,* or a combination of styles for the interviews?
- How does the researcher align ICT functions, features, and/or limitations with the selected e-interview style(s)?

Semi-structured and unstructured interviews were the dominant styles of interview chosen by the contributors to this book. Several researchers collected data in more than one way (with question-naires) or using more than one interview. In such cases, one interaction was typically more structured; that interaction was used to collect more background or demographic information. Four of the researchers (Dowling, Wilson, Bishai, Randall) chose to use unstruc-tured, conversational interviews.

Bishai, Deegan, Cabiria, Richter and Stanko, and Dowling con-tinued conversations over numerous interactions with partici-pants. These used asynchronous (e-mail) or near-synchronous (post and respond) technologies. Bishai, Cabiria, and Dowling studied sensitive, personal matters, and through multiple interac-tions built the trust and rapport needed for participants to openly discuss their feelings and perceptions. Their choices are mapped

Figure 12.8 Level of interview structure in cases (Salmons, 2010).

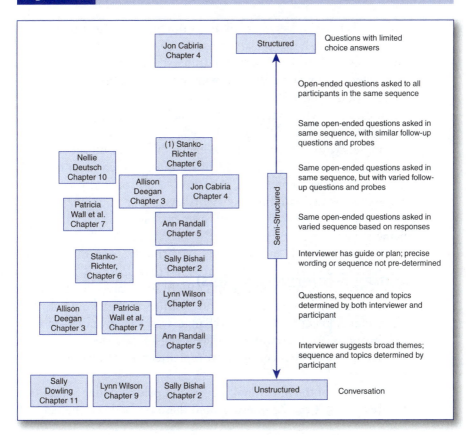

out in Figure 12.8. Some researchers are noted twice to reflect that fact that they used different approaches in various stages of the interview(s).

Selecting Information and Communication Technology (ICT) and Milieu

KEY QUESTIONS: SELECTING ICT & MILIEU

- Will the interview use text-based, audio, and/or visual communication options?
- Where will the interaction fall on the *Time-Response Continuum?*
- Will the interview setting be in a public or private online milieu?
- Is the choice of ICT aligned with research purpose, interview style, and access/preference of the research participants?

The book is organized into parts to differentiate the studies conducted with text-based social media (Bishai and Deegan), the studies conducted with text or voice and immersive environments (Cabiria and Randall) or simulations/evaluations of virtual environments (Stanko and Richter, Wall et al.), and studies conducted using a combination of web conferencing, e-mail, and face-to-face tools (Kraglund-Gauthier, Wilson, Deutsch, Dowling). As noted, the researchers who investigated phenomena that occur offline were less particular about the ICT selected, often opting for whatever technology the participants preferred, knew how to use, or could access. The researchers studying online behaviors, events, or phenomena chose to conduct interviews in the environment, platform, or technology being studied.

The selected ICTs and the ways participants used them meant the researchers communicated in ways that spanned the Time-Response Continuum (see Figure 12.9). In some cases, the researchers wanted synchronicity but found that the multitasking habits of participants meant that the exchange was synchronous or near synchronous. Sally Dowling and Lynn Wilson had the opportunity to have face-to-face meetings to complement asynchronous e-mail exchanges.

Almost all of the interviews occurred in private online spaces (see Figure 12.10). It can be inferred from these researchers' choices that

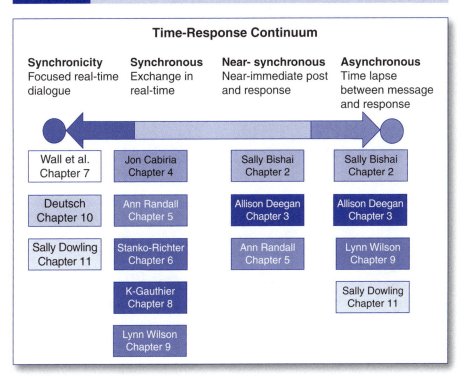

Figure 12.9 Cases positioned on the Time-Response Continuum.

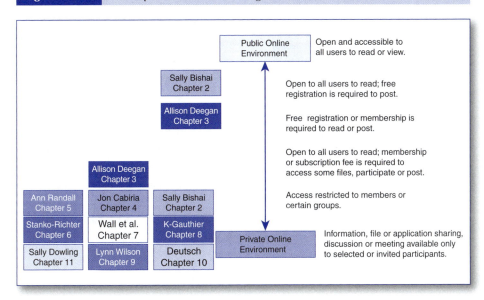

Figure 12.10 Cases positioned according to research milieu.

privacy is essential for in-depth interviews. In some cases, these spaces were specifically created for the purpose of the study. Wall et al. created an OpenSim. Stanko and Richter's research was part of the process for developing a virtual world, called the Collaboratory, for exclusive use as an online research milieu. The two researchers who used social media (Bishai and Deegan) communicated in semiprivate chat spaces.

Conducting the Interview

KEY QUESTIONS: CONDUCTING THE INTERVIEW

- Does the researcher have a plan for conducting the interview with either prepared questions or an interview guide?
- Does the researcher have a plan for the 4 interview stages: opening, questioning and guiding, closing, and following up?
- Does the researcher have a contingency plan in case there are technical difficulties?

Although some of the contributors are novice researchers, no one reported significant problems in the nuts and bolts of the actual interview. All were prepared with interview questions, guides, or topics. No one encountered participant dropouts or noncooperation. All were able to successfully collect data needed to complete the study— for some, more data was collected than anticipated. This suggests that the technologies did not present an impediment to the real dynamic of interviewer–interviewee rapport at the heart of the in-depth interview.

The most pertinent point to emerge from the cases related to interview conduct is the need for flexibility. Almost every researcher reported the need to change ICT or interview approach due to some kind of technical or access issue. The most notable was the situation faced by Deegan, who found herself "banned" from the Facebook community where she had not only the chat space for the interview but also the contact information for otherwise anonymous participants. Clearly, interviewers using proprietary spaces are most vulnerable.

Addressing Ethical Issues

KEY QUESTIONS: ADDRESSING ETHICAL ISSUES

- Has the researcher taken appropriate steps to protect human subjects, and where appropriate, their avatars or online representations?
- Has the researcher obtained proper informed consent?

Contributing researchers all had to gain approval from some kind of institutional review board and/or approval process. For many, the reviewers' lack of experience with or knowledge of e-interview research was the major obstacle. Multiple tries, and in some cases redefining or translating key terms allowed them eventually to gain the permission to conduct the research. Cabiria, Stanko and Richter, and Randall not only conducted their interviews in Second Life, but also reflexively explored virtual-world research issues for those who would interview avatars. Their discussions of the rights of avatars and protection of not only the human subject but the human subject's online identity will be important for future researchers.

Conclusions

The 10 cases collected in this volume provide a glimpse of possibilities and challenges, emerging best practices, and unanswered questions related to online interview research. Contributors to this book each truly built the bike while riding it. As individuals or research teams, they took nothing for granted and questioned the why and how of interview research at each step. Taking a collective view of their efforts, one cannot help but ask, what is next? It is also hoped that the world of scholarly publication will welcome the articles generated by e-interview researchers so the larger community can learn from and build on their work. Undoubtedly, given the expanded use of computer-mediated communications in professional, social, cultural, and personal life, more researchers and participants will find online interviews a natural way to interact for the purpose of data collection.

It is hoped that the E-Interview Research Framework will offer future e-interview researchers some questions and options to consider when designing, planning, and conducting studies. The E-Interview Research Framework will continue to evolve as new approaches to using new communications technologies raise new questions.

References

McCormick, J., Rodney, P., & Varcoe, C. (2004). Reinterpretations across studies: An approach to meta-analysis. *Qualitative Health Research, 13*(7), 933–944. (doi: 10.1177/1049732303253480)

Miles, M., & Huberman, A. M. (1994). *Qualitative data analysis: An expanded sourcebook* (2nd ed.). Thousand Oaks, CA: Sage.

Patton, M. Q. (2002). *Qualitative research & evaluation methods* (3rd ed.). Thousand Oaks, CA: Sage.

Stern, P., & Harris, C. (1985). Women's health and the self-care paradox: A model to guide self-care readiness: Clash between the client and nurse. *Health Care for Women International, 6,* 151–163.

Weed, M. (2005). "Meta interpretation": A method for the interpretive synthesis of qualitative research. *Forum: Qualitative Social Research, 6*(27), Art. 37.

Appendix

Suggested Resources for Qualitative Researchers

 Find more resources on the Study Site, including links to resources available online.

If you . . .	. . . then see these suggested resources:	Comments
Want to write a qualitative dissertation?	Bloomberg, L. D., & Volpe, M. (2008). *Completing your qualitative dissertation: A roadmap from beginning to end.* Thousand Oaks, CA: Sage.	
Want to choose a methodology appropriate to the study?	Creswell, J. W. (2007). *Qualitative inquiry and research design: Choosing among five traditions* (2nd ed.). Thousand Oaks, CA: Sage. Patton, M. Q. (2002). *Qualitative research & evaluation methods* (3rd ed.). Thousand Oaks, CA: Sage. Starks, H., & Trinidad, S. B. (2007). Choose your method: A comparison of phenomenology, discourse analysis, and grounded theory. *Qualitative Health Research, 17*(10), 1372–1380.	These books profile a number of methodologies, enabling you to compare and select the best one given your study's purpose. Once you select a methodology, you will want more specialized resources that focus more deeply on one approach.

(Continued)

(Continued)

If you . . .	. . . then see these suggested resources:	Comments
Want to learn more about qualitative research in general?	Anfara, V. A., & Mertz, N. T. (Eds.). (2006). *Theoretical frameworks in qualitative research.* Thousand Oaks, CA: Sage. Mason, J. (2002). *Qualitative researching* (2nd ed.). Thousand Oaks, CA: Sage. Ritchie, J., & Lewis, J. (Eds.). (2003). *Qualitative research practice: A guide for social science students and researchers.* London: Sage. Yin, R. K. (2011). *Qualitative research from start to finish* (4th ed.). Thousand Oaks, CA: Sage.	These books offer a broad overview of qualitative research.
Want to learn more about meshing qualitative and quantitative methodologies in mixed methods research?	Creswell, J. W. (2008). *Research design: Qualitative, quantitative and mixed methods approaches* (3rd ed.). Thousand Oaks, CA: Sage. Creswell, J. W., & Clark, V. L. P. (2007). *The mixed methods reader* (2nd ed.). Thousand Oaks, CA: Sage. Creswell, J. W., & Clark, V. L. P. (2011). *Designing and conducting mixed methods research* (2nd ed.). Thousand Oaks, CA: Sage. Hesse-Biber, S. (2010). *Mixed methods research: Merging theory with practice.* New York: Guilford.	*Mixed methods* is an umbrella term covering a variety of combinations of qualitative and quantitative methods. Creswell and Clark's *Designing and Conducting Mixed Methods Research* offers a detailed explanation of options for meshing or mixing methods—a must-read before deciding on a design. Hesse-Biber's *Mixed Methods Research* speaks to mixed methods from a qualitative stance.

If you . . .	. . . then see these suggested resources:	Comments
Want to learn more about analyzing qualitative data?	Bernard, H. R., & Ryan, G. (2009). *Analyzing qualitative data*. Thousand Oaks, CA: Sage. Elligson, L. L. (2009). *Engaging crystallization in qualitative research*. Thousand Oaks, CA: Sage. Miles, M., & Huberman, A. M. (1994). *Qualitative data analysis: An expanded sourcebook* (2nd ed.). Thousand Oaks, CA: Sage. Wertz, F. J., Charmaz, K., McMullen, L. M., Josselson, R., Anderson, R., & McSpadden, E. (2011). *Five ways of doing qualitative analysis*. New York: Guilford.	
Want to learn more about collecting data through interviews?	King, N., & Horrocks, C. (2010). *Interviews in qualitative research*. London: Sage. Kvale, S., & Brinkman, S. (2009). *InterViews: Learning the craft of qualitative research interviewing* (2nd ed.). Thousand Oaks, CA: Sage. Rubin, H. J., & Rubin, I. S. (2012). *Qualitative interviewing: The art of hearing data* (3rd ed.). Thousand Oaks, CA: Sage. Seidman, I. (2006). *Interviewing as qualitative research: A guide for researchers in education and the social sciences* (3rd ed.). New York: Teachers College Press. Weiss, R. S. (1994). *Learning from strangers: The art and method of qualitative interview studies*. New York: Free Press.	

(Continued)

If you . . .	. . . then see these suggested resources:	Comments
Want to learn more about using visual data?	Banks, M. (2001). *Visual methods in social research.* Thousand Oaks, CA: Sage. Pink, S. (2007). *Doing visual ethnography* (2nd ed.). London: Sage.	
Want to learn more about using (qualitative) online data collection?	Hine, C. (Ed.). (2005). *Virtual methods: Issues in social research on the Internet.* Oxford, UK: Berg. Markham, A. N., & Baym, N. K. (Eds.). (2009). *Internet inquiry: Conversations about method.* Thousand Oaks, CA: Sage. Salmons, J. E. (2010). *Online interviews in real time.* Thousand Oaks, CA: Sage.	
Want to find journals that specialize in publishing qualitative research?	International Journal of Qualitative Methods http://ejournals.library.ualberta.ca/index.php/IJQM/index The Qualitative Report http://www.nova.edu/ssss/QR/	
Want to learn about action research methodology?	Calhoun, E. F. (1993). Action research: Three approaches. *Educational Leadership, 51*(2), 62–66. Gray, D. (2009). *Doing research in the real world* (2nd ed.). London: Sage.	Action research involves close collaboration between researchers and subjects, who are often practitioners. It often aims to achieve benefits to the school or organization being investigated (Gray, 2009).

If you . . .	. . . then see these suggested resources:	Comments
Want to learn about case study research methodology?	Stake, R. E. (1995). *The art of case study research.* Thousand Oaks, CA: Sage. Yin, R. K. (2009). *Case study research* (4th ed.). Thousand Oaks, CA: Sage.	*Case study* refers to the collection and presentation of detailed information about a particular participant or small group, frequently including the accounts of subjects themselves (Palmquist, 2008). A setting or group treated as an integrated social unit to be studied "holistically and in its particularity" (Schutt, 2006, p. 292).
Want to learn more about using data from archives or documents?	Rapley, T. (2007). *Doing conversation, discourse and document analysis.* London: Sage.	
Want to learn about emergent research?	Hesse-Biber, S., & Leavy, P. (2010). *Handbook of emergent methods.* New York: Guilford. Leavy, P. (2009). *Method meets art: Arts-based research practice.* New York: Guilford.	
Want to learn about ethnographic research methodology?	Angrosino, M. (2007). *Doing ethnographic and observational research.* London: Sage. DeVault, M. L., & McCoy, L. (Eds.). (2003). *Institutional ethnography.* Thousand Oaks, CA: Sage.	Culture is central to ethnographic studies. Ethnographic researchers study cultures of individuals, groups, tribes, or

(Continued)

(Continued)

If you . . .	. . . then see these suggested resources:	Comments
	Fetterman, D. M. (2010). *Ethnography: Step-by-step* (3rd ed.). Thousand Oaks, CA: Sage. Gobo, G. (2008). *Doing ethnography.* Thousand Oaks, CA: Sage. Kozinets, R. V. (2010). *Netnography: Doing ethnographic research online.* Thousand Oaks, CA: Sage. Madden, R. (2010). *Being ethnographic: A guide to the theory and practice of ethnography.* Thousand Oaks, CA: Sage. Pink, S. (2007). *Doing visual ethnography* (2nd ed.). London: Sage. Sade-Beck, L. (2004). Internet ethnography: Online and offline. *International Journal of Qualitative Methods, 3*(2), Article 4.	communities. With roots in anthropology, this methodology has been used to study customs, patterns of behavior, beliefs, and creative expressions. These methods are used to study people in social or organizational settings.
Want to learn about grounded theory research methodology?	*Grounded Theory* Charmaz, K. (2006). *Constructed grounded theory: A practical guide through qualitative analysis.* Thousand Oaks, CA: Sage. Clarke, A. (2005). *Situational analysis: Grounded theory after the postmodern turn.* Thousand Oaks, CA: Sage.	Theory is "grounded" in the data from participants who have experienced the phenomenon. Situational analysis looks at the social *situation* while grounded theory looks at the social *process.*

If you . . .	. . . then see these suggested resources:	Comments
	Developing Models Jaccard, J., & Jacoby, J. (2010). *Theory construction and model-building skills: A practical guide for social scientists.* New York: Guilford. Van DeVen, A. H. (2007). *Engaged scholarship.* Oxford, UK: Oxford University Press.	
Want to learn about narrative research methodology?	Clandinin, D. J., & Connelly, F. M. (2000). *Narrative inquiry: Experience and story in qualitative research.* Thousand Oaks, CA: Sage. Janesick, V. J. (2010). *Oral history for the qualitative researcher: Choreographing the story.* New York: Guilford.	*Narrative research* emphasizes knowing through stories. Researchers using narrative inquiry see narrative as both the "phenomenon under study and method of study" (Clandinin and Connelly, 2000, p. 4). Narrative research approaches include life story or life history, interpretive biography or autobiography (Denzin, 1989).
Want to learn about phenomenological research methodology?	Giorgi, A. (2009). *The descriptive phenomenological method in psychology: A modified Husserlian approach.* Pittsburgh, PA: Duquesne University Press.	*Phenomenology* is the search for the ways participants experience and give meaning to an event, concept, or

(Continued)

If you . . .	. . . then see these suggested resources:	Comments
	Moustakas, C. (1994). *Phenomenological research methods*. Thousand Oaks, CA: Sage.	phenomenon (Gray, 2009). Phenomenological research methods provide a way to investigate human experience through the perceptions of research participants.
Want to network with other qualitative researchers?	Visit Methodspace, hosted by Sage Publications. Join (or start!) a group on a qualitative approach or issue at www .methodspace.org.	

Software for E-Interview Research

 Find more resources on the Study Site, including links to resources available online.

If you . . .	Then you may want to use . . .	. . . and here are some free or inexpensive options:
Want to collect data through text chat?	**Instant message or chat**	Yahoo, Google, ICQ, and other services allow for text chat as well as some file sharing.
Want to use visuals: drawing, showing images or artifacts?	**Multichannel meeting spaces.** Use the shared desktop, shared whiteboard, or shared applications features.	Most web conferencing services offer a free trial, or a basic version free. Most also offer institution-wide, enterprise-level packages.

If you . . .	Then you may want to use . . .	. . . and here are some free or inexpensive options:
		The ones listed here are accessible for individual users.
		BlackBoard Collaborate is the current name for Elluminate. (http://www.blackboard.com/ Platforms/Collaborate/ overview.aspx)
		LearnCentral (http://www .learncentral.org) offers a "free for 3" conferencing room for educators.
		Anymeeting (http://www .anymeeting.com) offers a free web meeting service.
		Vyew (http://vyew.com) has a free option and many collaborative features.
		WizIQ (http://www.wiziq .com) offers a free trial and inexpensive plans for individuals.
Want to see researcher/ participant(s)?	**Videoconferencing.** You can use desktop videoconferencing or videoconferencing rooms that allow for groups and other media.	The most popular desktop videoconferencing is Skype. It is free (www.skype.com). You can use a free or inexpensive system to record the call, such as eCamm (www .ecamm.com), VodBurner (www.vodburner.com), or IMCapture for Skype (www .imcapture.com).
		For a group interview or focus group, Vidyo (www .vidyo.com) is an option that can include groups,

(Continued)

(Continued)

If you . . .	Then you may want to use . . .	. . . and here are some free or inexpensive options:
		observers, and if needed a shared desktop or slides. Vidyo can connect desktop users, mobile tablet users, and/or videoconference rooms. Calls are recorded.
Want to learn how to create an avatar and get started in a virtual world?	**Second Life** is a virtual world with many commercial as well as educational options for participants.	Second Life is free. Log in to www.secondlife.com View what Second Life is at http://secondlife.com/whatis/?lang=en-US#Intro

Glossary

Application sharing: Multiple participants can interactively work in an application that is loaded on only one user's machine. Application "viewing" is similar to application "sharing"; however, although all users can see the document or image, only one person can actually manipulate or edit it.

Asynchronous communication: Communication that involves a delay between message and response, meaning it is not necessary to be online at the same time.

The Belmont Report: The basis for protection of human subjects regulations in the United States.

Beneficence: To do no harm and to reduce risks involved in research, a fundamental principle of research ethics.

Blog: See Weblog.

Chat: See Text message.

Computer-mediated communication (CMC): This term refers to human communication that occurs when messages are conveyed by computers.

Criterion sampling: Selecting all participants on the basis of criteria selected to align with the research purpose.

Emic: Stake defines emic issues as those that emerge from actors inside the case; they may occur when the researcher is an actor in the case (Stake, 1995).

Epoche: "Setting aside prejudgments and opening the research interview with unbiased, receptive presence" (Moustakas, 1994, p. 85).

Etic: Stake (1995) defines etic issues as those initiated or brought in by the researcher from outside the case.

Existing sample frame: Existing lists or collections of information about groups of people such as membership rolls or administrative records.

Follow-up questions: Follow-up questions build on interviewee responses to get a clearer or deeper understanding of the interviewee's response.

Human subject: A living individual about whom an investigator (whether professional or student) conducting research obtains the following: data through intervention or interaction with the individual, or identifiable private information (U.S. Department of Health and Human Services, 2005).

Immediacy: Communicative behaviors that reduce the physical or psychological distance between individuals and foster affiliation (Mehrabian, 1971).

In-depth interview: An in-depth interview is a qualitative research technique involving a researcher who guides or questions a participant to elicit information, perspectives, insights, feelings on behaviors, experiences, or phenomena that cannot be observed. The in-depth interview is conducted to collect data that allow the researcher to generate new understandings and new knowledge about the subject of investigation.

Information and communications technologies (ICTs): Umbrella term describing communication devices or applications including the following: cellular phones, computer and network hardware and software, satellite systems as well as the various services and applications associated with them.

Information and communications technology (ICT) literacy: Using digital technology, communications tools, and/or networks to access, manage, integrate, evaluate, and create information in order to function in a knowledge society (Educational Testing Service, 2002).

Media Richness Theory: Media Richness Theory (MRT) provides one way to classify different kinds of Internet communication by distinguishing between "lean" and "rich" media based on "the capacity for immediate feedback, the number of cues and channels utilized, personalization, and language variety" (Daft & Lengel, 1986, p. 580). Daft and Lengel argued that "rich media" allow people to provide and receive immediate feedback, check interpretations, and understand multiple cues via body language, tone of voice, and message content.

Media Synchronicity Theory: Media Synchronicity Theory (MST) offers a definition for *synchronicity* that distinguishes high-quality real-time communications from those interchanges that while ostensibly synchronous, do not entail an in-depth exchange or productive dialogue (Dennis, Fuller, & Valacich, 2008). Dennis et al. observe that while the medium may allow for immediate feedback, it may also allow for multiple activities and distractions that can detract from the communication partners' potential to really collaborate or solve problems.

Mediated immediacy: Communicative cues in mediated channels that can shape perceptions of psychological closeness between interactants; immediacy cues can be seen as a language of affiliation (O'Sullivan, Hunt, & Lippert, 2004, p. 471).

Methodologies: The study of, and justification for, methods used to conduct research. The term describes approaches to systematic inquiry developed within a particular paradigm with associated epistemological assumptions (Gray, 2009). Methodologies emerge from academic disciplines in the social and physical sciences, and while considerable cross-disciplinary exchange occurs, choices generally place the study into a disciplinary context.

MUVE, or multi-user virtual environment. See Virtual world.

Nonverbal communication: Aspects of communication that convey messages without words. Types of nonverbal communication include the following:

- Chronemic communication is the use of pacing and timing of speech and length of silence before response in conversation.

- Paralinguistic, or paralanguage, communication describes variations in volume, pitch, and quality of voice.

- Kinesic communication includes eye contact and gaze, facial expressions, body movements, gestures, and postures.

- Proxemic communication is the use of interpersonal space to communicate attitudes (Gordon, 1980; Guerrero, DeVito, & Hecht, 1999; Kalman, Ravid, Raban, & Rafaeli, 2006).

Online interviews: For the purpose of this book, the term *online interviews* refers to interviews conducted with information and communications technologies (ICT). The primary focus is on interviews conducted with synchronous technologies including text messaging, videoconferencing or video calls, multichannel meetings, or 3-D immersive environments. Asynchronous technologies such as e-mail, blogs, forums, wikis, social networks, or websites are used to prepare for, conduct, or follow up on the interview. Scholarly online interviews are conducted in accordance with ethical research guidelines; verifiable research participants provide informed consent before participating in any interview.

Purposive or purposeful sampling: A nonprobability sampling method in which participants or cases are selected for a purpose, usually as related to ability to answer central questions of the study.

Qualitative research: Methods of inquiry directed at providing an "in-depth and interpreted understanding of the social world of research participants by learning about their social and material circumstances, their experiences, perspectives and histories" (Ritchie & Lewis, 2003, p. 3).

Quantitative research: Methods of inquiry that analyze numeric representations of the world; the systematic and mathematical techniques used to collect and analyze data (Gray, 2009). Survey and questionnaire data are often analyzed in quantitative units (Yoshikawa, Weisner, Kalil, & Way, 2008).

Sample: The subjects or participants selected for the study.

Sample frame: Lists or collections of information about groups of people, either already existing or constructed by the researcher for the purpose of selecting the sample. For online research, sample frames help to ensure credibility and authenticity of participants through third-party verification, such as membership in a group or organization.

Sampling: Strategy for selecting cases or participants to study.

Second Life: A 3-D virtual world created by San Francisco-based software maker Linden Labs (Whatis.com, 2008).

Social Information Processing (SIP) Theory: SIP argues, "When most nonverbal cues are unavailable, as is the case in text-based CMC, users adapt their language, style, and other cues to such purposes" (Walther, Loh, & Granka, 2005, p. 37).

Social Media: (or social networking) describes a number of communications technologies that allow for various options and combinations of one-to-one, one-to-many, and many-to-many communication. There is usually an option to create affiliate networks of friends or members.

Structured or survey interview: Interviewers ask fixed-choice questions and record responses based on a coding scheme. All interviews ask the same questions in the same order, and interviewers are trained to maintain a consistent, neutral approach to questioning and responding to all participants (Fontana & Frey, 2003; Schaeffer & Maynard, 2003; Schutt, 2006).

Survey: An investigation into one or more variables in a population that may involve collection of qualitative and/or quantitative data (Gray, 2009). Data may be analyzed with qualitative or quantitative methods.

Synchronicity: See Media Synchronicity Theory.

Synchronous communication: Communication that occurs in real time, meaning it is necessary to be online at the same time.

Text messaging, instant messaging, and chat: In real time, people can communicate online by exchanging short written messages. Typically, the term "text message" is used when people write back and forth over mobile phones or devices, while "instant messaging" or "chat" refers to the same kind of communication on computers. Chat or messaging may require registration and/or log in to enter and post; it may be private or open to the public. One-to-one, one-to-many, or many-to-many individuals can converse in writing.

Video, web, or desktop conferencing: Videoconferencing is a live session between two or more users who are in different locations. Options include room systems that allow individuals or groups to see each other in an office, meeting room, or studio. Web conferencing, desktop conferencing, or video calls allow users to see each other using a web camera and computer. In addition to audio and video transmission, other meeting tools such as whiteboards and shared applications can be used to share visuals, slides, or other documents.

Virtual world: A virtual world is "a synchronous, persistent network of people, represented by avatars, facilitated by computers" (Bell, 2008 p. 2). Virtual worlds are also described as MUVE, for multi-user virtual environment or MUU, massive multiplayer universe. Second Life and Wonderland are popular immersive virtual worlds, as are many games. People joining Second Life or other virtual worlds create their own cartoonlike "avatar" that represents them in the 3-D world, and they can create buildings and campuses that may be realistic or based on fanciful imagination (Thorpe, 2008). Participants travel around the various online environments and interact with each other. Avatars can explore, meet other residents, socialize, participate in individual and group activities, participate in experiential and educational activities, and create and trade virtual items and services with one another. Second Life users can create buildings and campuses that may be realistic or based on fanciful imagination. Participation is free and open to anyone who registers; participants can choose to purchase virtual items or property.

Voice-Over Internet Protocol (VOIP): VOIP or Internet telephony are terms used to describe the techniques used to carry voice traffic over the Internet (infoDev, 2008). Using a headset or speakers and microphone, audio conversations can occur online in much the same way a telephone is used. Indeed, some telephone services, using conventional handsets, now use Internet instead of the usual telephone networks. With VOIP, the customer pays only for the Internet service. Increasingly, instant or text messaging applications are integrating desktop videoconferencing into the communications package.

Weblog (blog): A blog is a personal online journal where entries are posted chronologically. Users create their own weblogs as a way to share thoughts and ideas, and link to other websites and blogs to create families of sites with common interests. Microblogs use the same principle but allow for very short entries. Blogs can be text only or multichannel, with links to images or media. Some are public and others can be seen only by subscribers or friend lists.

Wiki: Unlike other types of websites that are designed, written, and posted by an individual or company for others' viewing, wikis allow multiple authors to add, remove, and edit content on a website. Users create social context on wikis, which can be public, such as the most global example, Wikipedia, the collaboratively edited global encyclopedia, or private, with access by members only.

References

Bell, M. (2008). *Definition and taxonomy of virtual worlds.* Paper presented at the New Digital Media (Audiovisual, Games, and Music): Economic, Social and Political Impacts, Sao Paulo, Brazil.

Daft, R. L., & Lengel, R. H. (1986). Organizational information requirements, media richness and structural design. *Management Science, 32*(5), 554–571.

Dennis, A. R., Fuller, R. M., & Valacich, J. S. (2008). Media, tasks, and communication processes: A theory of media synchronicity. *Management Information Systems Quarterly, 32*(4), 575–600.

Denzin, N. K. (1989). *Interpretive biography* (Vol. 17). Newbury Park, CA: Sage.

Educational Testing Service. (2002). *Digital transformation: A framework for ICT literacy: A report of the International ICT Literacy Panel.* Retrieved September 10, 2004, from http://www.ets.org/Media/Research/pdf/ICTREPORT.pdf

Fontana, A., & Frey, J. H. (2003). The interview: From structured questions to negotiated text. In N. K. Denzin & Y. S. Lincoln (Eds.), *Collecting and interpreting qualitative materials* (2nd ed.). Thousand Oaks, CA: Sage.

Gordon, R. L. (1980). *Interviewing: Strategy, techniques and tactics.* Homewood, IL: Dorsey.

Gray, D. (2009). *Doing research in the real world* (2nd ed.). London: Sage.

Guerrero, L. K., DeVito, J. A., & Hecht, M. L. (Eds.). (1999). *The nonverbal communication reader: Classic and contemporary readings.* Prospect Hills, IL: Waveland.

infoDev. (2008). *ICT regulation toolkit: Glossary.* Retrieved from http://www.ictregulationtoolkit.org/en/Section.560.html

Kalman, Y. M., Ravid, G., Raban, D. R., & Rafaeli, S. (2006). Pauses and response latencies: A chronemic analysis of asynchronous CMC. *Journal of Computer-Mediated Communication, 12*(1), 1–23.

Mehrabian, A. (1971). *Silent messages.* Belmont, CA: Wadsworth.

Moustakas, C. (1994). *Phenomenological research methods.* Thousand Oaks, CA: Sage.

O'Sullivan, P. B., Hunt, S. K., & Lippert, L. R. (2004). Mediated immediacy: A language of affiliation in a technological age. *Journal of Language and Social Psychology, 23*(4), 464–490.

Palmquist, M. (2008). *Writing guides: Case studies.* Retrieved July 18, 2008, from http://writing.colostate.edu/guides/research/casestudy/index.cfm

Ritchie, J., & Lewis, J. (Eds.). (2003). *Qualitative research practice: A guide for social science students and researchers.* London: Sage.

Schaeffer, N. C., & Maynard, D. W. (2003). Standardization and interaction in the survey interview. In J. F. Gubrium & J. A. Holstein (Eds.), *Postmodern interviewing.* Thousand Oaks, CA: Sage.

Schutt, R. K. (2006). *Investigating the social world: The process and practice of research* (5th ed.). Thousand Oaks, CA: Pine Forge.

Stake, R. E. (1995). *The art of case study research.* Thousand Oaks, CA: Sage.

Thorpe, S. (Ed.). (2008). *The use of story in building online group relationships.* Hershey, PA: IGI Global.

Walther, J. B., Loh, T., & Granka, L. (2005). Let me count the ways: The interchange of verbal and nonverbal cues in computer-mediated and face-to-face affinity. *Journal of Language and Social Psychology, 24*(1), 36–65.

Yoshikawa, H., Weisner, T. S., Kalil, A., & Way, N. (2008). Mixing qualitative and quantitative research in developmental science: Uses and methodological choices. *Developmental Psychology, 44*(2), 344–354.

Index

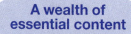